# IN SEARCH OF INDIAN-NESS:
## Cultures of Multinationals

# IN SEARCH OF INDIAN-NESS
## Cultures of Multinationals

DR. KANIKA AGGARWAL KHANDELWAL

**KANISHKA PUBLISHERS, DISTRIBUTORS**
**NEW DELHI-110 002**

KANISHKA PUBLISHERS, DISTRIBUTORS
4697/5-21 A, Ansari Road, Daryaganj
New Delhi-110 002
Phones : 2327 0497, 2328 8285
Fax : 011-2328 8285
e-mail: kanishka_publishing@yahoo.co.in

First Published 2009

ISBN 978-81-8457-115-8

PRINTED IN INDIA

---

Published by Madan Sachdeva for Kanishka Publishers, Distributors, 4697/5-21A, Ansari Road, Daryaganj, New Delhi-110 002, Typeset by Sunshine Graphics, Delhi, and Printed at Rajdhani Printers, Delhi.

**DEDICATED TO**

**My Husband Sumit,**
**for Being the Wind Beneath**
**My Wings...**
**and My Daughter Khushi,**
**for Just Being Her.**

# Preface

The world has shrunk and transformed itself into the proverbial 'global village.' As a result organizations now operate in more than one country, and the number and size of multinationals that span national boundaries has seen a phenomenal increase in the twentieth century. Expansion across national boundaries is not merely a step across a geographical line, but also a step into different political, economic, and social environments. Managers of multinationals confront a number of challenges that they never had to face when their operations were constrained within national borders. They not only face different legal, taxation, economic, and political systems, but they also must deal with varying national cultures, many of which are nothing like those in which they spent their entire lives.

The influence of the socio-cultural environment results in a set of beliefs and assumptions about human nature and organizational behaviour that employees carry with them as their cultural baggage when they join an organization. In recent years the role of the external environment, in particular socio-cultural values, has been acknowledged as having a strong influence on an organization's culture. A study of socio-cultural values gains further importance in the context of multinationals in India, where cultural and social diversities are to be assimilated into a larger unity. The effectiveness of these organizations would be more a function of their ability to adapt to the social environment than to insist on the same set of symbolic devices in every situation. Thus, cultural differences must be understood and managers must be sensitive to them in order to be successful in a global economy.

Undoubtedly, the rapid pace of change has brought many multinationals to India. They are carrying their technology and tools, but are they also carrying their 'cultural values'? Is the Indian soul ready to graft imported cultural values? Can MNCs be made more effective by constructing organizational cultures based on contextual Indian societal values? Will it contribute to commitment, health, or intention to stay in the job for employees? The present book attempts to find answers to these questions empirically in the context of three multinationals in India belonging to different national cultures.

Chapters 1, 2, 3, 4, 5 and 6 examine conceptualizations and theoretical perspectives on organizational culture, the Indian socio-cultural context, health at the workplace, organizational commitment, employee turnover and multinational organizations. Some research is also examined on factors affecting health at the workplace, organizational commitment and employee turnover and its linkages with the cultural context. Chapter 7 and 8 present the research strategy and finding of this work. Chapter 9 attempts to arrive at an emerging paradigm, linking societal values, organizational values and employee outcomes in multinational organizations. It also provides recommendations for managers of multinationals to design organizational interventions necessary to ensure their cultural fit.

I would like to thank all those who directly or indirectly helped make this work possible. This book is based in part on my Ph.D. research. Naturally, first and foremost, I wish to express my deep gratitude to my Ph.D Supervisor, Prof. Paramjeet Kaur Dhillon (Retired), for mentoring me at every step. I can never forget the education, encouragement and scholarly values I received from her when starting out in my academic career. My interest in the problem was aroused by some stimulating discussions with Prof. Anand Prakash, University of Delhi. I am also thankful to Dr. B.S. Nagi, who did several rounds of analysis uncomplainingly. I am also thankful to the management and employees of the organizations I studied. It is a pleasure to acknowledge the partial financial support I received from UGC, by way of Junior Research Fellowship. Thanks are also due to Mr. Madan from Kanishka Publishers, Distributors without whom this book may not have seen the light of the day.

It would be only befitting to mention Dr. Meenakshi Gopinath, Principal Lady Shri Ram College, for always inspiring me to push my limits. I would like to acknowledge the unconditional support and love provided by my friend and colleague Dr. Priti Dhawan. Over the years, I have been very lucky to have been associated with very bright students. I would like to thank each one of them for teaching me as much as I have taught them.

I am deeply appreciative of all my family members, who have provided me with a loving, supportive climate over the years needed to motivate me. My parents, Vinod and Kamini Aggarwal, for instilling in me standards of excellence and perfection (I am not claiming though that this work is perfect, by any means)! My father-in-law, Late Sh. Ramesh Khandelwal, would have been a very proud man today and I am sure he is blessing me from somewhere. My sincere thanks to my Bhabhi Neelam and Didi Aseema, for understanding my frenetic, often out-of-control, schedules. My sister, Saloni also deserves a special mention for being there for me.

Finally, last but certainly not the least, let me come back full circle to the one whose unstinting support was essential to this project: my husband Sumit and my two-year daughter, Khushi. Sumit, thanks for always standing by me. But for the love and patience of both of them, it would have been impossible for me to finish this work.

Thanks, everybody for the faith.

**Dr. Kanika Aggarwal Khandelwal**

# Contents

# List of Abbreviations

| | | |
|---|---|---|
| 1. | Analysis of Variance | ANOVA |
| 2. | Behavioural Health | BH |
| 3. | Dependent | Dep. |
| 4. | Education | EDU |
| 5. | Emotional Health | EH |
| 6. | Employee Health (Overall) | EH(O) |
| 7. | Experience Prior to Joining Present Organization | EXP |
| 8. | Family Structure | FS |
| 9. | Figure | Fig. |
| 10. | Group | G |
| 11. | Independent | Indep. |
| 12. | Individualism | IND |
| 13. | Job Involvement | OCJI |
| 14. | Loyalty | OCL |
| 15. | Marital Status | MS |
| 16. | Masculinity | MAS |
| 17. | Multinational Corporation | MNC |
| 18. | Number of Jobs Changed | NOJ |
| 19. | Number | N |
| 20. | Organization | Org |

| | | |
|---|---|---|
| 21. | Organizational Commitment | OC |
| 22. | Organizational Identification | OCI |
| 23. | Organizational Individualism | OID |
| 24. | Organizational Masculinity | OMAS |
| 25. | Organizational Power Distance | OPD |
| 26. | Organizational Uncertainty Avoidance | OUA |
| 27. | Pearson's Correlation Coefficient | r |
| 28. | Person-Organization Fit | P-O Fit |
| 29. | Physical Health | PH |
| 30. | Power Distance | PD |
| 31. | Promotion(s) Received | PRO |
| 32. | Societal Individualism | SID |
| 33. | Societal Masculinity | SMAS |
| 34. | Societal Power Distance | SPD |
| 35. | Societal Uncertainty Avoidance | SUA |
| 36. | Standard Deviation | SD |
| 37. | Tenure in the Present Organization | TEN |
| 38. | Turnover Intention | TI |
| 39. | Uncertainty Avoidance | UA |
| 40. | Variables | Vars. |

# 1
# Organizational Culture

## THE CONCEPT OF CULTURE

The concept of culture has a long tradition in behavioural sciences. Arguments about the definition of culture have had a long tradition in anthropology (Kroeber and Kluckhohn, 1952 identified 164 different definitions of culture existing in their search of the literature) and continue today. As a consensus of anthropological definitions, Kluckhohn (1951) suggested that culture consists of "patterned ways of thinking, feeling and reacting, acquired and transmitted mainly by symbols, constituting the distinctive achievements of human groups, including their embodiments in artifacts; the essential core of culture consists of traditional (i.e. historically derived and selected) ideas and especially their attached values."

Herskovits (1955) designated culture as the "man-made part of the environment." Using a metaphorical description, he adds, "it is the very air they breathe and the spirit which permeates their life. It is the totality of beliefs, norms, and values, which is related to the patterned regularity in people's behaviour. According to Keesing (1974), "cultures are systems (of socially transmitted behaviour patterns) that serve to relate human communities to their ecological settings." Hofstede (1980) treated culture as "the collective programming of the human mind which distinguishes the members of one human group from another." Emphasising the role of values, he says, "Culture.. includes systems of values; and values are among the building blocks of culture."

Thus, the concept of culture suffers from surplus meanings. Triandis et al. (1986) considered culture to be a fuzzy construct. According to Spiro (1951), "culture has no ontological reality...Culture is a logical construct, abstracted from human behaviour, and as such it exists, only in the minds of the investigator." On the other hand, for White (1948), culture determines everything that people do, feel, and think. For still others, culture is nothing but a bunch of independent variables which might "include basic institutions, subsistence patterns, social organizations, languages, and social rules governing inter-personal relations" (Segall, 1984).

The word "culture" is usually reserved for societies (in the modern world we call them nations) or for ethnic or regional groups, but it can be applied equally to other human collectivities or categories: an organization, a profession, or a family. Culture, whether organizational or national, is frequently defined as a set of taken-for-granted assumptions, expectations, or rules for being in the world. As paradigm, map, frame of reference, interpretive schemas, or shared understanding, the culture concept emphasizes the shared cognitive approaches to reality that distinguishes a given group from another (Adler and Jelinek, 1986).

## UNDERSTANDING ORGANIZATIONAL CULTURE CONSTRUCT

Organizational culture as a construct is a relatively recent addition to contemporary organizational behaviour literature. The term organizational culture first appeared casually in English-language literature in the 1960s as a synonym of 'climate' (Lewin, Lippitt and White, 1939). Early work utilized primarily the concept of climate and survey instruments. Schneider (1985) pointed that culture is now on the ascendance and climate is less popular. The term 'organizational culture' entered the U.S academic literature with an article in Administrative Science Quarterly by Pettigrew in 1979. A spate of articles/books claimed that organizational culture represents a path breaking "metaphor" or "paradigm" (Ouchi, 1981; Pascale and Athos, 1981; Deal and Kennedy, 1982; Peters and Waterman, 1982; Schein, 1985; Frost et al., 1985), while others feel that the idea of culture is overstated, and it is simply "old wine in a new bottle" (Parker, 2000).

There are very few areas of general consensus about organizational culture. These include the following (Ott, 1989):

- Organizational culture is the culture that exists in an organization.
- Each organizational culture is relatively unique.
- Organizational culture is a socially constructed concept.
- Organizational culture provides organizational members with a way of understanding and making sense of events and symbols.
- Organizational culture is a powerful lever for guiding organizational behaviour. It functions as "organizational control mechanism, informally approving or prohibiting some patterns of behaviour" (Martin and Siehl, 1983).

But beyond these five points agreement is very limited, and the points say nothing about what organizational culture is. Ott (1989), after reviewing the existing definitions of organizational culture from 58 different published sources, concluded, "There are as many definitions as there are researchers." He described organizational culture as a socially constructed, unseen, and unobservable force behind organizational activities. According to him, organizational culture is a hypothetical construct that must be inferred from the shared thoughts, feelings, values, and actions of organizational members. He suggested that organizational culture is a concept, construct, energy, or idea, rather than a thing that can be directly observed, measured, and manipulated. How one looks at culture to a large extent determines what it is.

Organizational culture has been likened to "one of those ink blots in which we see what we want to see" (Hampden-Turner, 1990). Barbara (1992) also emphasized that "organizational culture' serves also as an umbrella concept where almost all studies can find a place if their authors so wish." In a similar vein, Parker (2000) suggested, "organizational culture ends up as a 'dustbin category' that can collect all the non-structural elements of organizational functioning and can be reified as a noun with properties, types or functions. Culture can become a thing that is strong in some places, weak or non-existent in others." Similarly, Alvesson (2002) asserted, "culture is a tricky concept as it is easily used to cover everything and consequently nothing…I use the term 'organizational culture' as an umbrella concept for a way of thinking which takes a serious interest in cultural and symbolic phenomenon."

With most definitions of organizational culture, it is presumed that organizational culture is a "cue" for values, beliefs, norms, customs, or any other string of convenient identifiers chosen from cultural anthropology (Allaire and Firsirotu, 1984). Some illustrative definitions are as follows:

- Ideologies, a rationale for do's and don'ts . (Harrison, 1972).
- "The system of...publicly and collectively accepted meanings operating for a given group at a given time." (Pettigrew, 1979).
- A set of common understandings for organizing actions and languages and other symbolic vehicles for expressing common understanding. (Louis, 1980).
- "The collective programming of the mind which distinguishes the members of one organization from another." (Hofstede, 1980).
- The sum of rules observed by people for guiding their behaviour. (Rohner, 1984).
- Culture is the commonly held and relatively stable beliefs, attitudes and values that exist within the organization. (Williams et al., 1993).

Thus, the concept of culture seems to lend itself to very different understandings of its meanings: for instance, as ideology (Harrison, 1972), shared meanings (Pettigrew, 1979), common understandings (Louis, 1980), a set of shared core values (Deal and Kennedy, 1982; Peters and Waterman, 1982), basic assumptions (Schein, 1985), rules for getting along (Rohner, 1984; Schein, 1968; Van Maanen, 1976), or collective programming of the mind (Hofstede, 1980). Forms of culture include rituals and ceremonies (Trice and Beyer, 1984), stories and scripts (Martin et al., 1983; Wilkins, 1983), language or jargon (Pondy, 1983), logo and corporate jokes (Dandridge, Mitroff and Joyce, 1980).

## PERSPECTIVES ON ORGANIZATIONAL CULTURE

Researchers studying organizational culture have diverse perspectives to facilitate conceptual understanding as well as to guide research in the area of culture. This section presents four perspectives as given by Smircich, Deal and Kennedy, Schein, and Wilkins and Ouchi. However, they may not be taken as an exhaustive list of perspectives, but are only indicative of diversity of perceptions available on organizational culture.

**The Anthropological Perspective: Smircich**

Smircich (1983) distinguished the following five perspectives on organizational culture:

*(i)* ***Cross-Cultural Management:*** Culture as an independent variable. This line of research is concerned with variation in managerial and employee practices and attitudes across countries; and culture is considered to be a background factor (almost synonymous with country), an explanatory variable, or a broad framework influencing the development and reinforcement of beliefs.

*(ii)* ***Corporate Culture:*** Culture as an internal variable. Researchers holding this view believe that organizations are themselves culture—producing phenomena (Louis, 1980). The implication is that the cultural dimension in some way contributes to the overall effectiveness of an organization, and therefore organizational culture may be another critical lever or key by which strategic managers can influence and direct the course of their organizations.

***(iii)*** ***Culture as a Root Metaphor for Conceptualising Organization:*** Organizational cognition, organizational symbolism, and psychodynamics.

Culture as a root metaphor promotes a view of organizations as expressive forms, manifestations of human consciousness. The research work stemming from these foundations is as given:

*(a)* *A Cognitive Perspective:* Culture is seen as a system of shared cognition or a system of knowledge and beliefs. Culture is generated by the human mind by means of a finite number of rules or means of an unconscious logic.

*(b)* *A Symbolic Perspective:* In symbolic anthropology, culture is seen as a system of shared symbols and meanings (Geertz, 1973). The anthropologist's task is of interpreting the "themes" of culture-those postulates or understandings, declared or implicit, tacitly approved or openly promoted, that orient and stimulate social activity.

(c) *Structural and Psychodynamic Perspective:* From this point of view, organizational forms and practices are understood as projections of an unconscious process and are analysed with reference to the dynamic interplay between out-of-awareness processes and their unconscious manifestation.

Researchers pursue these five different themes for different purposes and their work is based on different assumptions about the nature of culture and organization.

**The Deal and Kennedy Approach**

Deal and Kennedy (1982) conceptualize culture as: "the way we do things around here." In their words: "In Culture There is Strength." They regard a strong culture as a powerful lever for guiding behaviour in that it helps employees do their jobs a little better, and the driving force behind continuing success in business. According to them, the ultimate success of a CEO depends to a large degree on an accurate reading of the corporate culture and the ability to hone it and shape it to fit the shifting needs of the marketplace.

Corporate culture is seen as being composed of the following elements:

(i) *Business Environment:* The environment in which a company operates determines what it must do to be a success, and is the single greatest influence in shaping a corporate culture.

(ii) *Values:* These are the basic concepts and beliefs of an organization; as such they form the "heart of the corporate culture." As the essence of a company's philosophy for achieving success, values provide a sense of common direction for all employees and guidelines for their day-to-day behaviour.

(iii) *Heroes:* If values are the soul of culture, then heroes personify those values and as such provide tangible role models for employees to follow. Heroes are pivotal figures in a strong culture and epitomize the strength of the organization.

(iv) *The Rites and Rituals:* These are the systematic and programmed routines of day-to-day life in the company. Rituals show employees the kind of behaviour that is expected of them, while ceremonies provide visible and potent examples of what the company stands for.

(v) *The Culture Network:* As the primary (but informal) means of communication within an organization, the cultural network, comprising of storytellers, spies, priests, cabals, and whispers is the "carrier" of the corporate values and heroic mythology.

Drawing on the terminology offered by Deal and Kennedy, Hofstede et al. (1990) opine that cultural differences manifest themselves in four ways: symbols, heroes, rituals, and values. In Figure 1.1, these are illustrated as the successive skins of an onion, indicating that symbols represent the most superficial, and values the deepest manifestation of culture. Symbols, heroes, and rituals have been subsumed under the term "practices", because they are visible to an observer although their cultural meaning lies in the way they are perceived by insiders.

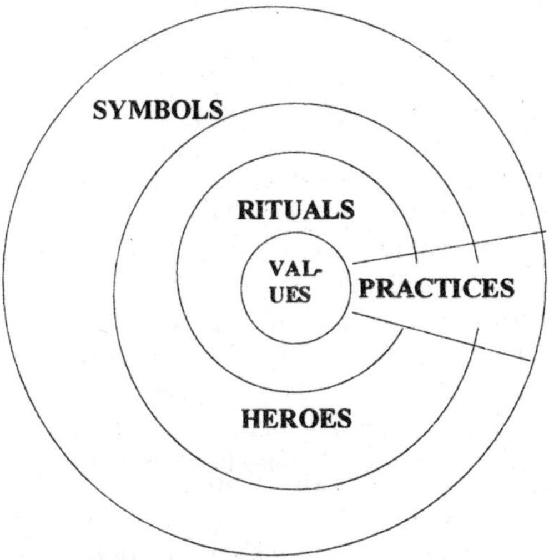


**Fig 1.1: Manifestation of Culture: From Shallow to Deep (Hofstede et al., 1990)**

Hofstede et al. (1990) tested this model in 20 units from 10 different organizations in Denmark and Netherlands. They concluded that in contrast to Deal and Kennedy ( 1982) and others like Peters and Waterman (1982) who insist that shared values represent the core of a corporate culture, shared perceptions of daily practices form the core of an organization's culture. They suggest that practices arise from shared values. The values of founders and key leaders shaped organizational cultures, and the way these cultures affect ordinary members is through shared practices. Thus, "founders' and leaders' values become members' practices".

**Culture as a "Layered" Phenomenon: Schein**

Analyzing culture from a broader perspective, Schein (1984, 1985) described three levels of organizational culture:

(i) *Visible Artifacts:* These are the visible behavioural manifestations of underlying concepts—the constructed environment of the organization, its architecture, office layout, manner of dress, visible or audible behaviour patterns, stories, etc. This level of analysis is tricky because the data are easy to obtain but hard to interpret.

(ii) *Values:* To analyse why members behave the way they do, we look for the values that govern behaviour. At this level, we may be seeing the 'ideology', 'philosophy', 'charter', or basic 'credo' of the organization.

(iii) *Underlying Assumptions.* What really drives or creates the values and overt responses are the learned underlying assumptions of level three. These are called assumptions rather than values, because we tend to be unconscious of them, to take them for granted and to view them as automatically true and non-negotiable. Whereas values can be debated and discussed, basic assumptions cannot. These are preconscious and taken-for-granted assumptions about broad human issues like relationship to environment, nature of reality, time and space, human nature, activity, and relationships.

These underlying assumptions actually determine how group members perceive, think and feel. Culture can thus be described as the pattern of underlying assumptions, a pattern that is implicit, taken for granted, and unconscious unless called to the surface by some process of inquiry, similar to that used by anthropologists. "The problem of deciphering a particular organization's culture... is more a matter of surfacing assumption" (Schein, 1984). Schein (1985) suggested that "only a joint effort between an insider and an outsider (using an iterative 'clinical' interview) can decipher the essential assumptions and their pattern of interrelationships."

Furthermore, Schein (1985) concluded that the manipulation of culture is the unique and essential function of leadership. At the "early" stages of the organization's development, this means culture's creation and establishment; in the "mid life" stage, an insight into the functioning of culture; and at "maturity," an ability to change, if necessary.

**The Utilitarian Perspective: Wilkins and Ouchi**

Wilkins and Ouchi (1983) "take the paradigmatic view of culture and call it clan" and define culture as shared social knowledge. Culture/clan is

*(i)* a general paradigm that helps participants determine what is in the best interest of the collective, and
*(ii)* the perception of goal congruence (the belief in a general or long-term equity).

Culture provides members of the organization with intellectual tools and a 'long memory' which guarantee their perception and evaluation of fair rewards in the long run and discourage them from short-term opportunistic behaviour. It can replace the need for close monitoring by *(i)* socializing employees into believing that their objectives in the exchange process are congruent with those of the employed, and *(ii)* by providing a general paradigm which facilitates the determination of what is best for the relationship.

They also underlined some conditions that encourage the development of clans: *(i)* long history and stable membership; *(ii)* absence of institutional alternatives, and *(iii)* interaction among group members to develop common interpretations of the ongoing events.

They also argued that, with respect to organizational performance, particular properties of local organizational culture are more important than others and that local organizational culture (clan) will be more critical to performance in one range of organizations than in others. They suggested that the clan would be more efficient under conditions of ambiguity, complexity, and interdependence of transactions. They, however, caution that the costs of developing and maintaining a clan (or organization-specific culture) are potentially significant and must be taken into account in assessing its efficiency.

## FUNCTIONS OF ORGANIZATIONAL CULTURE

A large number of functions have been attributed to organizational culture. Culture helps in locating what is important in both the external environment as well as important issues within the organization. Culture may provide a common purpose and a coordination of activities for members, they provide predictability in the social world and a common frame of reference. According to Hampden-Turner (1990), "the culture of an organization defines appropriate behaviour, bonds and motivates individuals and asserts solutions where there is ambiguity. It governs the way a company processes information, its internal relations and its values."

Schein (1985, 1990, 1992) suggested that the primary function of an organization's culture is to enhance the organization's responsiveness to the problems of external adaptation (those which help the group to survive in and adapt to the external environment), and internal integration (those which help an organization to integrate its internal processes in order to survive and adapt). He delineated the following effects of culture on organizational effectiveness and individual satisfaction:

- Determining and limiting strategy.
- Failure of mergers, acquisitions, and diversifications due to cultural mismatch.
- Failure to integrate new technologies due to the problem of meshing several occupational subcultures and/or changing the dominant organizational culture.
- Intergroup conflicts within the organization.
- Ineffective meetings and communication breakdowns in face-to-face relationships.
- Socialisation failures when the new member does not learn the culture of the host group, resulting in feelings of alienation, discomfort, and possibly unproductivity.

There is general agreement across the literature about four functions of organizational culture, summarized by Siehl and Martin (1984) as follows:

*(a)* It provides shared patterns of cognitive interpretations or perceptions;
*(b)* It provides shared patterns of affect, an emotional sense of

involvement and commitment to organizational values and moral codes;

(c) It provides and maintains boundaries, allowing identification of members and non-members, and

(d) It functions as an organizational control system, prescribing and prohibiting certain behaviours.

Agreement on a fifth function is not universal: organizational culture strongly affects organizational performance. The practitioner's emphasis on culture has been strongly influenced by its presumed association with strong corporate performance (Saffold, 1988; Denison, 1990). At a fairly simplistic level, two sets of relationships have captured the imagination: the first (Pascale and Athos, 1981) is a presumed association at a national level between Japan's industrial performance and its culture; the second is from the 'excellence' literature and is the presumed relationship between "strong culture"/"shared values" and business "success" or "excellence" (Peters and Waterman, 1982; Deal and Kennedy, 1982).

Brown (1998) summarised the most significant functions of culture as: conflict reduction, co-ordination and control, the reduction of uncertainty, motivation, and competitive advantage. Lawson and Shen (1998) likened organizational culture to the traditional construct of Chinese medicine, *Qi*, the vital universal energy that courses through each individual and consists of *yin* (dark force) and *yang* (bright force). According to Lawson and Shen, "organizational culture can be thought of an organizational *Qi* and that it serves the same functions and operates similarly in organizations as *Qi* is believed to do."

Using an emancipatory approach, Alvesson (2002) underlined the dark side of culture. He avers that culture limits opportunity, and acts as a counterforce to variation and autonomy. Culture not only serves 'positive' functions such as fulfilling people's needs for meaning, guidance, and expressiveness, but also leads to closure of mind and reduction of autonomy. Culture provides direction but also prevents us from 'seeing' and imagining. Culture reflects and reinforces not only (true) consensus but also domination.

This suggests that the strength of an organization's culture can be both an advantage and a disadvantage. Under stable conditions, widely shared and strategically appropriate values can significantly contribute to organizational performance. However, if the environment is changing, strong cultures can be a source of liability. Thus, no generalisations can be made about culture and effectiveness that do not incorporate the relation of the culture to the external environment (Denison, 1990).

## LINKING ORGANIZATIONAL CULTURE TO WIDER SOCIETAL CULTURE

Organizations are social cultures and therefore, understanding organizational culture without understanding the external, societal, cultural context within which organizations are embedded would be incomplete. Schein (1984) went on to say that "organizational culture paradigms are adapted versions of broader cultural paradigms." Cultural values provide elaborate and generalized norms both for the appropriate behaviour for the members and for activities and functions of the system (Enz, 1988; Chatman, 1991). It has been contended that while the structure of organizations seem to have many universal features, their functioning is affected by values that are culture specific (Prakash, 1994). Members of an organization in a given cultural environment would share a common set of assumptions, beliefs, and values, which originate from the local environment.

The work of some researchers who have linked organizational culture and the wider societal culture is examined below.

### Hofstede

Hofstede (1980) was among the first authors who researched differences in cultural values and thus shifted the unit of analysis from individual to society. He developed a model of national cultural patterns by studying a matched sample of 116,000 respondents of a multinational in 40 countries. He found striking cultural differences within a single multinational indicating that employee and managers bring their own ethnicity to the workplace. He argued that people carry "mental programmes" which are developed in the family in early childhood and reinforced in schools and organizations, and that these mental programmes contain a component of national culture. By means of theoretical reasoning and statistical analyses, Hofstede identified four main dimensions on which country's culture differ:

(i) *Power Distance (PD):* The extent to which a society accepts that power in institutions and organizations is distributed unequally. In cultures with high levels of PD, organizations are likely to be hierarchical, there are visible signs of status differences, the salary gap is high, and superiors are entitled to privileges.

(ii) *Uncertainty Avoidance (UA):* Indicates the lack of tolerance in a society for uncertainty and ambiguity, which expresses itself in higher levels of anxiety and energy release, greater need for formal rules and absolute truth, and less tolerance for people or groups with deviant ideas or behaviours.

(iii) *Individualism (IND)/Collectivism (COLL):* IND pertains to societies in which the ties between individuals are loose. COLL as its opposite pertains to societies in which people from birth onwards are integrated into strong, cohesive in-groups, which throughout people's lifetime continue to protect them in exchange for unquestioning loyalty. The major themes (Triandis et al., 1986) of individualism are being distinct and separate from the group, having an emphasis on personal goals, and showing less concern and emotional attachment to the in-groups. In contrast, collectivism conveys self-definitions as part of the group, subordination of personal goals to group goals, concern for the integrity of the group, and intense emotional attachment to the in-group.

(iv) *Masculinity/Femininity-Masculinity (MAS):* Pertains to societies in which social gender roles are clearly distinct (i.e. men are assertive, and focused on material success, whereas women are tender, modest and concerned with quality of life and people); femininity (FEM) pertains to societies in which social gender roles overlap (i.e. both are concerned with the quality of life).

These four dimensions together were found to account for 49 per cent of the variance in country means scores. In addition, the four dimensions show some significant and meaningful correlations with geographic, economic, demographic, and political national indicators. These dimensions affect the organizations as well as their members, for e.g., the dimensions of PD and UA affect organizational structure and processes, while IND/COLL and

MAS/FEM affect the individual and group behaviour in organizations. This has profound consequences not only for the behaviour of people within organizations and for the functioning of organizations as a whole, but also to the validity of the transfer of organization theories and working methods from one country to another.

**Ouchi**

Ouchi (1981) did not directly address the relation of organizational culture to societal culture. However, he examined how the successful Japanese system is different from the American and how firms might successfully modify their cultures. In particular, the following seven characteristics that differentiate the approach used by American (Theory A) and that of the Japanese (Theory J): employment with a firm, evaluation and promotion of personnel, career paths, decision making, control, responsibility, and concern for the personnel. Ouchi's theory Z is a combination of these theories designed to modify American corporate culture and help firms compete more effectively with the Japanese. For e.g., while short-term layoffs are quite common in American firms, layoffs are rare in Japanese firms. His Theory Z suggests that employment with a firm should be fairly long-term in order to develop a semi-permanent work force.

His Theory Z has drawn attention to culture specificity of organizational functioning, challenging the assumption about the universalitic nature of effective work organizations. The implicit conclusion seems to be that the "best" American firms should be concerned with developing the right corporate culture for their social and economic environments.

**Kanungo and Jaeger**

Kanungo and Jaeger (1990) emphasised the role of the environment in which the organization operates on its work culture. They asserted that "the effectiveness of an organization ... depends on how it adapts to its environmental demands by developing an appropriate corporate culture".

They provided a model (Figure 1.2) of how cultural values influence an organization's work culture which in turn influences the behaviour and practices of the management and employees. This organizational work culture shapes both the micro-level individual processes and macro-level organizational processes.

**Fig. 1.2: External and Internal Environment Factors Influencing Organizational Behaviour and Effectiveness (Kanungo and Jaeger, 1990)**

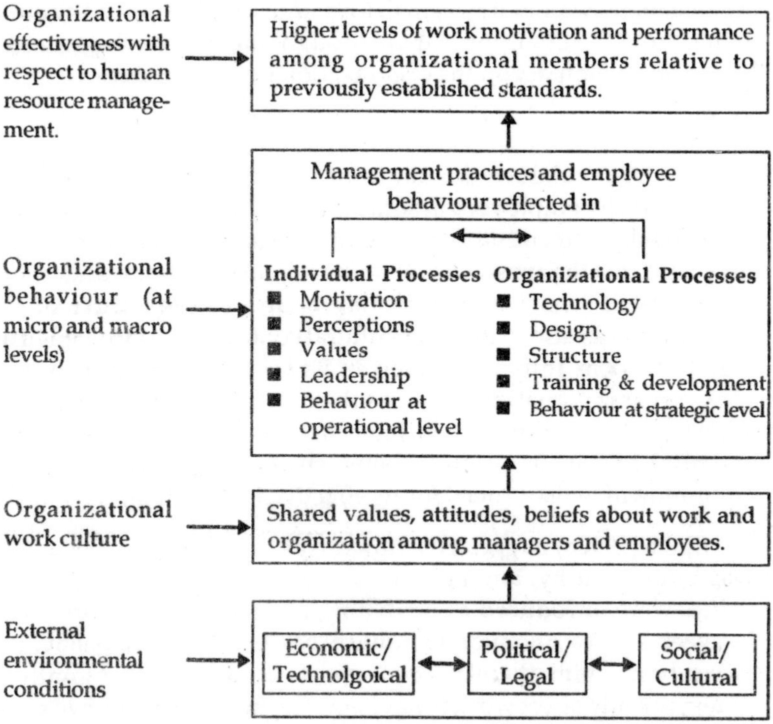


Kanungo and Jaeger identified three major aspects of the environment that influence the organization's internal work culture:

*(a)* *Economic and Technological:* comprising of prevailing labour market conditions, wage levels, development of infrastructure to support technology, and economic conditions like availability of investment capital, inflation rates, interest rates, taxes, etc.

*(b)* *Political and Legal:* comprising of factors like the stability of government, legal system, political interference, and bureaucratic hurdles.

*(c)* *Socio-Cultural:* determines collective norms and values, and individuals beliefs, attitudes and action preferences.

They particularly emphasised the importance of the socio-cultural environment "as a major determinant of organizational effectiveness both within a given country and across various countries in the world." Their model therefore suggests that the organizations are 'open systems' (Katz and Kahn, 1966) and cultural values from the environment are brought into the work place and have a strong impact on the organization's work culture.

**Sinha**

Sinha (1990a) conducted a study on work cultures in India and examined why employees in some organizations are committed to work, while their counterparts in others are alienated from it. He suggested that the answer lies in understanding the immediate work environment which is inextricably bound to the nature of the organization as also to its socio-cultural context. He conceived of an organization as fully embedded in its socio-cultural milieu, and views organizational culture as a sub-culture of the larger engulfing societal culture. Not only is integration within an organization essential but an integration between the organization and its environment is also crucial for its effective functioning.

Sinha (1990a) suggested a framework in which work behaviour was influenced by, among other factors, societal values. Societal values were introduced as mediating variables in the relationship between socio-economic and political context and work behaviour. According to him, there are two sets of social forces that jointly or independently affect work behaviour. The first consists of five social values, namely preferences for *(a)* hierarchical social structures and relationships; *(b)* social networking through own-other dichotomy; *(c)* Sneh-shradha (affection-deference) relationships; *(d)* personalized relationships; and *(e)* power differentials. The second set of functions affecting work behaviour pertains to developmental goals of *(a)* productivity and profit, and *(b)* social justice and welfare to the employees.

According to Sinha, the same socio-cultural values which interfere with productivity in a soft work culture (in organizations which have free access to unlimited government resources) are deployed in a synergetic culture (organizations which are self-reliant in resources) to facilitate work behaviours. Over a period of time, work behaviours turn into habits and habits assume the properties of values. Not only is work itself valued and thereby becomes central in one's life, but it starts being supported by work related values.

Work behaviours, work related values, and work centrality mutually support and constitute the focal variables of work culture. The social values, which still fail to play a facilitating role, lose their salience and become recessive.

**Pareek**

Pareek (1994) emphasised the organization-environment interface to be a vital process in transforming 'organizations' to 'institutions'. According to Pareek (1981), the main process with respect to institution building is "the influence—who influences more, the organization influences the environment, or the environment influences the organization. ....whether the organization merely reacts to the environment or it proacts with the environment so that it is also able to change the environment."

Pareek (1994) termed culture the "rim" (border, edge) of institution building. He defined culture as cumulative preferences of some states of life over others (values), response predispositions towards several significant issues and phenomena (attitudes), organized ways of filling time in relation to certain affairs (rituals), and ways of promoting desired behaviour and preventing undesirable ones (sanctions). People living in a society, by and large, imbibe these and are guided by them. Organizations have their own rituals, sanctions, values, and attitudes, and being part of a society, most of these are replica of the societal culture.

According to his paradigm (Figure 1.3), institution building requires a strong binding context of three cultures : organizational culture, societal culture, and political culture.

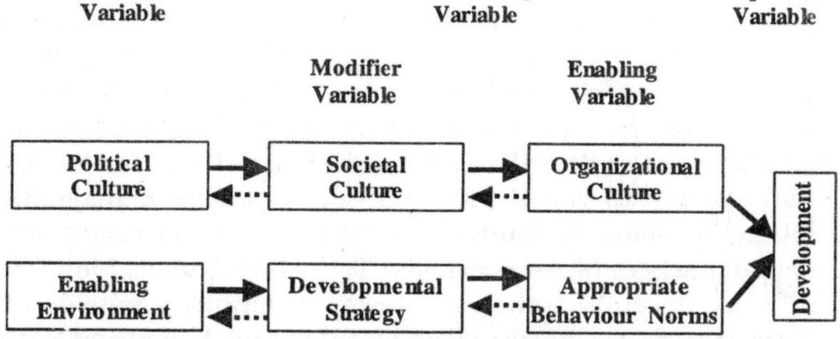


**Fig 1.3: Paradigm of Culture and Development (Pareek, 1994)**

This paradigm proposes that societal culture is a modifier variable, which modifies but does not determine the shape of the dependent variable. Societal culture is important in influencing the strategy of development, but organizational culture is seen as an enabling variable, which facilitates the dependent variable of development. However, political culture, independent variable in this paradigm, is the most important, more or less determining whether or not and how much development will take place. A symbiotic relationship is seen to exist between development and culture.

The preceding discussion indicates that work organizations are configurations of societal needs and objectives. "Society fashions them in its own image having prototypical properties of the larger culture. They are like mini cultures within the larger culture" (Sinha, 1997). Naturally, they have to reflect the major societal values and beliefs.

## ORGANIZATIONAL CULTURE, SOCIETAL VALUES AND WORK BEHAVIOUR

The society in which an organization operates provides the context for understanding the organization's culture. This is indicated by the well-documented comparison made between American and Japanese cultures, i.e. individualism in the U.S. as against collective orientation in Japan, and their implications for organizational culture (Ouchi, 1981; Schwartz and Davis, 1981). This section highlights the extent to which societal culture influences organizational processes, and the attitudes and behaviour of people in the organizations.

A substantial part of the literature dealing with comparative management suggests that there are some differences in attitudes between managers of various countries that are ascribable to the respective cultures. One of the earliest studies by Oberg (1963) showed that managers in Brazil are constrained by cultural factors from following the so-called principles of American management philosophy. Similarly, Lauter (1969), who conducted a study of the relative practices of American and Turkish managers, found that authority decentralization in Turkey is seriously impeded by constraints of a socio-cultural and legal nature. Kelley and Reeser (1973) suggested that Japanese-American managers in Hawaii might be influenced by their ancestral Caucasian culture. Similarly, Gallie (1978) suggested that the differences he observed in the attitudes of the workers in the same Oil Company in Great Britain and France were on account of the cultural differences between the two countries.

However, contrasting results were found by England and Negandhi (1979) who assessed the extent of national differences in perceptions of steelworkers in U.S. and India on the following issues: *(a)* employees' concern about various societal issues, such as crime and pollution; *(b)* importance of job content areas, such as security and good pay; and *(c)* nature of management styles, preferences, and willingness to participate in decision making. They found that national differences in workers perception existed only on such global issues as pollution, national economy, and housing problems, while national differences with respect to job content areas, factors influencing promotions and employee satisfaction, preferences and willingness to participate in decision-making were only marginal. Further, they also highlighted that the inter-country differences in employees' perceptions were as large or larger than the intra-country differences.

Laurent (1981) demonstrated strikingly that employees and managers bring their ethnicity to the workplace. After observing managers from 9 Western European countries and the U.S. working for companies in their native lands (e.g. Swedish managers working for Swedish companies), Laurent replicated his research in one MNC with subsidiaries in each of the 10 original countries. He assumed that managers working for the same MNC would be more similar than their domestically employed colleagues, but instead he found that managers maintained, even strengthened, their cultural differences. When working for a MNC, it appeared that Germans became more Germans, and Americans, more Americans. After replicating his research in 2 additional MNCs, he reached the conclusion that "employees maintain or enhance their culturally specific ways of working when placed within a multinational or global organization." Thus, far from eliminating or reducing national differences, organizational culture maintains or enhances them!

Beck and Moore (1985) explored the linkages between some important dimensions of a national culture (Canadian) and a commercial institution viz. the Chartered Banks. They conducted in-depth interviews with branch managers of the bank, based on critical incidents and metaphors. The underlying assumptions, attitudes and values held by these managers were located within the competing values framework constructed for the broader Canadian culture. The authors pointed out that identification of linkages between the host culture and organizational culture is the first step in understanding the deep significance of business behaviour in a given country.

Arogyaswamy and Byles (1987) suggested that the importance (or relevance) of culture to performance is contingency driven. The conditions that contributed to culture enhancing performance are its internal fit (cohesion and consistency among values and ideologies in the organization) and external fit (linkages to strategy and the environment).

Reddy (1988) argued that cultural values of the members of an organization influence its structure significantly, particularly in the Indian context. In Indian organizations, the cultural values most significant in influencing organizational structure were: dependent proneness, preference for personalized relations, status consciousness, and authority orientation. Similarly, Sinha (1988) commented on a greater penetration of social habits and cultural values into work organizations. According to him, Indian workers, who are by and large rural, bring to their organization, cultural norms and values in their most raw form.

Khandwalla (1988) suggested that the cultural context in which an organization operates is an important determinant of organizational effectiveness, as it serves as difficult to modify constraints on the organization, and influences an organization's strategic variables (goals and strategies), structural and technological variables, process variables (leadership, organizational climate, culture, change), and finally effectiveness variables.

Evan and Damanpour (1988) examined the thrust of current literature on organizational culture, and noted absence of explicit analytical effort to relate organizational culture to societal culture. They proposed linkages between societal culture, organizational culture and development, and argue that organizational effectiveness depends more on the degree of congruence between societal culture and organizational culture, than on each one alone, which in turn will significantly promote societal development.

Jaeger (1990) stated that culture has a two-fold impact on management practices. First, it will influence management behaviour, which might be said to be occurring "naturally." Thus, management behaviour will reflect values of the local culture. Second, culture will influence what is perceived and what is not perceived, and its evaluation. It is this process that will result in resistance to counter-cultural management behaviour.

Mendonca and Kanungo (1990) studied work culture in developing countries and its implications on performance management in organizations. They identified characteristics of the socio-cultural environment (viz. relatively high uncertainty avoidance, low individualism, high power distance, low masculinity, and low abstractive thinking) and internal work culture of the organization, and discussed reasons why such characteristics have facilitating or constraining effects in installation and implementation of the performance management process. They proposed organizational interventions to bring about a cultural fit so that the performance management process reflected the needs and aspirations of managers and their subordinates. They suggested that managers must function as nurturant-task leaders, envisaged as the traditional guru-chela relationship in the Indian context, to overcome the cultural constraints from realizing the full benefits of the performance appraisal process.

Kao, Sinha and Sek-Hong (1994) explored the impact of socio-cultural values and norms on the effective management of work enterprises. They suggest that the design of organizations and management practices cannot be imported wholesale but must develop indigenously within a specific cultural context. Further, nations which have developed at a faster rate have found ways of incorporating contextual societal values in designing their organizations, for e.g. the Japanese.

Bochner and Hesketh (1994) examined employees in a multicultural organization in Australia and found that those from high power distance cultures (e.g. Hong Kong, India) were less open with their superiors than employees from low power distance cultures (e.g. Finland). The former were less inclined to argue against their superiors' decisions and were more cautious about discussing work problems with a superior from a different ethnic background than the latter.

Evans, Hall and Schulli (1995) examined the influence of cultural values on managerial styles, with particular emphasis on Western (USA) and Asian (Hong Kong, Japan, and China) managerial systems. Specific differences in cultural values were found to exist in the areas of human nature, time, family relation, the relation between man and nature, and the supernatural and activity. Some of the major differences between Western and Oriental management styles were explained in terms of the paternalistic value orientation in Asian culture, with respect and obedience towards one's parents extended to include obeying one's boss. It was concluded that the management style is a function of level of industrialisation, but is tempered by cultural factors. Further, management development must be adapted to the requirements of the local culture and managerial style.

Mathur, Aycan and Kanungo (1996) analyzed the difference between the internal work culture of public and private sector organizations in India, to explain the differences in their effectiveness. They found that although there were no differences between managers of the two sectors in perceived socio-cultural characteristics (both being within the same culture), there were differences in internal work culture due to the influence of the enterprise environment (market, mission and ownership). While primary concern of the public enterprises was public security and welfare, that of the private enterprises was to obtain a good return on investment. Compared to public sector organizations, the internal work culture of private enterprises placed greater emphasis on internal locus of control, future orientation in planning, participation in decision-making and obligations towards others in the work context. Accordingly managerial practices in the private sector utilised more effective motivational techniques then those in the public sector. It can therefore be inferred that differences in enterprise environment led to differences in work culture and managerial practices, which may explain the observed differences in effectiveness between the two sectors.

Kim (1999), using the context of Korean organizations, emphasised that to understand Korean corporate culture, with its deep socio-cultural and historical roots, it is necessary to view it against the general cultural, economic and business scenario of the country. Korean social values of Confucianism (generosity, righteousness, etiquette, wisdom, and trust), the patriarchal system of extended large families and the collective community system is reflected in the corporate culture of collectivity-oriented values, strict hierarchies, and familism.

Schwartz (1999) proposed a theory of the types of values on which cultures can be compared and validated it with data collected from over 35,000 respondents (both urban school teachers and college students) in 49 nations from around the world. He identified seven types of values, structured along three polar dimensions: Conservatism vs. Intellectual and Affective Autonomy (dealing with the nature of relation between the individual and the group); Hierarchy vs. Egalitarianism (dealing with power differences); and Mastery vs. Harmony (dealing with the relation of mankind to the natural and social world). Further, Schwartz explicated the implications of national differences in cultural values for three aspects of work: work centrality, societal norms about work, and work goals. Work is likely to be experienced as central to life more in societies where Mastery and Hierarchy values are important and less in societies where Affective Autonomy, Egalitarianism, Harmony, and Conservatism values are important. Further, societal norms are expected to define work more as an entitlement where Egalitarianism and Intellectual Autonomy values are especially important. Finally, the types of work goals whose pursuit is encouraged and rewarded depend in part on the prevailing cultural value emphasized in a society, for e.g. the pursuit of power values is likely to be more acceptable in cultures where Hierarchy and Mastery values are emphasized.

Research evidence indicates that preferences for styles of conflict resolution are influenced by the values of individualism and collectivism. People from collectivistic cultures (e.g. Japan and possibly, India) show a greater preference for accommodation than do people from individualistic cultures, such as the U.S. (Kirkbridge, Tang, and Westwood, 1991; Ohbuchi and Takahashi, 1994; Gabrielidis et al., 1997). Verma (1986) reported that normative considerations and concerns of social consequences of one's actions characterise behaviour in a collectivistic society (India), whereas affective or self-oriented concerns are relatively more important in an individualistic society (USA).

Tinsley and Brett (2001) proposed that cultural differences in conflict management outcomes could be understood by the culturally based norms that managers have for resolving conflict. This hypothesis was tested in on 94 U.S. and 120 Hong Kong Chinese managers. It was confirmed that the traditionally American norms of discussing parties' interests and synthesising multiple issues were exhibited more strongly by American managers, while the traditionally Chinese norms of concern for collective interests and concern for authority appeared more strongly among Hong Kong Chinese managers. American managers were more likely to resolve a greater number of issues and reach more integrative outcomes, while Hong Kong Chinese managers were more likely to involve higher management in conflict resolution. Culture had a significant effect on whether parties selected an integrative outcome rather than an outcome that involved distribution, compromise, higher management, or no resolution at all.

Kirkman, Gibson, and Shapiro (2001) examined the role national culture and values play in determining employee receptivity to the implementation of Self-Managing Work Teams (SMWTs). The authors observed, interviewed, and collected survey data from 378 work teams working in 11 organizations located in 9 countries (Argentina, Belgium, Finland, France, Hong Kong, Indonesia, the Philippines, Puerto Rico, and the U.S.). Results showed that employees responded differently to the implementation of these teams depending on their values derived from the countries in which they live. Subjects were generally more receptive to the teamwork aspect of SMWTs when they valued collective interests more than individual interests; and to the self-management aspect of SMWTs when they valued equity in organizations more than status and power differences; valued work activities more the nonwork activities; and believed they (rather than external forces) controlled their personal and organizational outcomes. In another field survey of 81 Self-Managing Work Teams (SMWTs) in Belgium, Finland, the Philippines, and the United States, the same researchers found that teams higher in collectivism were also more productive, cooperative, and empowered, and teams that were more doing-oriented were also more empowered. The findings suggest that managers who are charged with implementing SMWTs should pay close attention to the predominant cultural values inherent in the teams they lead.

## SUMMARY

Despite apparent variations in the conceptualization of the term organizational culture, there are certain consistencies. Researchers have largely focused on the basic values, beliefs, and assumptions that are present in organizations, the patterns of behaviour that result from these shared meanings, and the symbols that express the links between assumptions, values, and behaviour to members of an organization. A number of different perspectives on organizational culture exist, ranging from anthropological, utilitarian, to approaches that emphasize levels and elements of culture.

Organizational culture, being a microcosm of the encompassing culture, reflects the dominant values and norms of the societal culture, reacting and responding to the socio-economic and political milieu. Although the extent of relationship between societal culture and organizational culture has not been established, research is clear that some relationship does exist between the dominant values and norms of the society and that of the organization. This spells out the importance of studying organizational culture within a context–the Indian socio-cultural context in our case.

# 2

# Indian-ness and Other-ness

## IDENTIFYING "INDIAN-NESS"

It is difficult to identify the main socio-cultural values in a society which has such a long history, diverse ethnic groups, religions, languages, castes, etc. Sinha (1999) laments the problems in understanding and analyzing the psychological characteristics of "the Indian people". While search for a distinctive mark of Indian-ness has been undertaken by many scholars, the attempts have not yielded any unambiguous picture. The Indian psyche is so varied and complex that no claim is made about the picture being complete or free from error. An attempt is made to review the literature on the basic Indian values, preferences, and behaviour dispositions drawing on religio-philosophical and cultural heritage, historical experiences, and the observations of social scientists, in particular those which are directly relevant for organizational functioning.

Taylor (1948) observed that Hindus stress the impersonality of a social order where status and formal obligations outweigh personal relationships. Passivity and conformity have often been considered as basic features of Indian psyche. It was suggested that the very nature of socialization and interactions in the family ensures that the Indian child learns to conform at the cost of personal initiative and capacity to make decisions. Koestler (1960) argued that the joint family system and caste system have been responsible for ingraining reluctance to take decisions and evade responsibility.

Narain (1957) presented a profile of Hindu character based on a variety of sources including ancient religious texts such as the

Bhagvad-Gita, as well as contemporary films and popular proverbs. He described Hindu character as passive and mild, marked by pessimism and asceticism "of the masochist and punitive variety", depressive rather than persecutory, with an id kept under very strict control, a weak ego, and an extremely strong superego.

There is some evidence to suggest that Indians have a high need for power (Hitchcock and Minturn, 1963), and that power maintenance in many instances is based on renunciation, giving away (*'dan'*), sacrifices and self-denial (McClelland, 1975). Sinha (1982) traced the backward linkages of the strong need for power: *(a)* physical proximity in which Indians live for generations, *(b)* pervasive poverty, and *(c)* the caste system.

Psychoanalytically oriented scholars like Lewis (1962), Carstairs (1971) and Spratt (1966) comment on the authoritarian Indian culture and project authoritarian features to Indians (certain amount of rigidity in social conduct, conformity to rules, emphasis on hierarchy, status orientation, etc.). Sinha (1973, 1980) too commented that Indians do manifest certain amount of rigidity in their social and interpersonal conduct, with social do's and don'ts being sharply defined and conformity to them demanded in many spheres of life. There does exist a strong need for power and status orientation among Indians. However, there is no conclusive evidence that Indians are highly anxious, insecure, cynical people with ego-alien sexuality and paranoid dispositions.

Nandy and Kakar (1976) believe that an emphasis on performance efficiency, duties and obligations is indicative of the secondary authoritarianism, a modern version of people's search for order to lean on others which expresses in subordinate's dependence on their leader and the leader's ego satisfaction in providing patronage. Similarly, Kakar (1971), after analyzing the authority patterns in Indian organizations, pointed out that they were dominated by the parental ideology of authority relations. He found that in an overwhelming number of cases (64%) the superior's right to command derived from the traditional-moral factors, though strongly supported by his personality. "In all cases the image of the supervisor was either nurturant or assertive, never impersonal or fraternal... it is the nurturant superior who is held to be the most effective."

In a similar vein, Sinha (1980), drawing upon Indian familial values of affection, dependency and need for personalized relationships, postulated that the 'nurturant-task' leader will be more appropriate and effective under the prevailing socio-cultural conditions. Pandey (1986) found that the superior-subordinate relationship in Indian work organizations is characterized by a great degree of dependence of subordinates who display a great deal of ingratiation in respect of their superiors. Chattopadhyaya (1975) also found this marked "dependence proneness" (Sinha, 1970) spanning from "mud huts to company board rooms."

The Indian approach to work is somewhat different from the Western approach. According to Shri Bhagvadgita, work was prescribed as 'duty' without any concern for the outcomes. However, this duty was not conceived of as socially neutral. On the contrary, duty meant meeting the obligation of one's relations, friends, and even strangers. According to McClleland (1975), "Indians perform work as a 'favour' to others. Work is believed to exhaust a person by draining out his energy which he believes to be precious and limited. Hence, he tends to conserve his energy which he can expend only in return for favour or tangible gains." However, such attitudes towards work are not peculiar to Indians. Early societies throughout the world viewed work as unpleasant and as something which was to be avoided. The attitude towards work underwent a change during the medieval period and later on with the rise of Calvinism in the Western societies. As a result of this, in theses societies work in itself became a value. This kind of change did not take place in the case of Indian society where work continued to be identified with livelihood (De, 1984).

Sinha's (1973) review of a number of studies showed that Indian industries have higher incidence of absenteeism than their Western counterparts, and surprisingly, without definite causes. Higher absenteeism with varying or flimsy causes seems to indicate that Indian workers do not get involved with their work. Ganesh (1982), similarly stated that work as "a concept and a culture has not been internalized in Indian organizations...There is very little concern for *(a)* quality of products and services, *(b)* timeliness, *(c)* costs, *(d)* people who work around, *(e)* employee's future, and *(f)* organizational process. Sinha (1985) claimed, "work in not intrinsically valued in India. There consists a culture of *aram* which roughly means rest and relaxation without (being) preceded by hard and exhausting work". Even today, as Sinha and Sinha (1990) pointed out, Indians view work as a duty to be performed for the sake of one's family.

A preference for showing off is another cultural value, which looks conspicuous in the backdrop of scarcity of resources. Foreign observers have been struck by the extravagance shown in this country. Dayal (1976) has termed this 'status-mindedness'. Individuals are recognized and respected according to their status, which is often ascribed than achieved.

Moddie (1987) delineated the Indian psyche from literary works in contemporary Indian languages and enumerated the following fundamental "Indian traits":

1. Indians' characteristic "tolerance of the good and the bad; the moral and ethical; the immoral and unethical; the efficient and the inefficient...leading to a characteristic ambivalence between word and deed."
2. An essentially narcissistic trait in Indian society, in the Freudian sense as highlighted by Spratt (1966), who found the Indian character narcissistic with a weak superego, and Kakar (1978), who endorsed the "heightened narcissistic vulnerability of the Indian male."
3. An undue allegiance to authority and hierarchy, springing primarily from parental authority patterns in the family, and caste patterns in society.
4. A strong trait of helplessness and a passive fatalistic yielding to *kismet*.

Some social scientists (Kapp, 1963; Weber, 1958) have argued that the passive helplessness of the Indian worker may be due to the influence of the Hindu doctrine of *(a) Moksha* (salvation) through renunciation of all material possessions (*sanyasa*) as an ultimate goal in life; *(b)* the illusory nature of the material world (*maya*); and *(c)* the experience of present life as an outcome of one's actions in the previous life (the 'law of *karma*' in an endless cosmic causal chain). According to Misra and Kanungo (1994), the feeling of helplessness and the attitude of fatalism are acquired through authoritarian practices in the family, the educational system, and the religious traditionalism of the Indian culture. Employees, owing to enduring influences of past socialization, bring with them their habits, norms, and expectations that guide their behaviour in the workplace.

Sinha (1988) identified basic Indian values after an extensive review of literature: *(a)* Hierarchical perspective; *(b)* Power play; *(c)* Preference for personalised relationships; *(d)* Social networking through own-other dichotomy; and *(e)* Collectivistic orientation.

Singh and Bhandarkar (1990) argued that organizations are embedded in the culture. "Successful organizational transformation is possible when the shifts are around these culturally prescribed values, beliefs, and norms." They reconfirmed the previously documented predominant Indian values, using slightly different nomenclatures: *(a)* Relationship orientation; *(b)* Proximity to power; *(c)* Sense of insecurity, anxiety, and fear; *(d)* Simple living and high thinking; and *(e)* High concern for survival.

Sinha (1990b) reviewed a wide range of literature to identify the dominant Indian values and their socio-ecological roots:

1. Embeddedness in one's in-groups. In contrast to the Western conceptualisation of "individuals", Indians are conceived to be "dividuals" (Marriott, 1976) and cannot be understood except with reference to their in-groups. Strong emphasis is placed on maintaining good relations with in-group members, caring and being cared for, forgiving their lapses, glorifying their achievements, etc. Singh and Paul (1985) label the cluster of interconnected behaviours as 'affective syndrome' and Roland (1988) characterises the pattern as 'affective reciprocity' - an intense emotionality in caring and being cared for without asking.
2. Harmony and tolerance. This indicates a preference to maintain harmony and to coexist despite differences. This helps maintain solidarity in in-groups, allows to tolerate, protect, and favour inefficient and even corrupt in-group members. A third-party mediation of disputes in order to save face rather than confrontation is another indication of this value.
3. Duty in contrast to hedonism. Hindu religion prescribes self-control over one's impulses in order to do what is right and proper. *Dharma* is operationalised as discharging one's duties.
4. Preference for personalised relationships even in "situations which demand an exchange relationship" (Sinha, 1990b).

Favouritism and nepotism are natural consequences of this preference.

5. Preference for hierarchy—Indians tend to arrange things, persons, relationships, ideas and almost everything hierarchically. The large power distance (Hofstede, 1980), status consciousness, centralization of decision making, need for a patron to depend upon, etc. are some of the manifestations of this preference (Virmani and Guptan, 1991).

An empirical investigation was conducted by Sinha et al. (1994) to ascertain the extent to which these five values have empirical support across three regions of India-the North (Patna and Varanasi), South (Bangalore and Chennai) and the Central (Lucknow, Kharagpur and Baroda). Some regional differences existed between the North and the South, with the former manifesting strong orientations to meet unjustifiable and inconvenient social obligations and to cultivate personalized relationships. A general factor of collectivism, however, was found common in all the three regions. This factor consisted of three major themes, namely *(a)* familialism, reflecting in-group embeddedness; *(b)* hierarchy, expressed in terms of caste and class differences; and *(c)* maintenance of relationships. This substantiated the findings by others that the Indian culture is collectivistic by nature (Hofstede, 1980; Sinha and Verma, 1987; Triandis, 1994). On the other hand, Tripathi (1988) who reviewed the studies on individualism and collectivism, found that Indians, particularly in achievement situations, are just as competitive as individuals from any Western society. Thus, both kinds of orientations seem to be present.

Chakraborty (1991) enumerated some of the idealized Indian values that are rooted in the ancient psycho-spiritual thoughts as: *(a)* the individual must be respected; *(b)* cooperation and trust; *(c)* jealousy is harmful for mental health; *(d)* '*chitta-shuddhi*' (purification of mind); *(e)* top quality product/services; *(f)* work is worship; *(g)* containment of evil; *(h)* ethico-moral soundness; *(i)* self-discipline and self-restraint; *(j)* customer satisfaction; *(k)* creativity; *(l)* the inspiration to give; and *(m)* renunciation and detachment.

Chakraborty (1993) has argued that these psycho-spiritual values have a normative role in transforming work organizations. Some evidence has been reported to suggest that workers and managers, by practicing yoga, meditation, controlling breathing process, and stilling their turbulent minds, can rise above their hedonistic and selfish desires, and view their work as a duty rather than an unavoidable burden. Work is presented as a "subjective" journey, a pilgrimage, and an inner transformation of mind which is rewarding in itself. The evidence, however, is not conclusive. There are doubts that this transformation process can be realised only in a few persons and may be quickly counteracted by more mundane concerns of the majority of employees. Moreover, not many organizations are likely to be transformed by these psycho-spiritual values.

However, later Chakraborty (1999) identified value paradoxes in the present Indian social milieu. He acknowledged an all-round shift from 'social values still prevalent in the wider society' (commitment and trust within the family, respect for age, simple living, sacred religiosity, etc.) to 'social dis-values of the smaller, privileged but rootless sector of society' (growing in-discipline, wastefulness, regionalism, consciousness of one's rights, etc.). He attributed this to shift from 'character-oriented education' to 'skills-oriented training'. Managers caught in this process tend to reveal varying degrees of ambivalence between correct beliefs on the one hand, and correct practices on the other.

Garg and Parikh (1995), similarly, commented on the Indian culture of transience' that emerges due to a clash between two distinct types of value systems: an agrarian and craft-based culture (anchored in affiliation) as opposed to an industrial and technological society (anchored in achievement). The contrast between the two ethos, has resulted in the fragmentation of the Indian identity, having implications for the work organization.

Chaudhari (2001) emphasised the need to develop an indigenous style of management ("Theory-I" management) that revolves around Indian culture and upbringing. The uniqueness of the Indian psyche makes it difficult for us to copy either the American philosophies of a contractual style of management or the Japanese organizational bonding style, and makes the need for an India-centric management approach very necessary. After a thorough research on more than 3000 managers across the country, he identified the following key character traits of Indians:

- Most Indians value emotional bonds and long-term relationships.

- Most Indians value growth opportunities and commitment.
- Our cultural roots (of tolerance etc.) often makes us complacent.
- Lack of patriotism at a macro level leave us aimless.

Granting that socio-cultural values do penetrate into organizational life, the basic issue is:

*(a)* Whether such values may be taken as given and hence the workplace should be designed around societal values (Sinha, 1990a; Kao, Sinha and Sek-Hong, 1994; Kao, Sinha and Wilpert, 1999).

*(b)* Or, should the workplace be structured according to some normative values and norms, relevant to organizational goals, with the assumption that the societal values will eventually yield to the new values (Udy, 1970, Tripathi, 1990).

This dilemma becomes even more confusing in the case of multinationals operating in India, where the socio-cultural beliefs may or may not be congruent with technological requirements or Western principles of management.

## COMPARING INDIAN-NESS WITH OTHER-NESS: IMPLICATIONS FOR WORK BEHAVIOUR

'*East is East and West is West, and never the twain shall meet...*' (Kipling, 1865-1936).

This famous quote suggests that there exist profound differences in thinking between East and West. Social scientists wonder 'will the twain really not meet', or with the globalization of business and the jet-age of travel, with frequent intermingling across national boundaries, the twain will meet somewhere. In a world that can only survive through global cooperation, such differences should be explored and understood. For illustrative purposes, in this section cultural pattern of America, France, Finland in comparison with India will be highlighted.

America today is at throes of change. With Barack Hussein Obama as the 44th President of United States of America, values of America will change, and perhaps change profoundly. An African-American, who is half-Muslim, with part madrasaa education, has won the 2008 presidential race by a landslide. The symbolism of a black in the White House, who 40 years ago was struggling to sit next to a white man on a bus, has shown that America has in it to finally give respect to a black man at the highest level possible. This highlights the American belief in equality and dignity. In fact, one theme running consistently in researches on the American national character is equalitarian aspects of American authority relations (Mead, 1940; Bateson, 1942, Fromm, 1947, Gorer, 1948, Splinder, 1948, Parsons, 1949, Erikson, 1950, Riesman, 1950, Lipset, 1960, McClosky and Schaar, 1965, Hofstadler, 1965). Karlins et al. (1969) gave a summary of three studies to trace changes in American values. Some of the values suggesting assertiveness and achievement (e.g. ambitious, aggressive, and efficient) show a decline by 1967 (e.g. industrious, alert); on the other hand, a lack of asceticism (e.g. pleasure loving) and materialism show a notable increase. Perhaps, the Obama-effect will be to add hope and a willingness to embrace change to this list.

Lipset (1963) emphasized two main values of equality and achievement for the Americans, from which many American characteristics can be derived. He stressed three aspects of equality: basic social equality, equality of opportunity, and prescriptive implications for non-interference by others. Some characteristics that can be derived from equality are: competition, status uncertainty, conspicuous consumption, 'other-directedness', 'popular culture', relative equality of children, humanitarianism, informality, and rejection of authority. Lynn (1991) compared "competitiveness" in 42 countries, and found that "competitiveness" scores for countries ranged from highest in the Indian subcontinent to lowest in European countries (France, Norway, etc.). On comparing India, France and USA, the scores were found to be highest for India (20.49), followed by USA (18.08), and lastly France (14.41). Lipset (1963) stressed the values of the French revolution- equalitarianism, as well as universalism and achievement.

Crozier (1964) recognised a cultural pattern of dependent individualism in France, meaning a need for strict authority of hierarchical superiors, while simultaneously stressing their personal independence from any collectivity. He noted that in contrast to the American bureaucracies, the French bureaucracies characteristically developed excessive centralization and extreme isolation between different strata by avoiding face-to-face relationships involving subordination, using impersonal rules and referring decisions upward in a centralized hierarchy. The Americans also used impersonal rules, which were more often procedural than substantive. Both countries, however, shared the value of equalitarianism leading to resistance to authority.

The influence of the French educational system on the maintenance of large power distances was commented upon by Marceau (1977). In French organizations, lower- and higher-level employees have different educational backgrounds and legal status: higher-educated employees are "cadres" and lower-educated employees "non-cadres", and transfer between the two groups is very difficult.

De Gramont (1969) listed some 'classically French traits' as the 'national vice', skepticism, uncooperativeness, and mistrust. According to him, "the most celebrated French trait is that of individualism". On the other hand is Coleman's (1941) review of generally recognized American characteristics: "bragging and boasting", "exaggeration", and "national conceit". Americans are not only judged "practical", but also "opportunist" (Peabody, 1985). Comparative studies have consistently shown the Americans to be optimistic, the French pessimistic (Inkeles, 1960). For purposes of comparison with Indian values, Sinha's (1999) comprehensive attempt at determining "the Indian national character" is reviewed. He pointed some "typical" value-preferences and patterns of behaviour like passivity and conformity, absence of "killer instinct", hierarchical structuring, dependence proneness, collective as contrasted with individual orientation, co-existence of contrasting values and behaviour dispositions, and resulting dissonance in work-life (Sinha and Sinha, 1990).

Leites (1969) suggested that carrying through decisions is a conflict dilemma for the French, for Americans this might be less problematic. He argued that the French view change as a danger, which can lead to immobilism, with action in the end only to avoid a worse outcome. They tend to avoid commitment to a decision, retaining freedom of choice and allowing for flexibility and "suppleness". There is more optimism that the situation may improve through waiting, again favouring last-minute action and improvisation. Similar results were reported by Pelissolo and Lepine

(2000), who studied a 602-subject community sample (263 men and 339 women; aged 15-88 yrs), representative of the French population and found that French were low on novelty seeking and higher on the need to avoid harm to oneself, when compared to Americans.

A cross-cultural study of personal values by England, Agarwal and Dhingra (1974) found that North American managers tend to be very pragmatic. Their personal values emphasise productivity, profitability, and achievement. Managers from India, on the other hand, tend to be less pragmatic and more moralistic. Their values emphasize equity, fairness, and the overall good of the work force.

Bass and Burger (1979), studied managers in 12 countries and found that: (1) French managers were less concerned about their subordinate's welfare; (2) Indian managers were most dependent on higher authority and followed bureaucratic rules; (3) Dutch managers were more co-operative with others, whereas the French were least; and (4) U.S. and Latin American managers emphasized greater interpersonal skills and competence than other nationalities. Further, different cultures had varying tolerance for risk taking, and produced managers accordingly. Managers' risk tolerance in different countries were given as: USA 89 per cent, France 61 per cent, Scandinavia 61 per cent, and India 50 per cent.

Pagès et al. (1979) remarked that French society as compared to U.S. society was characterized by a greater dependence of the average citizen on hierarchy and rules. The society of Finland, too, is less built on hierarchy and rules than in the USA. French academics are also more likely to stress intellectual rules and present broad conclusions unsupported by data, while American academics usually base their writings on extensive data, but present fewer conclusions. The French tend to reason by deduction, the American by induction (Hofstede, 1991).

Hofstede (1980) showed that French respondents, particularly technicians, attributed the most positive characteristics to a persuasive-paternalistic boss, i.e. they did not easily decentralize and did not stop short-circuiting intermediate hierarchical levels. On the contrary, Williams et al. (1966) showed that close supervision was associated with less positive attitudes to the boss among U.S. workers. Meade (1967) found that authoritarian leadership, as compared to democratic and laissez-faire leadership, maximized both morale and productivity in Indian school children, whereas the opposite had been found in the U.S.

Hofstede (1984), studied international differences in work-related values, and suggested that countries could be compared with respect to what motivates them. For instance, people of USA were motivated by personal, individual success, in the form of wealth, recognition, and self-actualization. France and Asian countries were motivated by security and belongingness, individual wealth being less important than group solidarity. In contrast, North European countries (including Finland) were motivated by success and belongingness, success being measured partly in the quality of human relationships.

French anthropologist d'Iribarne (1989) compared subsidiaries of the same French MNC in France, USA, and the Netherlands. He identified a different base philosophy (*logique*) in the three countries: honour in France, contractual relations in the U.S., and consensus in the Netherlands. He described the French principle of organizing as 'the rationale of honour', i.e. one's rank is less imposed by the group than determined by tradition: 'a strict rule but a lenient practice'. Another issue studied was a preference for resolving conflicts by compromise and negotiation. In France, there is occasionally a lot of verbal insult, both between employers and subordinates, but with a typically French 'sense of moderation', which enables parties to continue working together while agreeing to disagree. In sharp contrast is the way of handling conflicts in USA, where there is a feeling that conflicts should be resolved by a good fight: 'Let the best man win.'

Reiger and Durhane (1990) reviewed cultural dimensions in studies of organizations for developing and developed countries. According to their summary, India is characterized by personalism/paternalism (Kakar, 1971), emphasis on ascription/achievement (Nambudiri and Saiyadain, 1978) and fatalism (Narain, 1967); France by hierarchy and bypassing, formality norms, individual competitiveness, ability to command, and distrust of outsiders (Crozier, 1964); USA by individual competitiveness (Hsu, 1985) and ability to command (Pfeffer, 1981); and Latin America by elitism and social stratification (Whyte, 1969), emphasis on ascription/achievement (Harbison and Meyers, 1959) and fatalism (Gillin, 1960).

Comparative studies have shown Finland to be the least masculine, followed by France, and lastly the U.S. using various indicators like gender stereotypes (Fioravanti, Gough, and Frere, 1981), percentage of women in management ranks of subsidiaries in various countries of the same multinational (Ford, 1985), attitudes related to rejection of abortion as being positively related to masculinity (Inglehart, 1990), descriptions of actual self and ideal self from University students (Williams and Best, 1990); acceptance of homosexuality as being negatively related to masculinity (Halman, 1991), preference for maintenance of economic growth over preservation of the environment as being positively correlated with power distance and masculinity (Dunlap, Gallup and Gallup, 1993). In a similar vein, Hofstede et al. (1998) compared the percentage of women in both parliaments and governments of 22 developed countries and found that Finland had the highest percentage of women parliamentarians and government ministers (33.5% and 35% respectively), followed by U.S. (10.4% and 21.1% respectively) and then France (5.9% and 6.5% respectively), in keeping with the country's position on Masculinity and Uncertainty Avoidance. Moilanen et al. (2000) also reported Finland to be feminine and egalitarian. Sinisalo (1995) traced the changes in Finland's societal values over the years by comparing occupational plans of two cohorts, 1977 (778 Ss) and 1989 (607 Ss), of Finnish comprehensive school graduates, aged 16. It was found that traditional female occupations lost attractiveness during the 1980s while interest in creative, enterprising occupations rose, suggesting that Finland became lower on femininity after 1980s.

Peabody (1985) emphasized certain French values as: *(a)* a tendency to classification and codification; *(b)* belief in the power of ideas and in an intellectual caste appointed to guard them; *(c)* an emphasis on orderly thought and theoretical principles over experience; and *(d)* an emphasis on foresight before action and on control by the intellect. He summarized the differences between French and American nationalities with respect to five issues: (1) Social relationships: French tend to distinguish clearly between their public roles and "real self," while the distinction between "public" and "private" spheres is less clear cut for Americans. (2) Social rules: The Americans emphasise relatively general principles, while more specific substantive applications are left to be worked out for each concrete case. The French emphasize more on impersonal rules-more often substantive as well as procedural than Americans. (3) Control of hostility: French avoid public hostility by formal politeness and absence of public smiling. They regard the American spontaneous friendliness as superficial and hypocritical. (4) Impulse-control: For the French, impulses are not subjected to suppression by internalised inhibitions, instead, they are likely to be consciously recognized. In contrast, for the Americans, the impulse-control tends to be highly internalized. (5) Authority and hierarchical relations: In French society, due to the actual status differences, value of equality leads to resentment and avoidance by the subordinates. In contrast, Americans accept face-to-face subordinate relationships provided the subordination is minimized by informality, and is functionally specific.

Johnson (1985) while discussing the Western concept of "self", commented that stereotypically, Americans emerged as open, egalitarian, assertive, relatively unself-conscious, and not as attentive to nonverbal or contextual cues in the public presentation of self. The sense of heightened individualism affects the balance of family relationships and obligations. Children are socialized simultaneously to be obedient, to submit to rules which protect the rights of others, and to develop a progressive independence. Contrastingly, in India, the acknowledgement of interdependencies in family, work, and friendship relations is integral to successful social navigation. As Markus and Kitayama (1991) pointed out, self in India is defined more in terms of social relationships.

In a cross-cultural comparison of self-concepts among Indian and American college students, Dhawan et al. (1995) observed that while defining themselves Indian students made more references to social identities. While American students had a significantly larger proportion of responses for self-identity, their Indian counterparts described themselves more in terms of role, group, caste, class, and gender role identity.

Indians are believed to be more context sensitive than their counterparts in the West (Sinha and Kanungo, 1997). Indians decide the appropriateness of a behaviour by considering three aspects of context: *(a)* the person (i.e. *patra*) they are relating to; *(b)* the time (i.e. *kal*) at which a particular behaviour is to be performed; and *(c)* ecology (i.e. *desh*) or the setting of the behaviour.

The cultural assumptions in the USA may be summarized as: (1) Families/children are in the private domain. (2) Children/elder care, i.e. nurturance is rightfully the province of women, either because they do it better or because it is somehow their specific job. (3) In an individualistic, achieving society, balance between work and personal life is not a high priority goal, instead career and work success are more important. At least the first and third of these assumptions seen to be untrue in the Indian cultural context.

Juvonen (2000) reviewed a series of experiments that examined differences in failure accounts for American and Finnish students. The findings from the American sample of 4th, 6th, and 8th grade students show that by 4th grade (1) students understand that low ability and lack of effort attributions affect teacher and peer approval, and (2) that students vary their own failure accounts in ways that are consistent with their beliefs regarding linkages between attributions and social responses. It was found that Finnish students, unlike their American counterparts, were willing to portray themselves as low in ability, since they believed that it facilitated both teacher and peer approval as well as promoted perceptions of self-effacement and honesty.

Mark (1999) compared characteristics of the world's main business cultures in different countries, and summarized the differences between American and French cultures. He delineated the French business atmosphere, communication, and approach as *(a)* very hierarchical, *(b)* flexible, dynamic, and innovative task approach, *(c)* long-term view of business, *(d)* time planning more synchronic, with many interruptions, *(e)* relatively long working hours, *(f)* hard work and professionalism, although important, workaholism viewed negatively, *(g)* moderate orientation towards change and a particular affinity for technological advances, *(h)* relatively formal communication, *(i)* emphasis on verbal fluency and indirect, sophisticated approach, *(j)* high respect for authority, based on competence, *(k)* strong elite business network, *(l)* respect for senior executives, *(m)* tolerance for authoritative leadership, *(n)* intellectual approach to business with brainstorming and discussions, and *(o)* priority for establishing relationships first, and then getting on with tasks. In contrast, the American culture is *(a)* highly individualistic, which may make real teamwork difficult, *(b)* meritocratic and achievement oriented, *(c)* preference for flat hierarchies, *(d)* tough time-planners, *(e)* excessive working hours encouraged, *(f)* short-termism, *(g)* high service orientation, *(h)* relatively informal business communication, *(i)* factual and direct business tone, *(j)* task-oriented and extremely positive, *(k)* meetings with clear agenda and extensive written communication, *(l)* welcoming of new ideas and fresh approaches, *(m)* preference for decisive leadership, and *(n)* small business elite and encouragement to networking. Further, there is higher staff turnover in U.S. as compared to France. According to Mark, understanding of different business cultures is vital to those working in international teams.

In contrast, a few researchers have found universality of certain values in all cultures. Prominent among them were England and Lee (1974), who found that although there were inter-country differences among the personal values of managers, some values were universal. More successful managers appeared to favour pragmatic, dynamic, achievement-oriented values, while less successful managers prefer more static and passive values. Similarly, Kumar (1981) found similarity between characteristics of successful executives in India and the U.S., with high successful executives exceeding in intelligence, achievement orientation, domination, exhibitionistic tendencies, lack of defensiveness, relative unconventionality, optimism regarding career prospects, self worth, and perception of various organizational dimensions.

Schwartz and Bardi (2001) also noted that beyond the differences in the value priorities of national groups there is a widespread consensus regarding the hierarchical order of values. Benevolence, self-direction, and universalism values were found to be consistently most important; power, tradition, and stimulation values were least important; and security, conformity, achievement, and hedonism were in between.

## SUMMARY

This chapter shed light on the unique assimilation of both indigenous and universal values in the Indian socio-cultural context. Some indigenous 'Indian' values identified are: familial orientation, collectivism, dependence proneness, fatalism, personalized relationships, and harmony and tolerance. Some salient universal values that can also be culled out are: high need for achievement, power play, preference for hierarchy, and respect for authority, age and seniority. Although various constraints of Indian values and social institutions have been indicated by many Western scholars like Kapp (1963) and Weber (1958), the picture at times appearing impressionistic, stereotypical, and even caricature-like (Sinha, 1988), what is striking is a cheerful optimism on the so-called "Indian" values in the 90s and beyond (Chakraborty, 1991,1993; Sinha, 1990). Similarly, Sinha (1988), Tripathi (1988) and Pareek (1988) also acknowledge the uniqueness of Indian values and suggest different ways to bring out the best from them. It has been shown that Indian socio-cultural reality is not antagonistic to modernization and industrialization (Seth, 1988). Moreover, there is a growing realization that "Indian socio-cultural values are not dysfunctional to the functioning of organizations, provided that an optimum fit can be obtained between individual values and organizational values" (Prakash, 1994).

The cross-cultural comparison of values helps us understand *(a)* relativity of values; and *(b)* the influence of the wider cultural context on individual and organizational values. This chapter has highlighted the differences between socio-cultural values among four nations: India, America, France and Finland. It would suffice to say that these four cultural contexts are patterned along different lines, with some similarities and differences with one-another. For e.g. Hofstede (1998) argues that countries like Finland and the U.S. are so different (with reference to Masculinity/Femininity dimension), that they will continue to develop different responses to issues of organizational life, career, or international relations-in spite of the increasing impact of technology and its companion, the "global" market.

This raises some pertinent issues: *(a)* Are socio-cultural values of different nations stereotypical and differences in nationalities exaggerated? Do national differences have any relevance today when the world has transformed itself into a 'global village', with resulting homogenizing influences? *(b)* If not, does the contrast between Indian, American, French, and Finnish socio-cultural values have any relevance for functioning of both organizations and its members? And *(c)* To what extent does a match between Indian socio-cultural values and a multinational's culture influence employee outcomes like employee health, employee turnover, and organizational commitment.

# 3
# Health at the Workplace

## UNDERSTANDING HEALTH

Health is, undoubtedly, an indispensable quality in human beings. The growth of science, technology, materialistic predominance, and hazards and complexities of modern day living has caused a marked deterioration in mental health of people in modern societies. During the past few decades behavioural scientists have given due importance to health, particularly health at the work place.

The roots of the attempts to define mental health go back to Hippocrates' age. His notion of hysteria was essentially a mental health notion. Before the second half of the twentieth century, mental health was considered as the absence of mental illness. As a consequence, mental health was not considered in its more positive connotation. Soddy (1950) gave an operational description of individual mental health as the responses of the healthy person to life without strain, capable of both friendships and aggressiveness, consistent and self-reliant but can accept aid, and private beliefs being a source of strength. Argyris (1951), as an advocate of 'positive mental health' suggested that a person with positive mental health should have the ability to understand the realities which exist both externally and internally when he strives to be aware of acceptance of self. Conrad (1952) attempted to differentiate positive health from non-health and negative health. To her, "positive health consists of ways of living that are beyond the frontiers of mere social existence implied by negative health....this category (positive health) applies when there is evidence that the individual fully utilizes a capacity or is working in that direction." A qualitative distinction between mental health and mental illness was also established by Rumke (1955), who was of the view that "the understanding of the disturbances of a sick man hardly contributes to the understanding of normal man."

Maslow and Mittelman (1951) suggested the following criteria for normal psychological health: (1) adequate feeling of security; (2) adequate self-evaluation; (3) adequate spontaneity and emotionality; (4) efficient contact with reality; (5) adequate self-knowledge; (6) integration and consistency of personality; (7) adequate life goals; (8) ability to learn from experience; (9) ability to satisfy the requirements of groups; and (10) adequate emancipation from the group or culture.

Reviewing the psychological literature on mental health, Jahoda (1958) noted six aspects of positive mental health: (1) attitudes of an individual toward his own self; (2) growth, development, or self-actualisation; (3) integration; (4) autonomy; (5) perception of reality; and (6) environmental mastery. Schultz (1977) noted that there is no single description of psychological health on which all psychologists or personality theorists would agree. Perhaps the only point on which most theorists would agree fully is that "psychologically healthy persons are in conscious control of their lives." He outlined seven criteria of sound mental health: extension of self, warm relation of self to others, emotional security, realistic perception, skills and assignments, self-objectification, and a unifying philosophy of life.

The preamble of the World Health Organization's Charter defined health as "a state of complete physical, mental and social well-being, not merely the absence of disease or infirmity" (Monopolis, Moraitis, Kouvaris and Golanopoulou, 1977). The dictionary of Behavioural Sciences also defined mental health as a state of reality, good adjustment, feeling of well-being and actualization of one's potentialities and capacities.

Early theories of organizational behaviour laid strong emphasis on the 'economic' contract between employer and employee, negating the psychological or human aspects of the work life. But Hawthorne studies recognized the importance of human interaction as a critical part of the work situation. This historical incident encouraged psychologists to initiate researches concerning personal development and psychological well-being of employees.

Fountain (1945) was the first to use the term mental health in industry. Subsequently, Rennie et al. (1947) reviewed applications of psychiatry to industry in America during the 1930s. Most of the studies used the title 'Toward Industrial Mental Health' which suggests the development of the concept in industry (Murrell, 1978). Most of the early writings of psychologists tended to be theoretical and largely related to personality. None of these concepts is clearly related to the work situation, although Argyris (1964) discussed the integration of the individual into the organization. Buck (1972) suggested that "A mentally healthy worker has no special problem with his work, no worry about things related to the job, no reporting of getting angry over little things on the job and no feeling of worthlessness."

In 1962, Kornhauser gave new thought to the concept of mental health with direct practical industrial data. According to him, mental health comprises "those behaviours, attitudes, perceptions, and feelings that determine a worker's overall level of personal effectiveness, success, happiness, and excellence of functioning as a person." It concerns the complex continuations of inner and outer behaviour which result in what is judged to be satisfactory or less satisfactory psychological and social functioning. Kornhauser (1965) stated, "in so far as his entire job and life situation facilitate and support feelings of adequacy, inner security, and meaningfulness of his existence, it can be presumed that his mental health will tend to be good. He pointed out that mental health is a continuum running from high (good) to low or not good mental health; and it is not concerned with mental-ill-health or mental illness. Further, he showed that the proportion of the workers with high mental health steadily decreased as the work became less skilled. There was no difference between any levels of workers in terms of dissatisfaction regarding physical conditions of dust, dirt, heat, noise, etc., with all of them being equally dissatisfied. He concluded that physical conditions do not elicit positive or negative attitudes on the lower or higher mental health of his occupational groups.

Indian literature on the definition and criteria of mental health has been scant, apart from a few passing references like: "The concept of ideal social functioning is equivalent to 'positive mental health'" (Carstairs and Kapur, 1976) and "in the larger context, mental health is the other name for quality of life" (Wig, 1979). Mental health professionals, however, agree that positive mental health is not merely absence of mental illness but something different (Nagraja, 1983).

## FACTORS CONTRIBUTING TO (ILL)-HEALTH

A review of empirical research in the area of employee health indicates a relative lack of activity by I/O psychologists. Beehr and Newman (1978) postulated 2 reasons: (1) the belief that employee health is not considered as important as other work-related events such as job performance; and (2) the belief that physical rather than social or psychological events cause employee illness. Gradually, the recognition has occurred that health or illness is the result of the mind-body interaction, and the multidimensional environment has now been recognized as having an important influence on health. Two kinds of stressors have been identified as being potent in predicting employee health: organizational/job stressors and social/cultural factors at the workplace.

## ORGANIZATIONAL/JOB STRESSORS

Murrell (1978) suggested that the following characteristics may lead to mental health: job security, physical conditions of work, job surroundings, pay as distinguished from income, use of interesting work, repetitiveness and machine-pacing, the speed and intensity of work, social conditions such as supervision, relationship with coworkers or the company, job status and opportunities for advancement, the importance of the work being done, and the level of income.

After reviewing the literature related to specific work environment and mental health, Kasl (1978) reported that poor mental health was associated with:

1. Conditions at work: exposure to health and safety hazards, unpleasant work conditions, necessity to work fast and to expend a lot of physical effort, excessive and inconvenient hours.
2. Work itself: lack of use of skills and abilities, perception of job as uninteresting, repetitious work, especially on a constantly moving assembly line, role overload due to a discrepancy between resources and job demands.
3. Shift work: fixed afternoon and rotating shifts, which affect time oriented body functions, and load to difficulty in role

behaviour, if the role activities are normally performed during the time of day when the worker is on the shift.

4. Supervision: unclear or conflicting job demands, close supervision and no autonomy (Quinn, Seashore, and Mongione, 1971), lack of feedback from supervisor, reports of problem with supervisor (Buck, 1972).
5. The organization: working on the boundary of the organization.
6. Wages and promotion: inadequate income, perception of promotional opportunities as unfair or too slow, both over-promotion and under-promotion (Brook, 1973).

Researchers have identified various factors at the workplace that lead to poor physical and mental health. House and Rizzo (1972) found that role conflict led to tension and fatigue. Margolis, Kroes and Quinn (1974) found that non-participation at work and lack of role clarity were significantly related to physical and mental ill-health, escapist drinking, depressed mood, low self-esteem, life dissatisfaction, low motivation to work, and turnover intention.

Job satisfaction has also been found to be associated with mental health (Gechman and Wiener, 1975), health disorders (Rosse and Hulin, 1985), and stress (Rahman, 1989). Gavin and Axelrod (1977) found that underutilisation of skills, job insecurity, variation in workload, role conflict and ambiguity, and lack of participation produced high anxiety, depression, and irritation among managers. Martin (1984) found that inability to leave one's job along with role overload predicted acute and chronic mental health problems. In a study of 220 executives from New Zealand, McCormick and Cooper (1988) found that threat of job loss was the best predictor of mental health.

Quinn and Shepard's (1974) survey revealed that six measures of job stress had a significant positive correlation with three job satisfaction measures (job satisfaction, motivation to work, and intention to leave the job), and with three mental health measures (depressed mood, self-esteem, and life satisfaction). House et al., (1979) found that perceived job stress was consistently positively correlated with self-reported angina, ulcers, and neurotic symptoms, and with hypertension and other heart disease risk factors. Christopher's (1982) study on middle managers found a significant positive correlation between role conflict and physical and psychological strains. Frese (1985) examined the correlation between stress at work and psychosomatic complaints in a large sample of blue-collar workers, and found that objective conditions of work stress influenced the development of subjective stress and psychosomatic complaints. Mathieu and Hamel (1989), similarly, found role stress to exerted a negative influence on employees' mental health, which in turn tended to lower commitment as well as job satisfaction.

Hendrix (1985) in a study of 612, 18-74 year olds found that perceived stress was predicted by a combination of individual and job-related characteristics. Stress, in turn, affected individual and organizational health and effectiveness by causing increase in cold/flu episodes, somatic symptoms, and decreased job satisfaction.

In India, Srivastava (1983) examined the relationship between role stress and mental ill-health in a sample of white-collar employees. Role stress significantly correlated with various symptoms of neuroticism, e.g. free-floating anxiety, obsessive neurosis, phobic neurosis, neurotic depression, and somatic concomitants of anxiety. In another study, Banerjee (1989) found a negative correlation between organizational role stress and various dimensions of mental health in both manufacturing and non-manufacturing organizations. Similar results were reported by Jagdish and Srivastava (1989), who also found a significant negative relationship between perceived occupational stress and six symptoms of sound mental health (positive self evaluation, realistic perception, integration of personality, autonomy, group oriented attitudes, and environmental mastery).

Srivastava and Singh (1988) studied the relation of Organizational Role Stress (ORS) and mental health, and the moderating effects of approach and avoidance strategies, in 300 industrial supervisors. A significant positive relationship was noted between role stress and mental ill-health. The approach coping group reported more role stress, but scored lower on the measure of mental ill-health in comparison with the avoidance-coping group, suggesting that approach-coping behaviour alleviated and avoidance coping behaviour intensified the harmful effects of role stress on mental health.

Ganster and Schaubroeck (1991) reviewed and summarized literature on work stress with special focus on studies that examined the effects of work characteristics on employee health. Although convincing evidence that stressors cause health problems did not emerge, indirect evidence was strongly suggestive about the effect of work experiences on physiological and emotional responses.

In a sample of 74 adult nurses working in a psychiatric hospital, Thompson and Page (1992) found that subjects who reported higher emotional exhaustion and depersonalisation also reported a greater range of discrepant aspects of their job and expressed pessimism regarding improvement in the same aspects.

Kirckcaldy (1993) found that though the scores of 30 police officers on the Occupational Stress Indicator showed relatively high interpersonal job stress, their satisfaction with the job itself remained high. Total job stress was significantly negatively correlated with job satisfaction (-0.41), and significantly positively correlated with mental ill-health (0.56).

Ganster, Fox, and Dwyer (2001) tested the role of stressful demands and personal control to predict employee's health care costs in a sample of 105 full-time nurses. Both subjective and objective measures of workload demands were found to interact with personal control perceptions in predicting the cumulative health care costs over the ensuing 5-year period. Tonic elevations in salivary cortisol mediated the effects of demand and control on health care costs. Neither the job demands variables (both pace and amount of work) nor physiological reactivity measures, however, explained subsequent mental health.

Wilikinson (1997) identified the work environment as one of the main sources of stress. Its most marked affects occur if: *(a)* employees have no degree of control over their work; *(b)* employees perceive the work to be meaningless and not worthwhile; *(c)* employees fail to develop an affinity with fellow workers as a social support system and fail to identify with it through their work. According to him, the following stressors at work were critical to the physical and psychosocial well-being of employees:

*(a)* *The work environment:* this includes various hazards like excessive noise, exposure to toxic chemicals, etc., smoke-

filled atmosphere, building condition and layout, staff facilities, machinery and equipment.

(b) *The job:* this includes factors related to job design, shiftwork and internal rotation, work overload or sometimes even underload, role conflict, and role ambiguity.

(c) *The organization:* this includes the organization's culture (particularly a very demanding culture) and autocratic management styles.

(d) *Other causes:* like discrimination, limited authority, rapid changes in technology, etc.

Some working conditions, however, lead to better health even in people with most stressful jobs. Maddi and Kobasa (1984) compared the healthiest and least healthy middle managers at Illinois Bell in the high-stress period after its divestiture from AT & T, and found that no corporate level, type of job, or personality characteristics could predict that individual's health. Instead, they found three qualities to be present in healthy managers:

(a) *Commitment:* Healthy people have a sense of what they are doing is meaningful. They have a clear vision about where they are going that is largely in line with their basic values, allowing them to be involved and motivated in their work.

(b) *Control:* Healthy people feel free to take action to do what needs to be done to complete their job and achieve their vision.

(c) *Challenge:* Healthy people feel open to learning continually from others about how to do things better and improve their capabilities. They see change as an opportunity to develop their skills and to learn.

Jaffe, Scott and Tobe (1994) added a fourth factor based on research findings (Berkman and Syme, 1979) on the importance of social support:

(d) *Connection:* Healthy people feel that they can call on the help and support of other people, and that their coworkers are colleagues, not competitors.

These four C's-commitment, control, challenge, and connection-are all important for people who are effective at high-performance work.

**Social/Cultural Factors at the Workplace**

Furnham and Schaeffer (1984) examined Person-Environment (P-E) congruence at work and confirmed the hypothesis that employees who experienced low P-E congruence had higher level of mental distress.

Levi (1984) examined the relationship between work, stress, and health, and presented the ideal conditions of work and of the work environment. Work should provide a goal, a meaning, content and structure for life and give the worker a sense of identity, self-esteem, companions, friends, and material means. If the fit between workers and job is poor, and the worker is unable to control his work condition or copes ineffectively and lacks social support, potentially pathogenic reactions (cognitive, emotional, behavioural, or physiological) occur, and can lead to physical/ mental disease.

Repetti (1987) examined the relation between the social environment at work and mental health. Two aspects of social environment were used: (1) a common social environment perceived by all the participants in the same work setting, and (2) an individual social environment perceived by one individual in the same work setting. Data was collected in two phases. In the first phase, 302 volunteer employees from 37 bank branches filled Social Environment Survey. In the second phase, 70 female volunteer employees (out of 264 females in the first phase), completed the Psychological Well-Being Questionnaire. Results showed that there were significant correlations between the aggregate co-worker's ratings of common social environment and individual depression and anxiety. However, an individual's perception may mediate the social environment's outcomes.

Mishra et al. (1989) studied 600 executives from eight public and private sector organizations in India and found that both organizational climate and work environment explained 23.08 per cent of variance in mental health status.

Israel et al. (1989) studied 630 employees of a component-parts manufacturing plant and found that participation, influence and interpersonal relationships were consequential for various health outcomes.

Levi (1990) reported the increasing direct evidence of the causal relationship between work-related psychosocial stressors and incidence and prevalence of occupational morbidity and mortality. These stressors originate in the social structure and processes, affect human beings through psychological processes, and influence health through four types of interrelated mechanisms: emotional, cognitive, behavioural, and physiological. Health outcomes are moderated by situational factors (e.g. social support) and individual (e.g. personality) factors.

Phelan et al. (1991) studied 1500 married professional and managerial employees to investigate the associations of acute and chronic occupational and domestic stressors with diagnosed major depression and current depressive symptoms. Results showed that employees with more peer cohesion and supervisory support had less diagnosable depression, and fewer depressive symptoms. Regression analysis results showed that supervisory support was related to less current depressive symptoms even after controlling some demographic factors, clinical background, work factors, family situation, and a number of interactions between these variables. However, this was not true in the case of coworker support.

Repetti and Cosmos (1991) found a moderate relationship between social environment at work and individual job satisfaction and well-being among 299 bank workers. Job satisfaction was more strongly linked to quality of supervisory relationships than to relationship with coworkers. Contrary to expectations, the common social environment at work was a better predictor of job satisfaction than the individual social space, where supervisors and coworkers contributed equally.

Sanden and Johansson (1991) studied the influence of social isolation on employee health on 45 factory operators. Subjects' work was dominated by passive monitoring, and all tasks demanded continuous attention. Despite high job satisfaction, subjects reported pronounced fatigue after work. Three technical-organizational conditions were analyzed: computer support, collaborative work, and job complexity. Socially isolated subjects who supervised highly computerized processes reported more complaints, work difficulties, and somatic complaints than other subjects, as they were more dependent on technology, had less of an overview of their work, and had greater difficulty in switching from passive monitoring to active problem solving.

Cox (1991) was among the first to underline the importance of cultural factors in the health of an organization. He suggested that the organization would be unhealthy if its subjective and objective environments are inconsistent with one another, if the organization lacks a strong and penetrative culture, and the subjective organization lacks coherence and is not well integrated. The organization will also be unhealthy if any or all of its social psychological subsystems, which make up the subjective environment, are poor (or even lacking). He suggested that measures of work stress should be treated as potential moderators of the organizational culture-organizational behaviour relationship.

Sutherland and Davidson (1993) identified the potent role of organizational culture in producing stress of work overload and role insecurity, which in turn was associated with reduced mental health. They conducted a stress audit as a precursor to a stress management intervention programme, using interviews and postal questionnaires with 36 and 561 male construction site managers respectively. Job satisfaction was influenced by grade level, while mental health was affected by both grade of management and type of contract. Eight stressor factors were identified. The stress of work overload and role insecurity were associated with reduced mental health and high anxiety, and the stress of the organizational culture and climate was the strongest predictor of job dissatisfaction.

Cooke and Szumal (1993), using the Organizational Culture Inventory on 4890 subjects, measured 12 sets of shared behavioural expectations associated with three types of cultures: constructive, passive-defensive, and aggressive-defensive. These cultural norms were hypothesised to influence thinking and behaviour, motivation and performance, and satisfaction and stress of organizational members. Results showed that significant variance in individuals' responses was explained by their organizational membership, implying that differences in organizational culture influenced stress of employees.

Lindstrom (1994) delineated dependence on national and organizational culture and values as criteria for good work organizations. On the basis of empirical research, he associated job satisfaction, active life, and lack of subjective stress symptoms, with health and well-being. He also presented an overview of criteria for good work organization including such job characteristics as optimal quantitative and qualitative work loads, opportunities for control at work, clarified work roles balanced by other roles, and supportive social interaction. These can be promoted by using strategies such as mastery of work, management of change processes, support of employees by occupational health services, and emphasis on career stage and future perspectives. A clear link was found between organizational culture and employee health. According to Lindstrom, "typical for these job characteristics and interventive strategies as criteria for good work organization are their dependence on national and organizational culture and values."

Heaney, Price and Rafferty (1995) conducted a field experiment to increase social support, improve work team functioning, and enhance employee mental health. 1375 staff who worked in group homes for the developmentally disabled or mentally ill participated in a theory-driven training programme designed to increase psychosocial coping resources when coping with job demands. Results indicated that the programme enhanced work climate and reduced depressive symptoms and somatisation in those most at risk for leaving their jobs. It can thus be inferred that enhancing the work team climate fosters employee mental health, and perhaps also decreases their turnover intentions.

Schultz, Greenley and Brown (1995) studied such factors as environmental context, organizational structure, management processes, client severity, and staff characteristics as influencing work satisfaction and employee burnout. Survey data from 311 staff in 42 community mental health service organizations suggest that organization structure, culture, and management processes are important to work environment and in turn to satisfaction and subsequently, to burnout.

Thompson, Stradling, Murphy and O'Neill (1996) examined the role of human resource management issues affecting stress of social work staff. Questionnaires were distributed to 295 social worker in three local authority social services departments in northwest England. The identified differences among authorities studied in terms of the subjective experience of common stressors were explained using the role of organizational culture, and in particular the notion of a "culture of stress." This suggests important implications for social work agencies in which such an organizational culture has developed.

Tudor (1997) examined the effect of self-beliefs like self-efficacy, job involvement and work locus of control on work stressors (role conflict, job boredom, work frustration, and organizational climate) and strains (job satisfaction, organizational commitment, work anger, and work anxiety). The findings revealed significant relationships between self-efficacy and the stressors of role conflict and work frustration, and the strains of work anger and work anxiety. In addition, significant relationships were found between work locus of control and all the work stressors and strains. These findings suggested that self-efficacy, work locus of control, and job involvement are promising self-beliefs for dealing with the direct causes of workplace stress perceptions, going beyond the more traditional recommendations such as exercise, nutrition, deep breathing, meditation, and progression relaxation techniques. These results are significant since organizational climate is recognised as an important work stressor.

Warren (1997) attempted to uncover work organizational and psycho-social risk factors for stress-related and musculo-skeletal occupational illness. The investigation analysed a large questionnaire-based complimentary employer and employee data sets, the Monitor Study, collected in the Netherlands. The findings were: *(a)* Individual-level psychosocial and biomechanical stressor levels were strongly linked with strain, pain reports and health-related outcomes, but only moderately with musculo-skeletal strain. *(b)* Associations of organizational structure and culture with individual-level psychosocial and biomechanical stressors emerged as an etiology of risk factors. Industrial branch membership was strongly associated with increased levels of all 11 stressors analyzed. 'Discrepancy Variables', the differences between employer and employee estimates of risk level, hypothesized measures of organizational culture characteristics, were found to have a strong relationship with individual stressor levels.

Dick (2000) examined how the institutional context of policing influences the significance that acute stressors hold for police officers experiencing distress. 35 police officers referred to a stress counselling service underwent rational emotive behaviour therapy. Results showed that stressors reported included both operational and organizational acute stressors. Police organizational culture influenced ways in which officers perceived themselves and their environments and operated at the collective level to normalise some emotional responses and to pathologise others.

Peterson and Wilson (1998) presented a new culture-work-health model to provide a contemporary anthropological workplace health perspective. They argued for the inclusion of organizational culture in workplace health. The authors concluded that occupational health and organizational development professionals should focus their research and intervention efforts on understanding and addressing organizational culture from both individual's and organization's health perspective.

PROMOTING HEALTH IN THE WORKPLACE

Smith et al. (1986) suggest some ways of promoting workplace health:

*(a)* recreating a social, psychological and organizational environment in the workplace to encourage individual autonomy and participation by managers in their jobs;
*(b)* utilizing the social and interactive skills training that help to clarify role and interpersonal relationship difficulties within organizations; and
*(c)* creating an organizational climate to foster mutual interpersonal communication, openness and trust among managers and employees.

Research has suggested building an environment where trust and commitment can grow in fostering health of employees. Karasek and Theorell (1991) found that employees who experience better health even in high-demand environments, are those who have more control over how they do their work, participate in decisions, and have support from others.

Research has indicated that workplace health promotion has many benefits. The Canada Life Study (Cox, 1978) found that participation in programmes relating to worker health improvement led to a 22 per cent reduction in absenteeism and a 90 per cent reduction of staff turnover. Bertera (1990) found a 14 per cent decline in absenteeism over a two-year period and a return of $2.5 for very dollar invested by the end of the second year among blue-collar employees participating in a comprehensive health promotion initiative. Munroe (1994) evaluated perhaps the earliest and most comprehensive (targeting 30,000 employees) evaluation of a wellness programme undertaken in USA by the pharmaceutical giant Johnson & Johnson, and found that in addition to reduced absenteeism and increased employee morale, the annual rate of investment was approximately 30 per cent. Kerr (1996) found a 20 per cent decrease in sickness and early retirement rates in Ford Motor Company after implementing an extensive occupational health service.

Rosen (1984) noted the following benefits of health promotion programmes: *(a)* improving employee health and fitness; *(b)* reducing absenteeism; *(c)* decreasing medical and disability costs; *(d)* decreasing staff turnover; *(e)* improving employee mental alertness; *(f)* improving morale and job satisfaction; *(g)* enhanced corporate image; and *(h)* improved productivity. Many companies believe that employees who feel that the company cared about their well being were likely to be more productive and loyal in the long term.

Kogan (1997), however, cautions that health promotion may not necessarily be an easy way out to improve workplace performance efficiency and productivity. Organizational issues might be the cause of employee discontent and companies need to make an honest appraisal which takes into account the entire company structure and culture into account. Health promotion is not a panacea for all ills and companies need to be prepared to take action when other organizational issues become apparent as causes of employee ill health.

## SUMMARY

Research has focused on different aspects of the work place as potential predictors of employee health, namely close supervision and lack of autonomy at work, role conflict and ambiguity, role stress, job/occupational stress (Caplan et al., 1975; Johnson and Stinson, 1975), physical work-environment, supervisory support, stressful demands at work (Cooper and Marshall, 1980; Frese, 1978; Gardell, 1987; Margolis, Kroes, and Quinn, 1974; Karasek, 1979; Ganster and Schaubroeck, 1991; Kinicki, McKee, and Wade, 1996), etc. Job characteristics like job complexity and autonomy or control have been conceptualised as job stressors and have been shown to correlate with emotional reactions and health (Adelman, 1987). Specific work characteristics, such as workload demands and personal control are associated with elevated blood pressure and salivary cortisol (Fox et al., 1993) as well as CHD and depression (Theorell et al., 1998).

Very few studies have focused on employee health as the product of complex biophysical interactions. Only recently have researchers studied the role of "Person-Environment fit" (Furnham and Schaeffer, 1984), "social environment" (Repetti, 1987), "work climate" (Heaney, Price and Rafferty, 1995), "organizational climate" (Tudor, 1997), and even "organizational culture" (Cox, 1991; Sutherland and Davidson, 1993; Lindstrom, 1994; Warren, 1997; Peterson and Wilson, 1998; Dick, 2000). This suggests that greater attention needs to be given to social factors of an organization that may predispose an individual to poor physical and mental health. As Cooper and Locke (2000) remarked, "characteristics of jobs and the workplace social environment are implicated in the onset and progression of mental and physical health problems."

# 4
# Organizational Commitment

## CONCEPTUALIZING ORGANIZATIONAL COMMITMENT

The concept of organizational commitment has attracted interest of researchers for more than two decades now. Its enduring nature over time makes it more amenable for research, its normative content permits control of behaviour in organizations, and its linkages with organizational culture has useful implications for the organizations. In this connection, Parker (2000) claimed that: "Culturalism can be articulated as a movement from a concern with 'control' to a concern with 'commitment'—a humanistic development that 'hold the promise of satisfying the need of the spirit."

Literature has been characterized by a diversity of definitions and operationalisations of the concept of commitment. Commitment-like constructs have been defined in terms of identification and involvement in a particular organization (Porter, Steers, Mowday and Boulian, 1974; Porter, Crampon and Smith, 1976), behavioural intentions (Mobley, 1982), congruence between one's real and ideal jobs (Koch and Steers, 1978) or constraint (Johnson, 1973). Historically, two different approaches study the bases of commitment: the *side-bets orientation* and the individual-organizational *goal congruence orientation*. The first approach, Becker's (1960) side-bet orientation, regards commitment as behavioural rather than attitudinal, according to which, the individual is bound to the organization through extraneous interests (e.g. pension, seniority, etc.) rather than a favourable affect toward the organization. He describes commitment as the tendency to engage in "consistent lines of activity" as a result of the accumulation of "side bets" that would be lost if the activity were discontinued. Hrebiniak and Alutto (1972) supporting the exchange notion, defined commitment as "a result of individual-organizational transactions, and alterations in side bets or investments over time."

The second approach, individual-organizational *goal congruence orientation* focuses on the extent to which people identifying with an organization have personal goals that are in keeping with those of the organization. Emphasizing the role of "shared values," Hall, Schneider and Nygren (1970) defined commitment as "the process by which the goals of the organization and those of the individual become increasingly integrated or congruent." Sheldon (1971), too, defined organizational commitment as "an attitude or an orientation toward the organization which links or attaches the identity of the person to the organization." Buchanan (1974) conceptualized commitment as "a partisan, affective attachment to the goals and values, and to the organization for its own sake, apart from its purely instrumental worth." Porter et al. (1974) suggested that commitment is "the strength of an individual's identification with and involvement in a particular organization" (Porter et al., 1974). As defined by Mowday, Porter and Steers (1982), commitment is: *(a)* a belief in and acceptance of organization's goals and values, *(b)* a willingness to exert considerable effort on behalf of the organization, and *(c)* a strong desire to remain a member of the organization.

As researchers began to study organizational commitment from each of these two perspectives, it became clear that both these approaches were necessary. Meyer and Allen (1984) used the terms affective commitment and continuance commitment, respectively, to characterize Porters' and Becker's discrepant views of the construct. In their model of commitment, they added a third "distinguishable" component of organizational commitment-normative commitment. They defined these three components as follows: *(a)* Affective commitment refers to the employee's emotional attachment to, identification with, and involvement in the organization; *(b)* Continuance commitment refers to an awareness of the costs associated with leaving the organization; and *(c)* Normative commitment reflects a feeling of obligation to continue employment. Employees with strong affective commitment remain in the organization because they *want* to, strong continuance commitment because they *need* to, and those with strong normative commitment because they feel that they *ought* to do s^

Some other researchers who have also emphasized normative commitment view commitment as a belief about one's responsibility to the organization. Weiner (1982) defined commitment as "the totality of internalized pressures to act in a way which meet organizational goals and interests." Other authors (e.g. Presthold, Lane and Mathews, 1987) have identified personal norms as important contributors to behaviour, including terminating employment with the organization.

In conclusion, given the significant role of "shared values" in conceptualizing organizational commitment, one question becomes pertinent: Would organizational commitment be a function of the extent to which organizational values are aligned to societal values? Are employees affectively committed to their organization or have a sense of personal loyalty to some superior '*kartas*' in the organization?

There are three major issues related to the concept of organizational commitment:

1. The unitary frame of reference. A unitary frame of reference assumes, unrealistically that an organization consists of people with shared interests. The pluralist perspective recognizes the legitimacy of different interest groups and values (Mintzberg, 1983), and therefore asks the question "commitment to what?" As Coopey and Hartley (1991) put it "commitment is not an all-or-nothing affair, but a question of multiple or competing commitments for the individual." Reichers (1985), using a multiple-constituency approach, also emphasised that organizational groups such as top management, workers, customers and unions frequently pursue multiple, competing sets of goals and values, and employees may be committed to any or even all of these groups.
2. Commitment as an inhibitor of flexibility. Coopey and Hartley (1991) pointed that, "the problem of a unitarist notion of organizational commitment is that it fosters a conformist approach which not only fails to reflect organizational reality, but can be narrowing and limiting for the organization." They argued that if employees are expected

and encouraged to commit themselves tightly to a single set of values and goals, then they will not be able to cope with the ambiguities and uncertainties which are endemic in organizational life in times of change.

3. Whether high commitment really results in improved organizational performance. A growing body of research indicates that organizational commitment has immense utility as a determinant of positive behavioural outcomes such as "performance" (Meyer et al., 1989; Ornstein and Isabella, 1990; Mathieu and Zajac, 1990; Gbadamosi, 1995) and "prosocial behaviour" (Brief and Motowidlo, 1988). Further, the more committed the employee is to the organization, the greater the effort expended in performing tasks, and higher the willingness to share and make sacrifices (Steers, 1977). However, a review by Guest (1991) concluded that high organizational commitment is associated with low labour turnover and absence, but there is no clear link with performance.

Organizational commitment has positive personal consequences. Strong commitment to work is likely to result in conscientious and self-directed application to do the job, regular attendance, nominal supervision, and high level of effort. For e.g. Romzek's (1989) survey of work attitudes among public employees suggests that those who were most strongly attached to their organizations tended to enjoy highly successful careers and pleasant nonwork lives. Finally, organizational commitment also predicts withdrawal behaviour such as employee lateness, absenteeism and turnover (Porter, Steers, Mowday and Boulian, 1974; Koch and Steers, 1978; Steers and Rhodes, 1978; Mobley et al., 1979; Angle and Perry, 1981; Price and Mueller, 1981; Rusbult and Farrell, 1983; Cotton and Tuttle, 1986; Lee et al., 1992). Because turnover can be costly to organizations, commitment is generally assumed to be a desirable quality that should be fostered in employees

## FACTORS INFLUENCING ORGANIZATIONAL COMMITMENT

Since the 1960s, a large number of studies have sought to identify the antecedents, correlates and outcomes of organizational commitment, and they have resulted in long lists of variables. A review of the organizational commitment literature shows that two classes of variables: individual and organizational, have been used as antecedents of organizational commitment.

Some researchers have found demographic variables to be more powerful predictors of organizational commitment than organizational variables (Koch and Steers, 1978). Others have found the reverse to be true (Morris and Sherman, 1981; Angle and Perry, 1981). Yet another set of studies have found that the two sets of antecedents are equally effective in predicting organizational commitment (Buchanan, 1974).

### Organizational Commitment and Individual Variables

The demographic variables presumed to cause commitment comprise age and tenure (Sheldon, 1971), gender (Hrebiniak and Alutto, 1972), income, level of management, marital status, and education (inversely), need for achievement (Steers, 1977).

Age and tenure have generally been reported to be positively associated with commitment (Hall, Schneider, and Nygren, 1970; Lee, 1971; Sheldon, 1971; Hrebiniak and Alutto, 1974), and education has been reported to be negatively correlated to commitment (Morris and Steers, 1980; Angle and Perry, 1981). In a sample of service workers, Morris and Sherman (1981) reported that older employees, and employees with a greater sense of competence had higher levels of commitment. Dornstein and Matalon (1989) found that age and education in addition to several other variables like interesting work, coworker attitudes towards the organization, organizational dependency, employment alternatives, attitudes of family/friends, and importance to organization explain as much as 65 per cent of the variance in organizational commitment. Patel (1999) investigated the impact of age on job involvement and organizational commitment of nationalized and co-operative bank employees in India. Results showed that younger subjects (aged <35 yrs.) of both nationalized and co-operative banks exhibited less job involvement and organizational commitment than did middle-aged (aged 35-45 yrs.) and older subjects (aged >45 yrs.). The only significant difference between employees of the two kinds of banks were that middle-aged nationalized bank employees showed more commitment than did middle-aged employees of co-operative banks.

O'Reilly and Caldwell (1987) reported that workers who perceived fewer alternative options for employment tended to have higher organizational commitment. Stevens, Beyer, and Trice (1978) found that several worker characteristics like their tenure in the organization, and the extent of their ego involvement with the job predicted commitment.

Cain and Bruce (1987) studied organizational commitment, satisfaction and professionalism of newly employed managers. Changes during the first year were examined and a decline was observed in all three areas. The results confirmed a direct relation of all three areas with length of service.

Glisson and Durick (1988) analysed simultaneously the predictors of both satisfaction and commitment from the three categories of job characteristics, organizational characteristics, and worker characteristics on 319 workers in 22 service organizations. They found that job satisfaction and organizational commitment were each affected by a unique hierarchy of predictors. Results indicated two job characteristics, viz. skill variety and role ambiguity, to be the best predictors of satisfaction, while two organizational characteristics, leadership and the organization's age, were the best predictors of commitment. One worker characteristic, education, was found to be a significant predictor of commitment.

Singh (1990) conducted an in-depth study using 250 junior and middle-level executives belonging to seven private and public sector organizations of North India to explore prevalence and determinants of organizational stress, job strain, organizational commitment, job performance and satisfaction. Stress was observed to be the strongest predictor of organizational commitment, followed by personal and organizational factors.

Wallace (1993) assessed factors influencing the relationship between professional commitment and organizational commitment using meta-analysis. Results indicated a moderately strong positive association between the two. Further, the individual's position in the organization, the degree of occupational professionalisation, and the form of professional commitment had moderating effects on the true correlation between the two.

Cheng (1994) studied locus of control as an indicator of commitment and perceptions of organizational characteristics among 588 teachers from 54 secondary schools in Hong Kong.

Results revealed that subjects with a belief in internal control had a more positive job attitude in terms of organizational commitment, intrinsic satisfaction, extrinsic satisfaction, social satisfaction, influence satisfaction, role clarity, and feeling of job challenge. They also had more positive perceptions of principal's leadership, organizational structure, social norms, and organizational culture and effectiveness.

Sommer, Bae and Luthans (1996) examined antecedents of organizational commitment on 1192 Korean employees of 27 large Korean firms. The employee's position in the hierarchy, tenure, and age were all significantly related to commitment, while total tenure and education were not related. Further, as organization size increased, commitment decreased; as the structure became more employee focused, commitment increased; and the more positive the organizational climate perceptions, the more the commitment.

Chen and Francesco (2000) investigated the main effect of demographic variables on commitment and the moderating effect of gender and education on the relationship between commitment and turnover intentions based on a survey of 333 employees in China. Only position significantly influenced employees' commitment, while gender was found to moderate the relationship between commitment and turnover intentions.

### Organizational Commitment and Organizational Variables

The organizational variables comprise of task characteristics, pay, supervision, opportunity for advancement, participation (Denison, 1984), management support (Cook and Wall, 1980; Fukami and Larson, 1984), social support (Luthans, Wahl and Steinhaus, 1992), fairness of organizational procedures (Calorie and Sarnin, 1991; Chatman, 1989), socialisation practices (Kelley, 1992; Orpen, 1993) etc. Increasingly researchers have identified the potent role of an organization's culture in fostering commitment (Harris and Mossholder, 1996; Garr, 1998; O' Driscoll et al., 1998; Pool, 2000; Leib, 2000). While a complete review of this literature is unfeasible, a limited attempt is made only to present those studies which focus on organizational factors like organizational values, climate, culture, socialization practices, etc. as the causes of organizational commitment.

Louis, Posner, and Powell (1983) studied the role of socialisation practices used by employers in making newcomers feel effective (committed) organizational members. The results show that "daily interaction with peers while working" was the most important factor. Additionally, the impact of the first supervisor also plays a crucial role in helping newcomers feel effective. Among the socialisation practices adhered to, formal on-site orientation sessions had the greatest value in fostering loyalty to and identification with the organization. However, off-site residential programmes were strongly correlated with newcomers' positive job attitudes like job satisfaction, commitment, and tenure intention.

In an empirical investigation carried out by Posner, Kouzes and Schmidt (1985) with 1500 managers across United States, it was found that clearly articulated organizational cultures makes a significant difference to organizational and personal vitality. Shared values were found to be related to *(a)* feelings of personal success; *(b)* organizational commitment; *(c)* self-confidence in understanding personal and organizational values; *(d)* ethical behaviour; *(e)* feelings of job and personal stress, to the extent that organizational values were incompatible with personal values; *(f)* organizational goals; and *(g)* personal stakeholders.

Maeher (1987) found organizational culture to be strongly associated with personal investment (commitment). He found that employees were likely to be more personally invested in the organization when the company's values and beliefs were obvious to them. His study also concluded that organizational culture was a "controllable force" and advised corporate leaders to create and manage culture so as to enhance commitment.

DeCotiis and Summers (1987), using a sample of 367 managerial employees, found several aspects of the organization including perceived structure, process and climate, and job satisfaction to be predictive of commitment. Job satisfaction and organizational commitment were equally predictive of voluntary turnover. Organizational commitment was also found predictive of individual motivation and objective job performance.

The degree of agreement in values between production workers and their supervisors, and its impact on variables like organizational commitment, job satisfaction, tenure, and achievement outcomes, was assessed in a study by Meglino, Ravlin and Adkins (1989). 191 production workers, their supervisors (N=17), and 13 managers at a large industrial plant, completed questionnaires containing measures of job satisfaction, organizational commitment, and work values. Responses were later matched with the attendance and performance records of the production workers in the sample. The data strongly supported the conclusion that organizational commitment and job satisfaction are enhanced by value congruence, but produced mixed results on the achievement outcomes. For e.g., employees who had more congruent values were late less often but did not have significantly fewer absences. Value congruence between workers and their supervisors was not significantly correlated with workers' tenure; however, its effect on organizational commitment was more pronounced for longer tenured employees.

Vardi, Wiener, and Popper (1989) examined the value content of organizational mission as a factor in the commitment of members. The study was carried out on two manufacturing organizations, one having an organizational mission with a high value content, and the other whose mission was strictly commercial. They found the value related organization to elicit higher normative commitment among its members than the commercial one. This finding suggested that a major determinant of commitment was the congruency between individual and organizational values.

Peterson and Martin (1990) discussed the importance of how organizational cultures are built and reinforced, with particular attention to the interrelationships between mission, culture, leadership, rewards, and commitment in two different settings viz. schools and universities. They suggested that the basic structural configurations, the measurability of goals, the dispersion of authority, and the pull of external professional commitments may mediate the influence of culture on organizational commitment.

Box, Odom, and Dunn (1991) examined the impact of organizational values among 387 executives from transportation organizations using a questionnaire survey Both organizational values and congruence between personal and organizational values affected satisfaction, commitment, and cohesion. Subjects indicated that seven values should exist within their work environment: a belief in being the best, a belief in the details of execution, a belief in people as individuals, a belief in superior quality and service, and a belief in informality to enhance communication. Subjects also believed that most members of the organization should be innovators.

Luthans, Wahl, and Steinhaus (1992) empirically studied the role of social support for employee commitment among 19 banks and 85 tellers' (mean age 28.4 yrs.). Although there were some differences between the various dimensions of both the supportiveness climate and organizational commitment, in general results indicated a supportive climate to have a clear, positive relationship with teller organizational commitment.

Mishra (1992) investigated whether climate perception influences the feeling of organizational commitment and job satisfaction among 200 middle level and front-line executives (aged 29-42 yrs.) from public sector and private sector industrial organizations. There were significant differences between the two sectors with regard to climate-commitment and climate-satisfaction relationships on such dimensions as scope for advancement, monetary benefits, objectivity and rationality, recognition and appreciation, training and education, and welfare facilities.

Shaw and Reyes (1992) investigated elementary and high school teachers' organizational commitment and workplace value orientation. Two sets of schools (53 elementary and 51 secondary) were compared, and 265 elementary and 255 secondary teachers participated. The results indicated that workplace value crientation relates to teacher's commitment, with teachers in elementary schools displaying higher levels of commitment.

Kelley (1992) developed a conceptual framework that considered the impact of organizational socialization on customer orientation, and tested it on 249 customer-contact employees. The socialization outcomes included in the framework were employee perceptions of organizational climate, levels of motivation, and organizational commitment. Results suggested that organizational socialization had a positive impact on perceptions of climate, levels of motivation, and organizational commitment.

Orpen (1993) examined the impact of personnel practices on commitment among organizations with strong cultural norms.

Results from 80 employees from two firms indicated that recruitment and socialization practices were positively associated with employee commitment, but only in the firm with relatively strong cultural norms.

Orpen (1994) examined the relationship between perceived political climate and employees' work attitudes like organizational commitment and job satisfaction on 119 employees of a financial services firm. Employee's status was found to moderate the relationships between political climate and both commitment and satisfaction, with high status employees being less adversely affected than their low status peers in both cases.

Cheng (1995) studied the relationship between hierarchical fit in organizational value and employee effectiveness for Chinese employees in a large MNC in Taiwan using 170 high level managers, 261 professional staffs, and 335 shop floor operators. Results indicated that both organizational commitment and organizational citizenship behaviour were influenced by cooperative distances, e.g., the differences of the organizational value between the managers and staff, and between the managers and shop floor operators.

A longitudinal study by Major, Kozlowski, Chao, and Gardner (1995) examined the link between unmet expectations and socialisation outcomes: organizational commitment, turnover intention and job satisfaction. Data was collected from 248 new hires before organizational entry and 4 weeks after entry. Three role expectations—conflict, clarity, and acceptance—were measured. Results showed that met expectations, leader-member exchange, and team-member exchange were significant predictors of all outcomes.

Gunter and Furnham (1996) examined six biographical and 14 organizational climate perception correlates of 1041 employees' job satisfaction and pride in the organization, (similar to organizational commitment), in four public sector organizations. Analysis yielded correlations ranging from-0.12 to 0.51 between climate factors and job satisfaction. Correlations between climate and pride in the organization ranged from-0.08 to 0.53. A step-wise regression analysis revealed climate factors to be more significant than biographical factors as predictors of job satisfaction and pride.

Tantratian (1996) explored the association between organizational culture and commitment using 488 respondents from six small-to mid-size municipal police departments. Three dimensions of organizational commitment, viz. Continuance, Instrumental, and Normative, and five components of organizational culture, viz. Progressive, Coordinative, Outcome-oriented, Details-oriented, and Certainty-oriented, were measured. The results from multiple regression analyses demonstrated that a sizable part of the instrumental and normative dimensions of organizational commitment could be explained by the individual's perception of organizational culture. The individual's perception of the agency as having strong 'Liberal' values was related to lower levels of continuance and instrumental commitment and higher levels of normative commitment. Similarly, the perceived high Certainty-oriented values were associated with lower levels of Instrumental commitment and a high level of Normative commitment.

Chinnapan (1996) empirically studied the relation between organizational culture and employee commitment on 450 employees across 3 strata-150 workers, 75 clerical and 225 executives in a large automobile plant near Chennai. The hypothesis that more favourable the employee's perception of organizational culture, the higher the level of employee commitment was substantiated, with a correlation of 0.68. Four dimensions of organizational culture: reward system, organizational philosophy, conflict management, and decision-making emerged as significant predictors of EC, explaining 67 per cent of the total variance.

Harris and Mossholder (1996) explored the influence of 245 corporation managers' and executives' congruence with their organization's culture on their affective orientations toward the organization, in the context of an organization undergoing significant cultural transformation. Management style, the 'glue' binding the organization, and the dominant organizational characteristics were the attributes indicating culture. Job satisfaction, job involvement, organizational commitment, and job turnover intention were the affective outcomes measured. Results showed that organizational commitment and optimism about an organization's future explained the discrepancy between subjects' assessment of the current culture and their ideal culture.

In addition to personal characteristics and organizational characteristics, Luthans, Baack and Taylor (1987) introduced another factor as determinants of commitment, called the Person-Organization fit, which is basically an interaction between the individual and organizational characteristics. Warren (1997) explored the role of Person-Organization fit (P-O fit) in comparison to the role of organizational culture on organizational outcomes. A self-reported measure of P-O fit was calculated to assess individuals' perception of their fit with the organization. Results indicated that perceived P-O fit contributed, beyond culture alone, to the explanation of satisfaction, commitment, and intent to leave.

Khatib (1997) examined the relationship between organizational culture, subcultures, and organizational commitment. Two major concerns were: *(a)* differences in the perceptions of three custodial groups of their behavioural norms and shared values at the workplace; and *(b)* relationships between these two components of organizational culture and commitment. A survey was administered to 63 custodians located in three different workplaces belonging to three different supervisory teams in a land-grant university to assess their perceptions about behavioural norms, shared values and organizational commitment. All three groups reported similar perceptions about behavioural norms and shared values, irrespective of supervisory styles, and also reported a strong commitment.

Lee, Song, and Lee (1997) investigated the relationship of organizational commitment with occupational stress, personal strain, and stress coping ability among 306 male and female in various industries in Korea. Results from multiple regression analyses showed that role boundary, role insufficiency, organizational climate, and responsibility variables were significant predictors of organizational commitment.

Vashishtha and Mishra (1998) explored the potential moderator effect of social support on the occupational stress-organizational commitment relationship on 200 supervisors of a factory making auto scooters. Moderated regression analysis confirmed that social support did have a moderating effect on the occupational stress-organizational commitment relationship.

Rogg (1998) explored the relationships between the development of multiple commitments and important work organizational outcomes (organizational citizenship behaviour, job performance, turnover intentions). A number of variables were identified as important antecedents of multiple commitments, including perceived organizational support (especially for work), conscientiousness, work autonomy (control over schedule, methods, and outcomes), and conflict from outside influences (e.g., family) interfering with work. The results demonstrated the power of perceived organizational support to predict a range of important work outcomes.

Garr (1998) examined the relationship between organizational culture and organizational commitment. Specifically, the study was designed to determine whether level and type of commitment (Affective, Continuance, or Normative) varies predictably across culture patterns (Constructive, Passive-Defensive, or Aggressive-Defensive). Using 100 participants from legal, manufacturing, and government workplaces, the study found that Constructive cultures were related to higher levels of Affective commitment, and also accounted for the largest amount of variance in Affective commitment. Additionally, smaller differences between an organization's real and ideal Constructive and Passive-Defensive culture profiles were related to higher Affective commitment. Smaller differences between real and ideal Passive-Defensive culture scores also led to higher levels of overall commitment. Finally, high Constructive cultures and low Passive-Defensive cultures were more predictive of Affective commitment levels than tenure. The study thus clearly establishes organizational culture as a predictor of commitment.

O'Driscoll et al. (1998) examined the linkages between organizational culture and employee attitude and affect (psychological strain, job satisfaction, job involvement, and organizational commitment) in a study on managers and professionals from eight countries. Perceptions that the organization promoted employee-supportive values were associated with higher job satisfaction and commitment to the organization, along with reduced psychological strain. However, supportive values failed to buffer the impact of role stressors on employee attitudes, suggesting that organizational culture may be directly linked with employee attitudes and affect, but it does not serve to protect individuals from the effects of an adverse work environment.

O'Driscoll and Randall (1999) explored the role of perceived organizational support and satisfaction with rewards in explaining job involvement and organizational commitment (affective and continuance commitment) with 350 dairy workers in dairy cooperatives in Ireland and New Zealand using a mail questionnaire. Perceived organizational support was significantly linked with job involvement, affective and continuance commitment, although its relationship with continuance commitment was negative. Satisfaction with intrinsic and (to a lesser extent) extrinsic rewards was also found to be a salient predictor of job involvement and affective commitment, but not continuance commitment.

Schwepker (1999) examined the influence of the perceptual difference in shared ethical values between the salesperson and top managers (ethical conflict) on salespeople's commitment and turnover intentions. Survey responses from 152 salespeople in 26 firms suggested that ethical conflict was negatively associated with organizational commitment and positively with turnover intentions.

Pool (2000) examined the relationship between three organizational cultures and the role stressors within a business environment, in a study of 35 U.S. organizations with 238 executives. The results indicated that a constructive culture significantly reduced role stressors, thereby decreasing job tension and increasing job satisfaction, job performance, and commitment. The corporate culture's taproot is the organization's beliefs and philosophy in how it conducts business. When the beliefs, vision, objectives, business approaches and practices supporting a company's strategy are compatible with its culture, the culture becomes a valuable ally in strategy implementation and execution. When this is not accomplished, a company finds it difficult to implement the strategy successfully.

Lieb (2000) investigated the relationship between Organizational Culture (OC) and Performance Appraisal (PA) systems as perceived by 252 MBA and undergraduate students, on job satisfaction, organizational commitment and turnover intention. Using factor analysis, he developed a new scale of matching OC/PA items comprising of seven dimensions. However, no dimension was found to have a significant effect on Continuance, Normative or Total Organizational Commitment, General or Extrinsic Satisfaction. The results implied that OC and PA systems influenced turnover intention, and affective commitment, but not continuance or total organizational commitment.

Tain (2000) investigated the interaction of the cultural match between the individual and the organization to job satisfaction and organizational commitment. The results indicated that better the individual/organization fit, the higher the level of both job satisfaction and organizational commitment, regardless of the organizational culture studied.

Soh (2001) investigated organizational socialisation (particularly internalization of organizational beliefs and values) of newcomers and its relationship to some outcomes. A two-wave longitudinal field survey was conducted to examine change in perceptions, beliefs and values over a period of eight weeks for 718 newcomers (conscripts) in the Singapore Armed Forces which has a strong and homogeneous culture that emphasizes collectivism. The results showed that the newcomers' perceptions of the organizational culture did become more similar to those of their superiors between week 1 and week 8. Changes in collectivism that occurred at the individual level between week 1 and week 8 were systematically and positively related to organizational commitment. Newcomers who reported having positive experiences and superiors who engaged in pro-organizational (collectivism) culture behaviour showed an increase in their collectivism. Further, having self-concept related beliefs and values that were congruent with the organizational culture was directly related to perceptions of person-organization fit and indirectly related to organizational commitment, low stress and task performance.

**Cultural Influences on Organizational Commitment**

East-Asian studies have tried to determine if the variables associated with organizational commitment are universal or culture-specific. It has been suggested that the act of commitment is only a manifestation of the individual's own self, and the value considerations leading to commitment reflect value standards that are basic to the individual's existence as a person (Kidron, 1978). This view has been empirically demonstrated in studies relating work values to commitment and other related concepts like organizational identification and loyalty. Work values in turn have been found to be culturally determined (Hofstede, 1980; Cummings, Harnett and Stevens, 1971).

Lincoln, Hanada, and Olsen (1981) found that Japanese and Japanese American workers placed greater value on organizational paternalism than their U.S. counterparts. Yet there were no differences among employees in their level of personal ties to colleagues. Near's (1989) study of Japanese and U.S. workers found that social interaction, fairness, and job content influenced commitment, regardless of culture. Yet other variables remained culture-specific, for e.g. freedom on the job for Americans and age for Japanese.

Sopachitwattana (2000) noted absence of literature on organizational commitment, participative management and cultural values in Eastern Countries. He examined the questions: Are there differences between American expatriates and Thai managers in Thailand in commitment? Are the antecedents, participative management and cultural values, related to commitment among managers in MNCs in Thailand? Significant differences were found between American expatriates and Thai managers in levels of Continuance and Normative Commitment. Participative Management and Power Distance were significantly related to Affective Commitment. Participative Management and Long-term Orientation were significantly related to Continuance Commitment. Power Distance was significantly related to Normative Commitment for managers in Thailand.

Cho (2000) conducted two studies that addressed cross-cultural issues in organizational culture, and self-construal at the U.S. subsidiaries of Korean MNCs. The issue of how different organizational cultures influence employees' commitment in the U.S. and Korea was also examined. Unlike in Korea, organizational cultures of four U.S. subsidiaries did not significantly differ from each other inspite of belonging to different industries and different companies. Further, American employees with more interdependent self-construal and Korean employees with more independent self-construal showed more positive perceptions of organizational culture and higher organizational commitment.

Other researchers have found contrary results. Triandis et al., (1988) examined commitment in Japanese and American firms. Results suggested that commitment to the organization in both countries is contingent upon the expectancy of status enhancement not upon moral loyalty to the firm. The authors concluded that the role of cultural factors in the prediction of life time commitment has been exaggerated. In a study conducted in Singapore, Putti, Aryee, and Lang (1989) found that the same values that were related to organizational commitment in the West held true for Asia. This supports Marsh and Mannari's (1977) proposal that organizational commitment is based on universal values.

## INCREASING COMMITMENT

Jaffe, Scott and Tobe (1994) use the term 'empowerment' to define the processes that build commitment in the workplace. According to them "empowerment is personal power released within the context of organizational needs." Their advice to managers seeking to revitalize themselves, their work, and their organization is to rekindle commitment by empowering subordinates. Gbadamosi (1995) suggested that factors that enhance organizational commitment are high level of autonomy, challenging and interesting work, broad task design, investment in training and development, selection based on merit, fair appraisals, career progress or job advancement, high quality, supportive and friendly supervision, and effective reward management. The factors that inhibit commitment are: ambiguous roles, the use of punishment by the supervisor, alternative employment available, tension on the job, unfair performance appraisals, and a conviction that the organization is uncaring about employee's welfare. Thus, interventions designed to foster the former and remove the latter factors would increase commitment.

Bowditch and Buono (1997) suggested that if people are expected to exhibit greater commitment to their work, and the organization and its goals, they must be provided with an opportunity to fulfill valued personal goals such as a sense of autonomy, authority, and influence over organizational decision-making processes in return.

Chaudhuri (2001) suggested different ways to enhance the three different components (Meyer and Allen, 1991) of commitment. The affective component can be enhanced by increasing an individual's freedom at work, and by designing jobs in such a way that they are skill-enriched. The continuance component is largely a function of the tenure of an individual and the long-term benefits that are designed. The normative component is built by allowing individuals to participate more in matters relating to the organization. This creates a sense of obligation in the individual towards the organization and thus the individual starts feeling like an insider.

## SUMMARY

This section points to some main themes in our current knowledge of organizational commitment, most of which is based on Western employees in Western organizations. The antecedents of organizational commitment may be understood as falling into three major categories: *(a)* personal characteristics, including age, sex, education, organizational tenure, personality variables like need for achievement, sense of competence, protestant work ethic, and professionalism; *(b)* job characteristics, ranging from broad measures of job scope or motivating potential to specific measures such as task identity, role clarity, task challenge, feedback, responsibility, autonomy, and opportunity for social interaction; and *(c)* organizational characteristics, like organizational values, climate, culture, socialization practices, perceived pay equity, fair organizational practices, leadership skills etc.

While more research is needed to determine how many and which variables associated with commitment are universally valid, it is clear that the nature of culture influence on commitment is pervasive and needs to be explored. Commitment is a reaction between the employee and organization, but this reaction does not occur in a vacuum. It is influenced by personal, organizational, and cultural factors, and so researches on commitment need to take into account this relationship within a particular societal context.

# 5
# Employee Turnover

## UNDERSTANDING TURNOVER

Turnover, or employee withdrawal, is often studied in organizational behaviour. Turnover is an important and frequently used dependent variable in management research (Staw, 1984). A review by Steers and Mowday (1981) identified over 1000 turnover studies in the 20th century and at least 13 review articles in the last 25 years. Rice, Hill and Trist (1950) tracing new entrants, outlined three main phases in the turnover process: induction crisis, differential transit, and settled connection. A working definition of turnover was provided by Macy and Mirvis (1983): "a permanent movement beyond the boundary of an organization."

Studies have shown that the cost of replacing exempt employees, especially, senior managers and highly marketable personnel such as high-tech professionals and engineers, is substantial (Cooper and Burke, 2002). Other 'invisible' costs of turnover include the impact on the morale and productivity of work units, a possibility of a snowball effect, i.e. turnover itself causes more turnover (Mowday et al., 1982), delays on important projects, discontinuity of customer/client service with resultant negative impact on customer/client satisfaction, a loss of intellectual capital with the assumed possibility that a former employee may become a future competitor (Wagner and Hollenbeck, 1995). Finally, the damage that a sequence of short stays can do to an employee's own career chances and aspirations should not be overlooked (Fowler, 1996).

Campion (1991) suggested that in order to assess organizational consequences for employee turnover, it is important to consider three refinements: *(a)* avoidability: turnover is unfavourable to the extent that it is unavoidable through any action the organization believes it can take; *(b)* utility: turnover may be considered positive if the exchange results in more productive employees or if higher-paid employees are replaced with lower-paid employees; and *(c)* functionality: only the loss of good performers that the organization would rehire and who would be hard to replace is dysfunctional. Dalton et al. (1981), Watts and White (1988) made a distinction between functional turnover (when low performers quit) and dysfunctional turnover (when high performers quit). Some researches (Holenbeck and Williams, 1986; McEvoy and Cascio, 1987) have found turnover to have potentially beneficial effects. It must be remembered, however, that many good employees do also quit their jobs, and their loss is expensive for their organizations.

**Theoretical Models**

What causes job turnover? Why do some people develop strong commitment to continue on their jobs, while others fail to do so and quit their jobs? Theories of turnover process address the psychological experiences and choices individuals confront as they continue or withdraw from an organization. Some models or theories are being reviewed below.

March and Simon (1958), using equilibrium theory, developed a comprehensive turnover-participation model, including as key decision variables perceived desirability of movement, perceived possibility of intra-organizational transfer, and perceived ease of movement. According to them, "increases in the *balance of inducement utilities over contribution utilities decrease the propensity of the individual participant to leave* the organization, whereas decreases in that balance have an opposite effect." This inducements-contributions balance is a function of two major components: the perceived desirability of leaving and the perceived ease of movement from the organization.

Price (1977) utilized a psychological process similar to that of March and Simon and introduced a variety of sociological variables describing organizational conditions, for e.g., centralization, co-worker integration, formalisation, etc.

Mobley et al. (1979) developed a comprehensive process model of voluntary employee turnover identifying several probable antecedents of turnover in causal order. According to this model, (Figure 5.1) job dissatisfaction stimulates thoughts of quitting. Conditional causality rather than direct causality is implicit in the model. That is, job dissatisfaction does not lead directly to turnover, but does so conditionally on favourable search utility, successful search, attractive work alternatives, and action toward resignation. The intention to quit was suggested as the immediate precursor of actually quitting. Mobley also suggested that economic conditions, and hence the success of an initial search for alternative jobs, exert a strong impact on voluntary turnover.

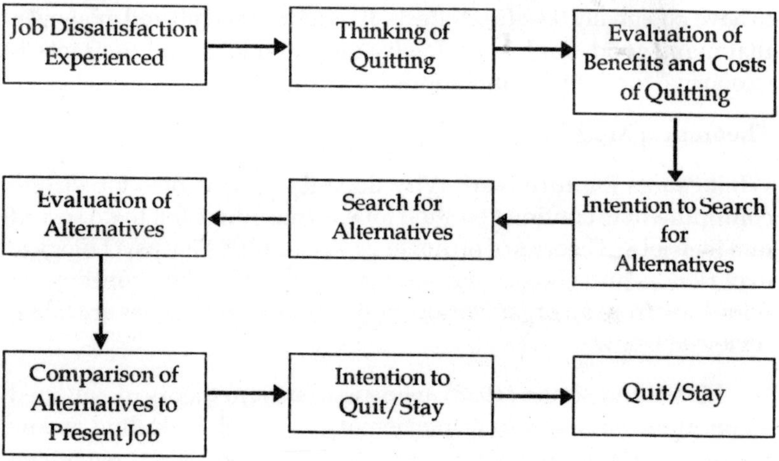


**Fig. 5.1: Model of the Turnover Process (Mobley et al., 1979)**

Farrell and Rusbult (1981), using an investment model, suggested that job commitment is a complex, multi-determined phenomenon, referring to the likelihood that an individual will stick with a job, and feel psychologically attached to it, whether it is satisfying or not. They asserted that job satisfaction should be greater to the extent that the job offers high rewards and low costs. Job commitment is said to increase with increases in job rewards, decreases in job costs, increases in investment size, and decreases in alternative quality. Finally, job commitment directly influences job turnover, with turnover resulting from decreases in level of commitment to the job.

Steers and Mowday (1981) using a cognitive framework, studied turnover by understanding the thought or decision processes related to the decision to stay or leave an organization. They suggested a complex 13-stage model of the process of voluntary employee turnover, including variables such as individual expectations, job experiences, affective responses to jobs, non work-related influences, intentions to stay, search for alternatives, and availability of alternatives as antecedents of turnover. In an abbreviated model, Steers and Black (1994) postulated that job attitudes (which are influenced by a host of individual and organizational factors, such as unmet job expectations, perceived inequitable rewards, poor supervisory relations, etc.) combine with nonwork influences (e.g. one's desire to stay home to raise a family, the transfer of one's spouse) to determine an employee's desire to stay or leave the organization (Figure 5.2).

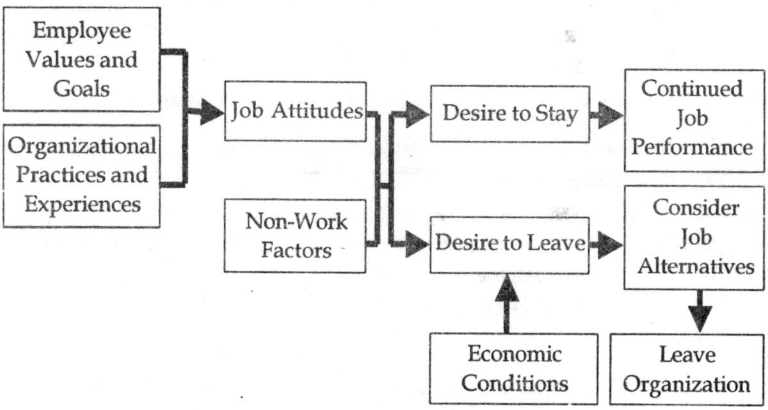


**Fig 5.2: Model of Employee Turnover and Post-Decision Accommodation Processes (Steers and Black, 1994)**

Fowler (1996) focused on "the early leaver" and outlined the following reasons as to why the initial employment period is a difficult one: *(a)* false expectations during recruitment; *(b)* inability to fit into the organization's culture; *(c)* unsatisfying relations with managers; and finally, *(d)* difficulty in adjusting to the immediate work group.

## CAUSES OF TURNOVER

Research has generally shown turnover to be moderately correlated with such variables as job satisfaction, organizational commitment, and intentions to leave (Michaels and Spector, 1982; Mobley, 1982;

Youngblood, Mobley, and Meglino, 1983). Because most studies have been correlational in nature, it is difficult to state conclusively what factors are responsible for the relationships. We will consider two main causes of turnover here: job dissatisfaction, and cultural/ socialisation factors.

**Turnover and Job Dissatisfaction**

Job dissatisfaction has been implicated as an important cause of turnover. Walker and Guest (1952) found high levels of turnover among employees dissatisfied with repetitive, machine-paced assembly-line jobs. Similarly, Porter and Steers (1973) found dissatisfaction to be a reasonably good predictor of absenteeism and turnover. Research reviews by Steers and Rhodes (1978), Mobley et al. (1979) have pointed to a relation between dissatisfaction, stress, and increase in absenteeism and turnover. Shaw (1999), too, found job satisfaction to significantly predict turnover intentions in 194 full- and part-time workers registered for MBA courses.

Porter and Lawler (1965) reviewed existing literature to investigate the role of organizational size on satisfaction and employee turnover. The type of organizations covered automobile dealerships, departments, and even work groups. They concluded that larger-sized subunits were related negatively to job satisfaction, and to the tendency to stay on the job by not being absent and not terminating employment.

Satisfaction with wages was suggested as being important in researches of job choices (Organization for Economic Cooperation and Development, 1965; Yoder, 1962), which revealed that: (1) organizations which pay higher wages are able to attract and retain high-quality labour; (2) turnover is high in organizations where wages are low relative to other companies in the area; (3) the stimulus to leave a company is greater when all the other employees are making more money; and (4) turnover is low in times of recession.

Dansereau, Cashman and Grean (1974), using two separate samples (222 office workers and 354 managers) reported that the strength of the predictive relationship of job satisfaction on turnover is moderated by the expectancy of finding a comparable job.

Mobley, Horner, and Hollingsworth (1978) collected survey data from 203 hospital employees to evaluate a heuristic model of employee turnover. The questionnaire included measures of general and facet job satisfaction, thoughts about quitting, the intention to quit, the perceived probability of finding another job, and biographical information. Turnover data were collected 47 weeks later. Regression analysis revealed significant correlations between job satisfaction and thinking about quitting and intention to search, but not to actual turnover. As hypothesised, intention to quit exhibited the only significant coefficient with actual attrition.

Miller, Katerberg, and Hulin (1979) investigated the contributions of withdrawal cognition, job satisfaction, and career mobility in predicting turnover using two independent military samples of 235 and 225 National Guards members. Measures of job satisfaction, thoughts of quitting, intention to search for an alternate job, intent to quit, age, tenure, and perceptions of job opportunities were related to re-enlistment decisions made within 6 months of attitude assessment. Results showed that job satisfaction and career mobility (age, tenure, job opportunities) influenced turnover only through withdrawal cognitions (intent to quit and to search for a job, thoughts of quitting).

Motowidlo (1983) examined the effects of pay satisfaction and pay expectation (in another job) on withdrawal cognition and turnover by 89 sales representatives. Both correlated with withdrawal cognition, but pay expectation did not contribute explanatory variance after pay satisfaction. Only withdrawal cognition and pay satisfaction were significantly correlated with actual turnover. Thus, effects of pay on turnover were mediated primarily by pay satisfaction and intentions to quit.

Carsten and Spector (1987) conducted a meta-analysis to determine the relation between satisfaction-turnover correlations across studies and unemployment rates at the times those studies were conducted. They hypothesised that low relations would be found in studies conducted during times of high unemployment and limited employment opportunity and vice-versa. Results supported the hypothesis: correlations were found that ranged from -.18 to -.52 between unemployment rates and the magnitude of satisfaction-turnover relations across studies. Further, the behavioural intention-turnover relation was also moderated by economic alternatives.

Aryee, Wyatt, and Ma-Kheng (1991) studied the antecedents of turnover intentions among 245, 30-35 year old professional accountants in different employment settings in Singapore. Questionnaires measured organizational commitment, professional commitment, skill utilization, realization of professional expectations, job satisfaction, and turnover intentions. Job satisfaction, realization of professional expectations, and professional commitment contributed to professional-organizational commitment. Skill utilization emerged as a significant predictor variable in the nonprofessional setting. Further, organizational commitment and job satisfaction were found to be the main predictors of turnover intentions.

Quarles (1994) used path analysis to analyze the effects of Satisfaction with Promotion Opportunities (SWPO), satisfaction with Promotion and Reward Evaluation Criteria (SWPREC), Organizational Commitment, and job satisfaction on employees' expressed Turnover Intention (TI). Subjects were 64 internal audit supervisors and 62 non-supervisory professional staff-level auditors. SWPO had a direct positive effect on job satisfaction and an indirect effect on TI for both groups. For supervisors, SWPO had both a direct and indirect effect on job satisfaction; for staff-level subjects, SWPREC had both a direct and indirect effect on TI. Results show the pervasive influence of satisfaction with promotion opportunities and criteria on job satisfaction and TI.

Omundson, Schroeder and Stevens (1996) compared 860 Euro-Americans and 119 Hispanics on Type A personality, job satisfaction, and turnover intention among certified public accountants. Results indicated personality, but not job satisfaction, to be significantly associated with occupational setting and level of decision-making authority. Turnover intention was not associated with occupational setting but was associated with level of decision-making authority.

Siu and Cooper (1998) investigated the effects of locus of control and organizational commitment on the relationship of sources of stress with psychological distress, job satisfaction, and quitting intention of 122 Chinese employees (66 males, 54 females, and 2 unclassified) working in Hong Kong firms. Results suggested that locus of control and commitment had strong direct effects (externals were dissatisfied with the job itself and thought of quitting the job quite often; employees who had a high commitment had higher job satisfaction) and moderating effects (the stressor-strain relationships were significant in externals, and commitment buffered most of this relationship).

**Turnover and Organizational Culture Influences**

Porter, Lawler, and Hackman (1975) considered a high rate of turnover as problems of individual-organization interaction in many work environments, particularly in the early months after a person joins an organization. The kind of socialization influences that act on the individual may affect how well he fits into the organization.

Youngblood, Mobley, and Meglino (1983) used a longitudinal design to analyse the turnover process among a cohort of 1445 U.S. Marine Corps enlistees over a 4-year period. Significant predictors of early turnover were found at the time of organizational entry and were indicative of individual and anticipatory socialisation differences. The study demonstrated that changes in satisfaction over time are related to turnover.

Butler, Lardent, and Miner (1983) proposed that turnover may be due to certain motivational propensities of the individual in interaction with aspects of organizational structure and process, i.e. people are less likely to quit their jobs when their motives are consistent with the demands of their organizations. For e.g., among managers in bureaucratic, hierarchical organizational structures, the people most likely to separate are the ones with low levels of managerial motivation. This hypothesis was tested on *(a)* 502 individuals of the U.S. Military Academy, 189 of whom separated in a 4-year period after testing, and *(b)* 251 individuals from The Officer Candidate School, 29 of whom failed to complete the 15-week course. Results indicated that lack of congruence between individual motives and that of the essentially hierarchical military education and training context, predicted turnover for both samples.

In a study of 2300 Black and White enlisted U.S. Army Personnel, Butler and Holmes (1984) found that the likelihood to stay in the organization was partly determined by the degree of congruence between the employee's personal beliefs about racial separation, and the army's policy of thorough integration. The degree of fit between personal values and those of the organization was an important factor in continuation of employment.

Steel, Shane and Kennedy (1990) investigated the effects of social-systems factors (participation in decision making, group cohesiveness, and communication climate) on absenteeism, turnover, and job performance, on 101 full-time civilian employees of the Air National Guard. Job performance was rated through self-appraisal and supervisory appraisal. The three social system variables were found to be highly intercorrelated. Affective, motivational, and behavioural work outcomes covaried with the features of the psychosocial work environment.

Chatman (1991) tracked the early careers of 171 entry-level auditors in U.S. public accounting firms and assessed the congruence of their values with those of the organization. Results suggested: *(a)* recruits, whose values match those of the firm, adjust to it more quickly; *(b)* those who experience the most vigorous socialization fit the firm's values better than those who do not; and *(c)* recruits whose values most closely match the firms' feel more satisfied and intend to and actually remain with it longer.

O'Reilly, Chatman and Caldwell (1991) studied the relationship between person-culture fit and certain work outcomes on 224 graduate students, 395 accountants, and 730 middle-level government employees. Their hypothesis was that Person-Organization Fit (POF) is related to work outcomes viz. organizational commitment, job satisfaction, intent to leave, and turnover. POF predicted job satisfaction and organizational commitment a year after fit was measured and actual turnover after 2 years.

Vandenberghe (1999) examined the relation between the level of congruence between an organization's culture and its new employees' (average tenure of 5.31 months) value preferences, on 565 subjects in a health care industry in Belgium. As expected, the congruence between the values of the hospital and nursing recruits' preferred values was predictive of nurses staying one year after congruence was measured.

Van and Annelies (2000) examined the effects of two measures of fit on newcomers' commitment and turnover intentions. 154 newcomers', 101 supervisors' and 104 peers' perceptions of organizational culture (P-O fit) were compared and with their preferences for organizational culture (P-P fit). Subjects' culture preferences and perceptions yielded two dimensions of organizational culture: concern for people and concern for goal accomplishment. Results revealed that newcomers' concern for people P-P fit with their supervisor was related to organizational commitment and turnover intentions.

Delobbe and Vandenberghe (2001) examined contributions of four training devices on socialization of newcomers in the banking industry: mentoring, formal courses, self-learning devices, and job rotation. The socialization outcomes measured were attitudinal variables such as job satisfaction, organizational commitment and intent to stay, and the relative fit between newcomers' perceptions of organizational culture and those reported by tenured managers of the firm (person-culture fit). A survey was conducted in four Belgian banks and included 201 newcomers and 247 tenured managers. Results of hierarchical regressions revealed that training intensity, whatever the device, did not explain a significant amount of variance in job satisfaction, organizational commitment and intent to stay. On the other hand, training devices had no effect per se on person-culture fit. They concluded that, more than the objective intensity of training, the newcomers' subjective appraisal of training explained socialization outcomes.

Wanous, Poland, Premack, and Davis (1992) conducted a meta-analysis of the effects of met expectations on newcomers' attitudes and behaviours. They found mean (corrected) correlations of 0.39 for job satisfaction and for organizational commitment, 0.29 for intent to leave, 0.19 for job survival, and 0.11 for job performance. They suggested a met-expectations hypothesis, namely that confirmation of employees' pre-employment expectations about the nature of their jobs leads to higher levels of job satisfaction and organizational commitment, and reduced likelihood of turnover. The reverse, i.e. 'reality shock' results in lower levels of satisfaction and commitment and increased turnover.

Irving and Meyer (1994) questioned the met-expectations hypothesis (Wanous et al., 1992) due to methodological problems. They conducted a longitudinal study to examine the separate and joint contribution of expectations and experiences to the prediction of job satisfaction, organizational commitment, and intent to leave during the first year of employment. The findings suggested that to lower turnover intentions, it is advisable to focus more on providing positive work experiences than on confirming expectations.

In an investigation of the relationship between organizational culture and employee retention, Sheridan (1992) examined the retention rates of 904 college graduates hired in six public accounting firms over a 6-year period. The variation in organizational cultural values had a significant effect on the rates of turnover. Subjects voluntarily stayed 14 months longer in the culture emphasising interpersonal relationship values than in the culture emphasising work task values. The relationship between the employees' job performance and their retention also varied significantly with organizational culture values. The cultural effects were stronger than the combined exogenous influences of the labour market and the new employees' demographic characteristics.

Ostroff (1993) investigated the effect of organizational climates and personal orientations on attitudes and behaviours (job satisfaction, job performance, employee absenteeism, employee turnover, job involvement, and occupational adjustment) of 533 teachers from 29 secondary schools. Results indicated that work responses could be explained by a joint, additive function of organizational climates and personal orientations. Using a sample of 101 middle managers, Orpen (1995) examined the effects of perceived downward and upward communication quality on employee turnover intentions. Results confirmed the importance of communication quality, but suggested that its effects on valued outcomes like job satisfaction and intentions to remain in the organization were moderated by organizational commitment, being much stronger among employees attached to the particular organization.

Vukotich (1996) examined organizational culture from 150 current as well as 150 former members of a major consulting firm. Aspects of culture were believed to play a major part in whether individuals choose to stay with or leave an organization. Differences in perceptions of cultural styles were observed between current and former members. Current members felt the organization was managed in a participative and person focused manner. Former members saw the organization as being bureaucratic, focusing on tasks, and demanding long hours. He suggested that by designing appropriate strategies for modifying the culture, turnover can be dealt with.

Abrams, Ando, and Hinkle (1998) conducted two studies to predict turnover intentions in Japanese and British Commercial and Academic Organizations. As expected, the authors found that identification with the organization substantially and significantly predicted turnover intentions in both countries. Attitudes predicted intentions only in Study 2, and subjective norms significantly predicted intentions across both studies. However, subjective norms were a significantly stronger predictor of turnover intentions in a collectivist setting in the Japanese Organizations.

Fletcher (1999) examined the relationships between organizational commitment, job involvement, the psychological contract, organizational culture, and the process of employee voluntary turnover. Participants in this study were managerial and service employees of a large southwestern organization. Turnover data was assessed each month for a period of six months after the initial administration. Results indicated a significant negative association between voluntary turnover and employee perceived obligation to employer. Demographic variables that were significant were gender, age, ethnicity and salary, with a significant negative relationship between age, salary and voluntary turnover, and a positive association between gender, ethnicity and turnover.

Peters (2000) examined the effect of six variables (attributional style, role conflict, role ambiguity, supervisory support, and spouse, friends and family support) on propensity to leave for male and female consultants. Results indicated that attributional style, social support and role stress were found to contribute to a propensity to leave in both male and female consultants. Supervisory support had a positive direct effect on role ambiguity, a negative direct effect on role conflict, and a negative indirect effect on propensity to leave via role ambiguity and role conflict.

Ellett (2000) explored some individual and organizational factors in explaining retention of professional staff in public child welfare agencies. Measures of intent to remain (employed) in child welfare settings, human caring, self-efficacy beliefs, and professional organizational culture were developed to explore linkages among the study variables. Results showed that intention to remain employed was largely explained by staff members' positive perceptions of administrative support and beliefs about work tasks.

Parkes, Bochner, and Schneider (2001) investigated the effect of a national culture dimension affecting organizational values: individualism-Collectivism (I-C) on three organizational outcomes viz. tenure, satisfaction, and commitment, using 581 volunteers from two matched organizations (hospitals and management consultancies) in Australia and in South-East Asia. Two types of fit were analyzed: Interactions between individual I-C and national culture, and individual I-C and organizational culture. Both national and organizational differences were found with respect to I-C. In support of person-nation fit hypotheses, collectivists were more committed to their organizations and had longer tenure than individualists in Asian, as compared to Australian Organizations.

## REDUCING TURNOVER

Cascio (1982) suggested that organizations seeking to reduce turnover ought to look at recruitment, selection, and early socialisation practices, job content, compensation practices, leadership and supervision, career planning and development, and alternative schedules. Similarly, Zippo's (1982) recommendations for reducing turnover are: raising salaries, instituting orientation and exit interviews, increasing benefits, training supervisors, and improving selection and placement.

Rusbult and Farrell (1983) extended their investment model for the control of turnover. They suggested that programmes to reduce attrition may benefit by increasing pay relative to competing firms, by providing workers with realistic job previews, by job redesign and other programmes intended to eliminate aversive elements of work, by promoting employee-firm linkages through home loan assistance, employing spouses, and so on, and by offering unique advantages (e.g. job sharing) not available elsewhere.

Research has emphasized the importance of Realistic Job Preview (RJPs) in controlling some turnover. McEvoy and Cascio (1985) investigated the relative effectiveness of Realistic Job Preview (RJPs) and job enrichment/redesign as turnover reduction strategies. Their meta-analysis, based on 20 experiments indicated that job enrichment techniques were about twice as effective at reducing turnover as RJPs. Buckley et al. (1998) suggested that the application of an Expectation Reducing Procedure (ELP), which is not job specific and is relatively content free, unlike RJPs, may yield similar benefits of reducing expectations. They suggested using ELPs in conjunction with RJPs in the newcomer socialisation process to reduce turnover.

Henry, Keys, and Schaumann (2001) underlined the importance of value-based job analysis intervention to improve the fit between new employees and the organization in reducing turnover. Using a case study in a recreational rehabilitation serving people with developmental disabilities, they described the benefits of implementing value-based recruitment, selection and training procedures as reducing unwanted staff turnover from 26 to 8 per cent and improving the quality of staff performance.

## SUMMARY

Turnover represents a sizeable cost for most companies, both in terms of actual costs and damage to the organization's reputation as an employer. While some turnover may be unavoidable or even desirable, it must be remembered, however, that many good employees do also quit their jobs, and their loss is expensive for their organizations. Thus, it is especially important for organizations to identify their better employees through performance appraisal programmes, and if these employees show low job satisfaction, commitment, and involvement, to try to remedy the situation.

Early research tended to focus on such determinants of employee turnover like job satisfaction, pay, withdrawal cognition, organizational commitment, job involvement, economic conditions, and a host of biographical factors. Only recently the role of individual motivational-organizational fit (Butler, Lardent and Miner, 1983), Person-Organization Fit (P-O fit) with regards to value congruence (O'Reilly, Chatman and Caldwell, 1991; Vandenberghe, 1999); met-expectations (Wanous et al., 1992; Irving and Meyer, 1994), content of organizational socialisation (Chao et al., 1994), organizational culture (Sheridan, 1992; Ellett, 2000) and very recently national culture dimensions (Parkes, Bochner, and Schneider, 2001) have been implicated in turnover.

# 6
# Multinational Corporation

## UNDERSTANDING MULTINATIONAL CORPORATION (MNC)

The phenomenon of globalization has had a dramatic effect on organizations. Whether or not they operate internationally, competing in a globalized economy has affected almost everyone in the new millennium. With the emergence of a truly global economy, domestic firms cannot insulate themselves from the effects of foreign competition. Large business organizations increasingly see their markets as international rather than purely domestic. The precipitating factors have been not only developments like rapid technological change, global transport and improved communication, but also attitudinal shift that perceives the new world as a smaller place.

In a way, multinational organizations have been with us for a long time. The Venetian city-state in the 15th century was heavily involved in international finance, and larger international trading companies like the Dutch East India Co. and the Hudson Bay Co. developed commercial operations in many continents as early as the 17th century. In legal form and structure, MNCs do not seem to be very different from the traditional types of private foreign investment with which nations have been familiar for over a century, yet they are in some ways a distinct form of enterprise of relatively recent origin. It is in the late 19th and the early 20th centuries that witnessed the growth and proliferation of multinationals, along with developments in the capitalist world economy. Globalisation expands the search for complementary capabilities to virtually the whole world. Texas Instruments, for instance, operates in India because the skilled and inexpensive labour available here adds value to TI's products.

Attempts to evolve a precise definition of what is known as a MNC have not met with much success. The United Nations Study titled "Multinational Corporations in World Development" (1973) used the term MNC in a broad sense to cover all enterprises which control assets, factories, mines, sales offices and the like in two or more countries. This is a very wide definition and would cover a lot of insignificant and routine activities such as those of international airlines. A narrower definition stipulating, for example, a certain minimum scale of operating would tend to be arbitrary and perhaps leaves out some which should be included. The U.N. document has taken size and concentration as the basic criteria for identification of MNCs and listed 650 industrial corporations with sales exceeding $300 billion in each case. The Government of Canada has fixed a minimum number of four or five countries across which a single business enterprise straddles as the basis of criterion for defining a Multinational Enterprise. Lilienthol (1960), probably the first author to use the term 'multinational firm', draws a wider parameter when he defines MNCs as corporates which have their home in one country but operate and live under the laws and customs of another country as well. According to Business International (1965), a firm becomes multinational when foreign operations account for at least 35 per cent of its total sales and profits. MacDonald and Parker (1965) consider a firm to be multinational if 20 per cent of its assets are overseas. The U.S. Tariff Commission Report (1973) points out that an enterprise can qualify itself a multinational if it has at least 25 per cent participation in the share of the foreign enterprise. Perlmutter's (1969) typology of the multinational business corporation on the basis of geographical orientation of activities suggested three classifications: ethnocentrism (home country oriented), polycentrism (host country oriented), and geocentrism (world oriented).

Gordon, Mondy, Sharplin and Premeaux (1990) define a MNC as an organization that conducts a large part of its businesses outside the country in which it is headquartered and has a significant percentage of physical facilities and employees in other countries. They usually operate through subsidiary companies in countries outside their home nation. Their operations create interrelationships between countries and cultures as well as between economic and political systems. They believe that organizations designated as multinationals should meet the following criteria:

1. Conduct operations in at least six different countries.
2. Have at least 20 per cent of the firm's assets and/or sales from business in countries other than that where the parent company is located.
3. Have and demonstrate an integrated, global managerial orientation:
   - Resources of the enterprise are allocated without regard to national boundaries.
   - National boundaries are merely a constraint that enters into the decision-making process; they are not part of the definition of the company itself.
   - The firm's organizational structure cuts across national boundaries.
   - Personnel are transferred throughout the world.
   - Management takes on a broad, global perspective; they view the world as interrelated and interdependent.

In India, the definition of MNC as appearing in Foreign Contribution Regulation Act, 1973, is as follows: "a corporation incorporated in a foreign country or territory shall be deemed to be a multinational corporation, if such corporation *(a)* is a subsidiary or a branch or has place of business in two or more countries or territories; *(b)* carries on business or otherwise operations in two or more countries' territories." A number of measures were taken in India in the early 1980s to liberalize the control environment and to increase the use of high technology and the computerization of industries. The Industrial Policy (1991) of the government reflected a quantum leap toward liberalization. The protective umbrella once placed over the economy is being withdrawn to a large extent, with foreign equity not only being allowed to exceed 51 per cent, but also permitting 100 per cent foreign-owned subsidiaries. Licensing is being abolished in most sectors. The private sector is being allowed entry into the areas once forbidden to it.

The term multinational organization is in many ways incorrect and misleading (Pandey, 1991). It would be better to describe it as transnational, because its activities are spread across national boundaries, than the term multinational which carries the suggestion that its ownership or control is shared by many nations, as many purists allege. Further, it operates not as a corporation but as a series of corporations, constituted in different countries but having a common affiliation and unified control. To further compound the confusion, the two terms multinational and transnational are also being used interchangeably (Encyclopedia Britannica, 2000).

Rollinson and Broadfield (2002) define a multinational organization as "one that is primarily located and managed from the country of its origin, but produces goods or services in relatively autonomous subsidiaries to meet the needs of the local market." On the other hand, a transnational organization is one that operates simultaneously as an international, multinational, and global organization, with some transnationals being remarkably similar to globalised organizations, while others more like multinationals.

Advocates of the multinationals often see them as positive forces in economic development, creating jobs and bringing capital, technology, and expertise to communities or countries that might have difficulty developing these resources on their own account. Their critics, on the other hand, tend to see them as authoritarian juggernauts that are ultimately out to exploit their hosts for all they can get. Particularly, with respect to the Third World, critics see multinationals as modern plunderers, exploiting natural and other resources for their own ends. Mostly the MNCs have been castigated for introducing inappropriate technology in labour-surplus nations, hammering the growth of local enterprises, and for interference in national politics of less developed countries. The argument identifies the horns of a major dilemma, in that the policies that serve the interests of a multinational firm may not be in the best interests of the community or country in which the firm is located.

## CULTURAL CONSIDERATIONS FOR THE MNC

### "The Business of International Business is Culture" (Hofstede, 1995)

The competitive global market has brought about new rules for survival, joint ventures and a network of contracted relationships, and strategic alliances that often cross cultural borders. Thus, following the process of globalisation, organizations no longer have distinct physical entities (Miles and Snow, 1984) as headquarters of an organization can be located in one country, manufacturing in another, sales and distribution in a third, and service close to the customer in a non-local market. Each distinct part of the business is responsible for day-to-day operations, whereas the corporate office is responsible for the overall financial control and the overall strategic development (Hill, Hitt, and Hoskisson, 1988). Culture probably plays a different role in organizations that vary in matters such as local versus international operations, foreign participation in equity, and technological complexities. The changes in the world market have made cultural changes in work context clear.

Most MNCs cover a range of different businesses and/or product/market divisions, in a range of countries. Along with the increasing pace of technological competition and the expansion of global markets, such ecumenical participation defines a new global reality. Expansion across national boundaries is much more than a step across a geographical line. It is also a step into different political, economic, social, and cultural environments. Managers of multinationals confront a number of challenges that they never had to face when their operations were constrained within national borders. They face different legal, taxation, economic, and political systems. But they also must deal with varying national cultures, many of which are nothing like those in which they spent their entire lives (Black and Porter, 1991).

Managers in multinational firms are often confronted with the need to bridge cultural distance in an attempt to improve their relationship with subordinates. They have to bridge both national and business cultures. The MNC must deal with the environment of the parent country, in which the headquarters are located, and the host country, in which the operational firm resides. Some researchers (Gordon, Mondy, Sharplin and Premeaux, 1990) have asserted that management of a MNC is directly impacted by societal concerns. Customs, beliefs, values, and habits of each society will vary. If the MNC is to operate in many nations, it will be required to adapt some of its managerial practices to the specific and unique expectations and situations of each nation.

Adapting one's behaviour to more closely approximate that of another culture has often been advocated as a way to improve international business relationships (Black and Mendenhall, 1990). Thomas and Ravlin (1995) found that cultural adaptation by the foreign manager (Japanese) was positively related to subordinates (American) intention to trust and perceptions of managerial effectiveness. This also moderated the relationship between perceptions of similarity and intentions to associate . Comprehensive acculturation training has been proposed by Mendenhall and Oddou (1985) to help expatriate managers adjust to the host culture's social and business environment.

According to Hofstede (1991), the structure of a multinational should follow culture. Davis and Newstrom (1989) suggest that the best results occur when neither the home country's nor the host country's traditional practices are used. Instead, a third set of practices contingent upon situational needs is developed that integrates the most workable ideas from both sides of existing practices. This clearly indicates that understanding the effects of culture on human behaviour is critical to the business success of MNCs. As asserted by Adler and Jelinek (1986), the role of societal culture must be incorporated within the organizational culture paradigm to make it more relevant for the MNC. By careful attention to societal culture, managers of multinationals can more effectively help to create an organizational culture in harmony with societal culture.

Expatriate managers often find that organizational behaviour practices of one country cannot be transferred directly to another, especially if the host country is less developed (Mendenhall and Oddou, 1985). Successful management of a MNC requires that managers understand the needs, values, and problems of employees in the host countries. Thus, as pointed out by Hofstede (1980) and Kanungo and Jaeger (1990), it is necessary for managers of multinationals to perform cultural transposition of ideas to make them fit the values of their subordinates. As suggested by Hofstede (1991), "culturally a manager is the follower of his followers: he has to meet the subordinates on these subordinates' cultural ground."

## SUMMARY

Models for understanding and managing people need to be adapted to the particular culture, level of development, and employee need structure of a host country. Cultural differences must be recognized and understood and one must be sensitive to them in order to be successful in a global economy. The multinationals operating in a foreign culture face a major challenge: whether to accept or try to change local cultural habits in host countries? This dilemma of the multinationals in India, which are the new transplants in a traditional cultural soil, presents an interesting research proposition. Would the culture of multinationls uphold Indian values or would have national values dominate? Against the backdrop of the preceding theory, and the changing scenario of the contemporary politico-economic world order, this book explores the consequences of diverse cultural encounters for organizational behaviour.

# 7
# The Research Strategy

When the first wave of liberalization in the nineties in India brought in the multinationals in droves, on the lookout for attractive markets and valuable human resources, it seemed that they would be able to replicate their worldwide success stories very quickly. However, most cross-border ventures resulted in failures as the subsidiaries of multinationals tended to function by centrally established systems and procedures, overlooking the unique cultural milieu of India, the host country, and the very different business environment that existed. The influence of the socio-cultural environment results in a set of beliefs and assumptions about human nature and organizational behaviour that employees carry with them as their cultural baggage when they join an organization (Kanungo and Mendonca, 1994). This is all the more true because of the collectivistic nature of the Indian culture, (Bond, 1988; Sinha and Verma, 1987; Triandis, 1994), where organizations are conceived to be more deeply embedded in the societal culture. It has been observed that Indian organizations "have 'fuzzy' boundaries. Essentially organizations have come to represent settings in which societal forces interact" (Ganesh, 1982). As observed by Sinha (1998), culture does enter through the back door to surreptitiously undermine the systems and distort managerial practices.

The increasing presence of multinationals in India presents an opportunity to examine the role of Indian societal values in organizational cultures and its consequences for organizational members. Thus, the broader socio-cultural context determines the immediate organizational culture of a given organization, which will regulate the behaviour of its employees in specific ways, which in turn, will influence the realization of organizational goals. This line of reasoning creates an interesting situation in the case where people from alien cultures are involved in running the organization. It would perhaps, lead to gaps, discrepancies, and discontinuities between the culture of the people and the culture of the organization, and may lead to poor health, lower organizational commitment, and turnover intention. The present book attempts to explore the nature of these relationships, in the context of MNCs in India belonging to different national cultures.

## METHOD

The conceptual framework for the present study has its roots in the model of culture fit proposed by Kanungo and Jaeger (1990). According to their model, external environment influences organizational culture, which in turn shapes management practices and employee behaviour reflected in individual processes and organizational processes, which leads to organizational effectiveness (job and organizational commitment of employees and their work performance). In this work, employee health, turnover intention, and organizational commitment are seen as consequent (dependent) variables, which are affected by antecedent (independent) Indian societal values directly as well as through the intermediate variable organizational culture. Further, societal values and personal variables of employees are proposed to influence organizational values.

To examine the impact of societal values on organizational culture, Hofstede's framework will be used. Hofstede's framework is recognized as a significant landmark in cross-cultural research (Triandis, 1982) and is widely used by researchers (Kanungo and Jaeger, 1990; Mathur, Aycan and Kanungo, 1996). Using an extensive survey, Hofstede identified 4 main dimensions on which country's culture differ:

1. Power distance is the acceptance of power hierarchy in institutions.
2. Uncertainty avoidance denotes the extent to which a society feels threatened by uncertainties and ambiguous situations.
3. Individualism/Collectivism describes people to be individualists, taking care only of themselves and their

families. They are collectivists when they distinguish between ingroup and outgroups and expect their ingroups (relatives, clans, organizations) to look after them, in exchange for being loyal to them.

4. Masculinity/femininity perceives a person as being masculine when s/he values assertiveness, acquisition of money and things, and feminine when quality of life and caring for others are emphasized.

Further, Hofstede asserted that "organizations are culture bound" and that national cultural values have consequences for organizational functioning. For e.g., high power distance in organizations translates into greater centralization, hierarchical structures, visible signs of status differences between various levels of the organization, and deference and lording behaviour. Thus, the four value dimensions identified by Hofstede are potentially well-suited to a comparison at both the societal and the organizational level. Both the Indian socio-cultural values and the organizational values are analysed on these four dimensions, identified by Hofstede (1980).

OBJECTIVES

1. To assess employee's perception of the Indian societal values on 4 dimensions, viz. societal power distance, societal uncertainty avoidance, societal individualism, and societal masculinity, in three MNCs.
2. To analyze and compare the organizational values as perceived by employees of three MNCs on 4 value dimensions, viz. organizational power distance, organizational uncertainty avoidance, organizational individualism, and organizational masculinity.

   - To study the effect of age, education and gender on perception of organizational values in three MNCs separately.
   - To study the effect of tenure, promotion(s) received, and number of jobs changed on perception of organizational values in three MNCs separately.

3. To understand the organizational values of three MNCs (as exemplified in organizational stories), and the espoused

and practiced values as perceived by organizational members.

4. To understand the extent to which Indian societal values have influenced organizational values of three MNCs.
5. To examine and compare the various outcome variables: employee health, turnover intention, and organizational commitment of employees of three MNCs.
   - To study the effect of age, education, gender, marital status, and family structure on employee health, turnover intention, and organizational commitment in three MNCs separately.
   - To study the effect of tenure, number of jobs changed, and promotion(s) received on employee health, turnover intention, and organizational commitment in three MNCs separately.
6. To investigate the relationships between the various independent variables (Indian societal values, organizational values, and personal variables) and dependent variables (employee health, turnover intention, and organizational commitment), separately in three MNCs.
7. To examine how Indian societal values, organizational values, and personal variables determine the outcome variables of employee health, turnover intention, and organizational commitment, separately in three MNCs.

## ORGANIZATIONAL SETTING

The present study was conducted in three large multinational organizations in India, chosen from the same area of business, viz. telecommunications to keep factors like nature of business and business environment constant. Multinational organization has been operationalized according to the definition given by Hofstede (1980): "By multinational organizations I mean organizations active in several countries but in which there is one dominant 'home' national culture to which most key decision makers of the organizations belong." Examples are IBM (American) or Mitsubishi (Japanese). These 3 MNCs belong to 3 different national cultures: French, American, and Finnish. To maintain anonymity, these organizations will be addressed as A, B and C respectively.

**Organization 'A': French Multinational**

*Company Profile*

With its extensive product portfolio and international positions, Organization 'A' is a key player in the globalisation of the telecommunications sector. As one of the world's very first providers of telecom solutions, Organization 'A' is a leader in its markets: internet, high-speed access, terrestrial and submarine optical networks, and intelligent networking. Its product portfolio includes all the essential components for building a communications network: network systems, access and transmission solutions, and a range of products designed for companies, communities and individual consumers. The organization's ultimate goal is to satisfy each customer's needs, from basic phone services to the most sophisticated multimedia networks. Its major business segments are: networking, optics, e-Business, space and components, and Nexans (cable activities).

Headquartered in Paris and with a strong presence in 130 countries, Organization 'A' with to 76,000 employees (2008) generated revenue of $ 22.6 billion in 2007. increase of 36 per cent over 1999. It has activities widely distributed throughout Europe, America, and Asia. The Group's long-term vision and its high level of technology are key factors in the success that has earned Organization 'A' the leading position it holds today. Innovation, the ability to develop and encourage the rapid growth of new technologies, is recognized as one of the keys to its success. An emphasis on R&D is a clear indication of the corporation's commitment to the future, but it is the lifeblood of today's business since about 60 per cent of "A's" revenues comes from products that did not exist just two years ago!

"A's" strategy has two aspects. First to establish and carefully manage a strong patent portfolio to secure its future. Second, to translate those assets into business success. Their commitment towards quality excellence incorporates *(a)* Environmental Management Systems, and *(b)* Software Process Improvement.

*Company Values*

The values espoused by Organization 'A' are: "Customer focus, Innovation, Teamwork, and Accountability."

### *Company History*

The company was set up on May 31, 1898 by French Engineer Pierre Azaria as Compagnie Générale d'Electricité (CGE) with the aim of taking on the likes of AEG, Siemens and General Electric. In 1985, a merger took place between this company and Thomson Télécommunications. In 1995, Serge Tchuruk became Chairman and CEO. He restructured the company focusing on telecommunications. In 1998, the company was renamed "A," as it is presently known.

### *Organization 'A' in India*

The organization's initial presence in India was through a partnership with Indian Telephone Industries forged in the early 1980s. In 1991, 'A' created a joint venture with an Indian partner, buying back its shares in 2000. 'A' now has a fully owned subsidiary, 'A India Ltd.,' which offers the complete suite of telecom solutions and services to meet the challenges of the Indian market. In India, it has offices in Gurgaon, Bangalore, and Chennai, employing about 2000 employees in all. The office at Gurgaon has a total strength of about 350 employees, of which 160 are white-collar employees.

## Organization 'B': American Multinational

### *Company Profile*

Organization 'B' is a global leader in providing integrated communications solutions and embedded electronic solutions. These include: software-enhanced wireless telephone, two-way radio and messaging products and systems, as well as networking and Internet-access products, for consumers, network operators, and commercial, government and industrial customers. They also provide end-to-end systems for the delivery of interactive digital video, voice and high-speed data solutions for broadband operators; embedded semiconductor solutions for customers in the networking and computing, transportation, wireless communications and digital consumer/home networking markets; and embedded electronic systems for automotive, industrial, transportation, navigation, communication and energy systems markets.

Organizations "B's" business units include: Global Customer Solutions Operations, Integrated Electronic Systems Sector, Networks Sector (comprising of Broadband Communications Sector,

Industrial Solutions Sector, Commercial, Government and Industrial Solutions Sector, and the Global Telecom Solutions Sector), Personal Communications Sector, and Semiconductor Products Sector.

In 2007, Organization 'B' posted net sales of $36.6 billion, It employs 66,000 employees in over 70 countries (2008). It has activities widely distributed throughout America, Europe, Asia, Russia, and Egypt.

*Company Values*

The organization's key beliefs are "constant respect for people" and "uncompromising integrity." This means "we treat others with dignity, as we would like to be treated ourselves."

*Company History*

The company was founded by Paul V. Galvin as the Galvin Manufacturing Corporation, in Chicago, Illinois, in 1928. Its first product was a "battery eliminator," allowing consumers to operate radios directly from household current instead of the batteries supplied with early models. In the 1930s, the company successfully commercialized car radios under the brand name "B", a word suggesting sound in motion. During this period, the company also established home radio and police radio departments; instituted pioneering personnel programmes; and began national advertising. The name of the company was changed to "B, Inc.", in 1947.

Its historical feats include making the first hand-held two-way radio for the U.S. Army Signal Corps. in World War II, commercially manufacturing the first fully transistorized Handie-Talkie, and manufacturing a transponder aboard the Apollo 11 lunar module that relayed astronaut Neil Armstrong's first words from the moon.

Under the Leadership of Robert W. Galvin, Paul Galvin's son, 'B' expanded into international markets in the 1960s and began shifting its focus away from consumer electronics. The colour television receiver business was sold in the mid-1970s, allowing the organization to concentrate its energies on high-technology markets in commercial, industrial and government fields. By the end of the 1980s, it had become the premier worldwide supplier of cellular telephones.

### *Organization 'B' in India*

The organization was incorporated in India on 23 June 1989 in collaboration with an Indian company and "B International Development Corporation" of the United States of America, to manufacture data communication equipment such as modems, multiplexers and networking products. The company commenced commercial production on 21 October 1990. The company now has a fully owned subsidiary called "B India," diversified into the following major lines of businesses: cellular infrastructure group, information systems group, land mobile products sector, and messaging systems products group. In India, it has offices in New Delhi, Bangalore, Calcutta, Bhubaneshwar, Chandigarh, Mumbai, Poona, and Patna, employing about 2100 employees in all. The office at New Delhi has a total strength of about 390 employees.

## Organization 'C': Finnish Multinational

### *Company Profile*

Organization 'C' is the world leader in mobile communications. They are not only the world's largest mobile phone manufacturer, but also leading suppliers of almost every aspect of the new mobile world, ranging from corporate and personal innovations, through to mobile, fixed and IP networks. It offers intelligent and user-friendly home products. Whether it be wireless, broadband, cable, or satellite technology, 'C' delivers cutting-edge home devices that take full advantage of today's leading technologies and bring feature-rich applications as well as services to the home. Recently, it opened up television to internet sofa surfers through their infotainment devices, which combine internet, digital T.V., and broadcast services.

'C' is a front runner when it comes to supplying data, video and voice networks and related services for their operator customers and Internet Service Providers. They are a leading developer of mobile Internet applications and solutions with an aim to be a pioneering partner in the era of mobile Internet and mobile multimedia. They aim to exceed the customers' needs through excellence in three key areas – design of products and solutions, services, and the state-of-the art technology.

Organization 'C' consists of 'C' Networks, 'C' Mobile Phones, 'C' Ventures Organization, and the research unit – 'C' Research

Centre. 'C' Mobile Phones is Europe's largest and the world's second-largest manufacturer of cellular phones, covering all of the world's major digital and analog standards.

In 2007, Organization "C's" net sales totaled $ 64.76 billion. It employed over 120,000 people (2008). By the end of the year 2007, 'C' had 14 manufacturing facilities in 9 countries around the world, a strong R&D presence in 10 countries, and offices in 30 countries, generated revenue that exceeded the state budget of its home country Finland.

### *Company Values*

The organizations' core values are: "Customer Satisfaction, Respect for the individual, Achievement, and Continuous learning." Employees are expected to behave according to these four values "which inform every issue that we as a company approach – whether it's business, employment, the environment, or society at large." It is believed that whatever the service, "our watchwords are speed, openness and quality."

### *Company History*

"C's" history dates back to 1865, when the Finnish Mining Engineer Fredrik Idestam established a wood-pulp mill in Southern Finland and began manufacturing paper. Since then, the company has evolved dramatically, growing first into a conglomerate encompassing industries ranging from paper to chemicals and rubber, and streamlining in the 1990s into a dynamic telecommunications company.

The groundwork for the shift to telecommunications was laid in the 1960s, when the company's electronics department was researching radio transmission. In the decades that followed, it's mobile phones and telecommunications infrastructure products reached International Markets, and by the 1990s, 'C' was established as a global leader in digital communication technologies.

### *Organization 'C' in India*

An industry leader worldwide, 'C' set up their 100 per cent owned subsidiary of the U.S. $8.5 billion 'C' Group of Finland, an International Telecommunications and electronics group with close to 80 per cent of their operations in telecommunications, in India in

1994, and launched cellular services in 1995. It soon commissioned India's first operational GSM cellular network at Calcutta, followed by the Madras network. The company's main Indian office was officially inaugurated in New Delhi on 27 November 1996, by the President of Finland, and President and CEO, "C" Group.

Organizationally, 'C India' follows a low hierarchy, matrix form of organization that gives tremendous operational freedom to each employee. The group practices a core culture of learning and excellence with a developmental attitude towards its people. Each employee is considered a global company resource and is expected to be internationally mobile. In India, it has offices located in New Delhi, Calcutta, Chennai, Bangalore, Ahmedabad, Hyderabad, Cochin, Coimbatore, Pune, and Chandigarh, employing about 900 employees in all. The office at New Delhi has a total strength of about 95 employees.

SAMPLE

Sampling was done in two phases. In the first phase a sample of 202 executives were drawn from three multinational organizations. The method of selection was non-probability incidental sampling, that is, executives who were present on the days the investigator visited the organizations and were willing to co-operate, were selected. The criteria for the selection of the sample included at least 6 months tenure of the employee in the present organization, minimum educational qualification of respondents being graduation, residing in Delhi or its satellite cities (Gurgaon, NOIDA, etc.) for at least the past one year.

An organization-wise sample distribution is shown below:

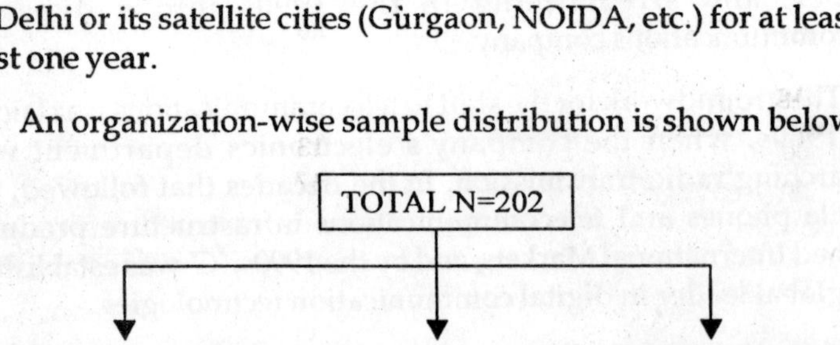


In the second phase, 60 executives were selected, using purposive sampling, 20 from each organization, for an in-depth interview session. The executives to be interviewed were chosen by the respective HRD departments of each organization. Interviews were conducted to provide the necessary backdrop to complement the quantitative information obtained from questionnaires.

Table–7.1 : Provides a Description of the sample.

**Table–7.1**
**Description of the Sample**

| *Sl. No.* | *Demographic Variables* | *Organization 'A' (N=65)* | | *Organization 'B' (N=71)* | | *Organization 'C' (N=66)* | |
|---|---|---|---|---|---|---|---|
| | | *Freq.* | *%* | *Freq.* | *%* | *Freq.* | *%* |
| **1.** | **Gender** | | | | | | |
| | Females | 24 | 36.92 | 19 | 26.76 | 20 | 30.30 |
| | Males | 41 | 63.08 | 52 | 73.24 | 46 | 69.70 |
| **2.** | **Marital Status** | | | | | | |
| | Unmarried | 21 | 32.31 | 16 | 22.53 | 17 | 25.76 |
| | Married | 44 | 67.69 | 55 | 77.47 | 49 | 74.24 |
| **3.** | **Education** | | | | | | |
| | Graduation | 24 | 36.92 | 13 | 18.31 | 16 | 24.24 |
| | Engineering | 31 | 47.69 | 31 | 43.66 | 22 | 33.33 |
| | Post Graduation | 10 | 15.39 | 27 | 38.03 | 28 | 42.43 |
| **4.** | **Family Structure** | | | | | | |
| | Nuclear | 51 | 78.46 | 45 | 63.38 | 54 | 81.82 |
| | Joint | 14 | 21.54 | 26 | 36.62 | 12 | 18.18 |
| **5.** | **Age** | | | | | | |
| | Below 25 | 9 | 13.85 | 13 | 18.31 | 11 | 16.67 |
| | Between 25-35 | 42 | 64.62 | 37 | 52.11 | 43 | 65.15 |
| | Above 35 | 14 | 21.53 | 21 | 29.58 | 12 | 18.18 |
| **6.** | **Tenure in Present Organization** | | | | | | |
| | 0.5-2 years | 34 | 52.31 | 32 | 45.07 | 24 | 36.36 |
| | 2.1-4 years | 14 | 21.54 | 21 | 29.58 | 15 | 22.73 |
| | 4.1 or more years | 17 | 26.15 | 18 | 25.35 | 27 | 40.91 |

*Contd...*

| Sl. No. | Demographic Variables | Organization 'A' (N=65) | | Organization 'B' (N=71) | | Organization 'C' (N=66) | |
|---|---|---|---|---|---|---|---|
| | | Freq. | % | Freq. | % | Freq. | % |
| 7. | **Experience Before Joining Present Organization** | | | | | | |
| | 0-1 year | 5 | 7.69 | 12 | 16.90 | 5 | 7.57 |
| | 1.1-3 years | 25 | 38.46 | 16 | 22.53 | 17 | 25.76 |
| | 3.1-5 years | 11 | 16.92 | 15 | 21.13 | 15 | 22.73 |
| | 5.1 or more years | 24 | 36.92 | 28 | 39.44 | 29 | 43.94 |
| 8. | **Number of Jobs Held Prior to Present** | | | | | | |
| | 0-1 | 18 | 27.69 | 27 | 38.03 | 25 | 37.88 |
| | 2 | 23 | 35.39 | 24 | 33.80 | 18 | 27.27 |
| | More than 2 | 24 | 36.92 | 20 | 28.17 | 23 | 34.85 |
| 9. | **Promotions** | | | | | | |
| | Not promoted | 48 | 73.85 | 34 | 47.89 | 22 | 33.33 |
| | Promoted | 17 | 26.15 | 37 | 52.11 | 44 | 66.67 |

Table 7.1 reveals that the percentage of women executives is largest in Organization 'A,' followed by Organization 'C,' and lastly organization 'C'. About two-third executives in Organization 'A' are married, while the number of married executives is even greater in Organization 'B' and 'C'. Since the three organizations belong to telecommunications sector, almost half of the respondents are engineers. Organization 'B' has the maximum per cent of engineers, followed by Organization 'A' and lastly 'C'.

The profile of executives of Organization 'A' depicts that majority have an age range of 25-35 years, are married, live in nuclear families, had experience (maximum had between 1.1-3 years) prior to joining their present jobs, more than half have spent less than two years in the present organization, and about three-fourth have not been promoted. The profile of executives of Organization 'B' reveals that about half of them have worked for less than 2 years in this organization, and slightly more than half have been promoted. Organization 'B' has the maximum per cent of executives aged over 35 years, maximum per cent of males, maximum engineers (many are engineers along with management degrees), and maximum living in joint families (about 37%). Majority of executives of Organization

'C, on the other hand are Post-Graduates (CAs, MBAs, etc.), have an age range of 25-35 years, about 40 per cent have a tenure of 4 or more years in the present organization, and a majority had worked for 4 or more years before joining this organization, highest per cent live in nuclear families and highest per cent of respondents (about 67%) have been promoted, at least once.

## MEASURES

"Just as the organizational culture perspective is encountering problems of *youthfulness*, so also are its favoured research approaches" (Ott, 1989). According to Ott, as "there is no consensus on what organizational culture is......it is impossible to have agreement on its research methodologies." Measures used by researchers range from straightforward research tools like questionnaires, inventories, structured and unstructured individual and/or group interviews, to longitudinal qualitative research methods like ethnography (Van Maanen, 1983). A very small number of organizational culture researches have combined qualitative and quantitative methodologies. The present study attempts to fill this gap by using a multifaceted methodology incorporating both qualitative (interviews) and quantitative research methods (questionnaires). The usefulness of such an approach is that it makes a fuzzy field somewhat accessible.

### *Quantitative Measures*

1. *Indian Societal Values Scale*

This questionnaire incorporates statements given by Hofstede (1980) describing four dimensions along which dominant value systems in forty different countries can be compared and which affect human thinking, organizations, and institutions in predictable ways. These four dimensions can be described as follows:

*(i)* Societal Power Distance (SPD) is "the extent to which a society accepts the fact that power in institutions is distributed unequally."

*(ii)* Societal Uncertainty Avoidance (SUA) is "the extent to which a society feels threatened by uncertain and ambiguous situations by establishing more formal rules, not tolerating

deviant ideas and behaviours, and believing in absolute truths and the attainment of expertise."

*(iii)* Societal Individualism (SID) "implies a loosely knit social framework in which people a value set in which people are supposed to take care of themselves and their immediate families only, while collectivism is characterized by a tight social framework in which people distinguish between in-groups and out-groups; they expect their in-group (relatives, clan, etc.) to look after them, and in exchange for that they feel that they owe absolute loyalty to it."

*(iv)* Societal Masculinity (SMAS) expresses "the extent to which the dominant values in society are 'masculine' that is, assertiveness, the acquisition of money and things, not caring for others, the quality of life, or people."

The statements given by Hofstede (1980) to describe each of these above-mentioned dimensions of national culture, were modified to make them more relevant to the Indian socio-cultural context. In the initial stage of adaptation of the scale, a number of statements were taken under each dimension, with some worded negatively and some positively. Originally 66 statements were included in a Likert-type questionnaire having 5 response categories. On this prepared questionnaire, views of twenty people from diverse fields—army, management, academicians, business, housewives-were taken, since the aim was to tap Indian societal values. Accordingly, some statements were deleted and some modified such that the refined questionnaire now included 58 items distributed amongst the four value dimensions as follows:

(a) *Societal Power Distance:* This was measured through 13 items, of which 7 were positive and 6 negative.

(b) *Societal Uncertainty Avoidance:* This was measured through 15 items, of which 10 were positive and 5 negative.

(c) *Societal Individualism:* This was measured through 14 items, of which 6 were positive and 8 negative.

(d) *Societal Masculinity:* This was measured through 16 items, of which 9 were positive and 7 negative.

The original questionnaire (Appendix II-ii) was administered to 60 employees working in an Indian organization in order to analyse and validate the items.

### *Reliability*

The reliability of the questionnaire was calculated by the Spearman-Brown formula using the split-half method, using scores on the odd and even items of the test. The split-half reliability was found to be 0.68.

### *Validity*

This tool is found to have face validity, since it measures what it purpots to measure. Content validity is evident; most of the items and area assessed by the scale are found to be important by previous investigators, including Hofstede (1980) and Mathur, Aycan and Kanungo (1996). Hofstede (1980) validated the said four dimensions using a number of geographic, demographic, economic, and political national indicators, such as wealth (GNP per capita), economic growth (GNG: 10-year average growth in GNP), latitude, population size, population growth, population density. Further, he found that the stability coefficients of scores by country, computed as Spearman rank correlations of mean country scores between the first and the second survey rounds (in 1968 and in 1972) varied from 0.12 to 0.95.

### *Item Analysis: Maximizing Reliability and Validity*

Item analysis (Anastasi, 1982) was carried out to determine which items best measure the construct that the test was designed to measure, and the discriminatory power of each item. To compute the discriminatory power of each item, the method of extreme groups was employed. Two methods were used for making 2 extreme groups: *(i)* dividing the sample according to medians calculated for each of the 4 dimensions, and *(ii)* using upper and lower 27 per cent of the total sample (Kelley, 1939). After applying t-test to both the groups, only those items were retained that discriminated the high and low scorers at .05 level of confidence. (Results of item analysis are reported in Table IV of Appendix).

Further, the internal consistency of the scale was worked out by correlating each of the scale item to dimension-wise subtotals. Since the total test measures four different value dimensions, dimension-wise item-subtotal correlations were calculated (Murphy and Davidshofer, 2001) instead of calculating item-total correlations. 30 items were found to have significant correlations at the .05 level, while 25 among these were significant at .01 level. The correlation coefficients of the selected items varied from 0.33 to 0.69 (Appendix II-iii).

Analyzing the results of both measures of item discrimination and item-subtotal correlations, 25 items which were significant on all three were selected for the final form. This scale has been published (Khandelwal and Dhillon, 2003) and has been used by researchers subsequently. The scale (Appendix II-i) has following number of items under each value dimension.

**Table–7.2**

**Item Classification of Indian Societal Values Scale**

| *Sl. No.* | *Dimensions* | *No. of Items* | *No. of Positive Items* | *No. of Negative Items* | *Item Numbers* | *Range of Scores Possible* |
|---|---|---|---|---|---|---|
| 1. | SPD | 7 | 4 | 3 | 1,4*,6,8*,11,15,22* | 7-35 |
| 2. | SUA | 5 | 5 | – | 3,7,12,16,19 | 5-25 |
| 3. | SID | 6 | 2 | 4 | 5*,9*,13,20,23*,24* | 6-30 |
| 4 | SMAS | 7 | 4 | 3 | 2,10*,14*,17,18*,21,25 | 7-35 |

*Note:* * These items are scored in the reverse direction.

### *Scoring*

A 5-point response scale was used to score the subject's responses as follows: Agree=5, Agree to some extent=4, Undecided=3, Disagree to some extent=2, and Disagree=1.

Total scores for the four dimensions are obtained separately and are not additive in nature. The total score on each dimension is a simple mean value across the items under that dimension. Thus, scores can range from 1-5. Higher scores indicate greater Power Distance, greater Uncertainty Avoidance, greater Individualism, and greater Masculinity at the societal level.

2. *Organizational Values Questionnaire (Adapted from Hofstede, 1980)*

Organizational values of each multinational organization were assessed on the following four cultural dimensions:

(*i*) Organizational Power Distance (OPD). Power Distance in the workplace can be observed in centralization, tall organization pyramids, large wage differentials, visible signs of status differences, low qualification of lower strata, etc.

*(ii)* Organizational Uncertainty Avoidance (OUA). High uncertainty avoidance in organizations is reflected in are more structuring of activities, more written rules, larger number of specialists, standardisation of organizations, lower labour turnover, less ambitious employees, higher satisfaction scores, more power through control of uncertainty, more ritual behaviour, etc.

*(iii)* Organizational Individualism (OID). High individualism in organizations translates into primarily calculative involvement of individuals with organizations, organizational policies and practices allowing for individual initiative. In collectivistic cultures, in which the work group is the ingroup, employees are expected to act according to the interest of their group, which may not always coincide with their individual interests.

*(iv)* Organizational Masculinity (OMAS). High masculinity in organizations is characterized by seeing organizational interests as a legitimate reason for interfering with people's private lives; fewer women in more qualified and better-paid jobs; structuring jobs on the basis of individual achievement rather than permitting group integration.

According to Hofstede (1980), the four national cultural dimensions have 'predictable consequences for organizations.' Taking a lead from this, the statements given by Hofstede (1980) to describe consequences of cultural dimensions for organizations, were modified by the investigator to make them more relevant for Indian employees working in organizations. In the initial stage of adaptation of the scale, a number of statements were taken under each dimension, with some worded negatively and some positively. Originally 45 statements were included in a Likert-type questionnaire having 5 response categories. On this prepared questionnaire, views of twenty experts from the field of psychology and management were taken. With the changes incorporated, a refined questionnaire was prepared, which included 39 items (Appendix III-ii), distributed amongst the four value dimensions as follows:

*(a)* *Organizational Power Distance:* This was measured through 10 items, of which 4 were positive and 6 negative.

(b) *Organizational Uncertainty Avoidance:* This was measured through 11 items, of which 5 were positive and 6 negative.
(c) *Organizational Individualism:* This was measured through 11 items, of which 5 were positive and 6 negative.
(d) *Organizational Masculinity:* This was measured through 7 items, of which 2 were positive and 5 negative.

Item-analysis, reliability, and validity-coefficients were calculated using the scores of 100 employees working in 3 different MNCs.

### *Reliability*

The reliability of the questionnaire was calculated by the Spearman-Brown formula using the split-half method, using scores on the odd and even items of the test. The split-half reliability was found to be 0.72.

### *Validity*

The validity of the dimensions, as empirically demonstrated by Hofstede has already been explained earlier.

### *Item Analysis: Maximising Reliability and Validity*

Item analysis (Anastasi, 1982) was carried out to determine which items best measure the construct that the test was designed to measure, and the discriminatory power of each item. As in the case of Form 1, to compute the discriminatory power of each item, the method of extreme groups was employed, by the upper and lower 27 per cent of the total sample (Kelley, 1939). After applying t-test, only those items were retained that discriminated the high and low scorers at .05 level of confidence. 28 items were found to be significant at the .05 level, while 24 out of these were significant at the .01 level. (Appendix III-iii).

Further, the internal consistency of the scale was worked out by correlating each of the scale item to dimension-wise subtotals (Murphy and Davidshofer, 2001). 34 items were found to have significant correlations at the .05 level, while 30 among these were significant at .01 level. The correlation coefficients of the selected items varied from 0.31 to 0.74 (Appendix III-iii).

Analysing the results of item discrimination and item-subtotal correlations, 25 items which were significant on both measures were selected for the final form. The final questionnaire (Appendix III-i) has following number of items under each value dimension.

**Table–7.3**
**Item Classification of Organizational Values Questionnaire**

| *Sl. No.* | *Dimensions* | *No. of Items* | *No. of Positive Items* | *No. of Negative Items* | *Item Numbers* | *Range of Scores Possible* |
|---|---|---|---|---|---|---|
| 1. | OPD | 7 | 3 | 4 | 1,3*,5*,10*,13,20*,22 | 7-35 |
| 2. | OUA | 5 | 3 | 2 | 7,9*,11,16,18* | 5-25 |
| 3. | OID | 6 | 3 | 3 | 2*,4,6*,8,15*,24 | 6-30 |
| 4 | OMAS | 7 | 2 | 5 | 12*,14,17*,19*,21*,23,25* | 7-35 |

*Note:* * These items are scored in the reverse direction.

***Scoring***

A 5-point response scale was used to score the subject's responses as follows: Agree=5, Agree to some extent=4, Undecided=3, Disagree to some extent=2, and Disagree=1.

Total scores for the four dimensions are obtained separately and are not additive in nature. The total score on each dimension is a simple mean value across the items under that dimension. Thus, scores can range from 1-5. Higher scores indicate greater Power Distance, greater Uncertainty Avoidance, greater Individualism, and greater Masculinity at the organizational level.

3. *General Health Scale (Cooper and Sawaf, 1997)*

This scale measures the general health of employees, including physical (e.g., back pain), behavioural (e.g., smoking), and emotional (e.g., constant worrying) symptoms.

***Scoring***

A 4-point response scale was used to score the subject's responses the basis of how often they had experienced the mentioned health symptoms: The seven response categories and the values assigned to each category is as follows: Never=0, Once or twice a month=1, Every week=2, and Nearly every day=3.

Scores in each section: physical symptoms, behavioural symptoms, and emotional symptoms were added to obtain a total score of general health symptoms. Higher scores thus indicate greater health symptoms, and thus are indicative of poor health.

***Reliability and Validity***

According to the authors, it is extensively researched, nationally norm-tested, statistically reliable, having been tested on thousands of executives, managers, and professionals in more than a hundred organizations in service, technology, and manufacturing industries in the US and Canada.

4. *Organizational Commitment Scale (Buchanan, 1974)*

This 23-item scale measures organizational commitment of employees, viewed as "a partisan, affective attachment to the goals and values of an organization, to one's role in relation to goals and values, and to the organization for its own sake, apart from its purely instrumental worth." This is measured through three components:

*(i)* Identification, tapped through six items, is viewed as "adopting as one's own the goals and values of the organization."
*(ii)* Job Involvement is measured through six items intended to measure "psychological immersion or absorption in the activities of one's work role."
*(iii)* Loyalty, is viewed as the "feeling of affection for and attachment to the organization", and is measured by an 11-item sub-scale.

The seven response categories and the values assigned to each category is as follows: Strongly disagree=1, Moderately Disagree=2, Mildly Disagree=3, Undecided=4, Mildly Agree=5, Moderately Agree-6, and Strongly Agree=7.

***Scoring***

The 23-item scale contains seven reverse-scored items. Scores in each section: Identification, Job Involvement and Loyalty are added to obtain a total score of Organizational Commitment. Higher scores indicate greater Identification, Job Involvement and Loyalty, and thus are indicative of greater Organizational Commitment.

*Reliability and Validity*

Buchanan (1974) obtained responses from 279 managers from eight organizations, and coefficients alpha of 0.86, 0.84, 0.92 and 0.94 were recorded for the three sub-scales and the total scale respectively. The intercorrelations between sub-scales are as follows: Identification and Involvement 0.65, Identification and Loyalty 0.74, Involvement and Loyalty 0.58. A number of perceived organizational characteristics, for example the extent to which one's work was thought to be generally accepted as important to the company, were also observed to be significantly associated with individual managers' Commitment scores.

5. *Intention to Turn Over (Cammann, Fichman, Jenkins and Klesh, 1979; Seashore, Lawler, Mirvis and Cammann, 1982)*

In the field of turnover research, behavioural intentions have rapidly come into vogue and are becoming increasingly indispensable to empirical and theoretical work linking turnover behaviour to psychological antecedents. The present work focuses on turnover intent in the belief that intent represents the single best predictor of turnover (Kraut, 1975; Fishbein and Ajzen, 1975; Triandis, 1977; Mobley et al., 1978; Michaels and Spector, 1982; Steel and Ovalle, 1984). The Michigan Organizational Assessment Questionnaire contains a number of scales to measure work attitudes and perceptions, and one of them is the intention to turn over. This includes a three-item index of employees' intention to leave their job.

*Scoring*

This 3-item scale contains 1 reverse-scored item and the responses are on a five-point scale, ranging from 1-5. The mean value across the items constitutes the scale score. Higher scores indicate a higher turnover intention.

*Reliability and Validity*

Items and scales of The Michigan Organizational Assessment Questionnaire have been developed through a series of substantial empirical analyses, after administering it to several thousand employees from many organizations. The coefficient alpha is reported as 0.83 (N>400). Correlations of –0.58 and –0.27 are reported with the authors' measures of Overall Job Satisfaction and Job Involvement respectively.

6. *Personal Data Schedule*

Relevant information about the respondent's age, sex, education, marital status, family structure, years of experience in the present organization, work experience prior to joining present organization, number of jobs changed, and number of promotions received in the present organization was recorded by means of this schedule.

***Qualitative Measures***

Quantitative research methods risk missing the essence of culture as a whole and can easily become mechanistic. Hence qualitative measures were also used in order to illuminate and validate the quantitative data. The qualitative phase of the research consisted of interviewing.

A semi-structured interview schedule was prepared (Appendix I) with 2 objectives:

*(a) To Elicit Organizational Stories as Manifestations of Organizational Values*

The importance of stories in organizational research has started being recognized only recently Using stories as elements of organizational culture is an interpretivist approach, seeking to identify the meanings and symbolism of stories for organizational members (Martin et al., 1983; Allaire and Firsirotu, 1984; Mahler, 1988; Meek, 1988; Hansen and Kahnweiler, 1993; Gabriel, 1998), the underlying aim being to understand the core organizational values, as exemplified in organizational stories. An attempt was made to uncover organizational stories by means of loosely structured interviews, seeking to evoke stories the respondents had heard, or memories of critical events which were then presented as stories. Gabriel's (1998) approach of temporarily forgetting one's research role and becoming a fellow traveller on the narrative, engaging with it emotionally, displaying interest, empathy and pleasure in the storytelling process, was followed for eliciting stories.

*(b) To Understand the Espoused and Practiced Organizational Values*

To delve into the core of culture, formed by values, an attempt was made to uncover the espoused and practiced organizational values of each of the 3 MNCs as perceived by organizational members by means of a focused enquiry.

PROCEDURE

Three multinational organizations were selected from the same nature of business, i.e. telecommunications belonging to three different national cultures, i.e. French, American, and Finnish. Data collection in the three organizations was begun only after completing all essential formalities like seeking permission to conduct the study from the concerned authorities, and preparing the necessary tools.

In all 3 organizations, initially HRD department was contacted, which provided the lists of names of executives in various departments, and gave a brief introductory letter to the investigator. All the executives were then personally contacted and rapport was established after giving them a brief outline of the aim of the study. In order to obtain their honest responses, they were informed that their identity would not be disclosed, and the responses obtained would be kept confidential and used strictly for research purposes. The questionnaire schedule was administered only after answering all their queries, allying their fears and apprehensions, and building a trust.

In Organization 'A,' initially 90 executives were contacted out of which 15 did not seem to be motivated to take time their busy schedules, and hence were dropped from the list. The questionnaires were distributed to 75 executives, out of which 68 were received back (after persistent reminders). Only 65 were found usable (3 had incomplete information), and hence only these were retained for the study.

In Organization 'B,' initially 90 executives were contacted out of which 10 were extremely busy in travelling, and hence were dropped from the list. The questionnaires were distributed to 80 executives, out of which 72 were received back, of which 71 were found usable.

In Organization 'C,' only 78 executives could be contacted (because of relatively smaller size of the organization). The questionnaires were distributed to 73 executives, out of which 66 were received back (after persistent reminders) and all were usable.

Some executives complained about the length of the questionnaire, but after persuasion agreed to co-operate. Respondents were assured that the study had not been commissioned by the management, and that their participation was to be on an entirely voluntary basis.

As regards interviews, the list of interviewees was obtained from the HRD departments of each organization. In all, a total of 60 interviews were conducted over 38 visits to the three organizations, after fixing prior appointments. The 60 interviews ranged from a minimum of 15 minutes to a maximum of one hour forty minutes, although most interviews lasted between 45 and 75 minutes.

Throughout the periods of data collection, a concerted effort was made to spend as much time informally with the respondents as possible. During the interviews I also took notes about the conversation which were written up afterwards. Indeed, some of the most valuable parts of the interview took place after the formal interview was over and the notebook shut, the closing intimacies of the conversation being prefixed with a silent or explicit "Well, if you really want to know what I think..." Needless to say, a visit to the toilet to write as much as I could remember followed almost immediately. An analysis of the issues that came up during informal chats and various other subtleties was helpful for understanding the nuances of culture.

Finally, while completely unstructured observation time within an organization was impossible (due to lack of permission-it was eye-opening to see how bureaucratic MNCs could be!), I treated each visit as an opportunity to see the organization at work. If I had an interview, I would arrive early and stay on long after the interview was conducted. I would also wait happily between interviews so much so that the receptionist started suspecting that I had nothing better to do! This was, in a sense, the most useful time I spent since it enabled me to 'feel' the organization. Waiting outside managers' offices, often for long periods of time, allowed me to take copious notes about noticeboards, clothing, noise, furniture layout, office decoration, and so on—small details that seemed to illuminate so much. By paying attention, watching, listening carefully, an attempt was made to understand the observable level of organizational culture—visible artifacts (Schein, 1985), viz. the organization's codes of behaviour, dress code, symbols, etc.

Data collection was spread over a period of five-six months. After the data collection, all participants were sincerely thanked for their cooperation, and formal letters sent to HR departments of all 3 organizations thanking them.

**Precautions for Data Collection**

The following precautions were taken during collection of data:

- A good rapport was established and maintained with each respondent throughout the period of data collection.
- Only those executives who were willing to co-operate and respond honestly to the schedule were included in the sample.
- An attempt was made, as far as possible, to get a fair representation of executives from the three organizations.
- Care was taken to ensure that no item was omitted by the respondents, by chance or otherwise.

ANALYSIS

Raw data was tabulated for each variable being studied, separately for each organization. This data was subjected to different statistical analysis at various levels—univariate, bivariate, and multivariate levels in order to achieve the objectives of the study.

1. Descriptive Statistics. At the univariate level, the analysis included 'means' as a measure of central tendency and 'standard deviation' as a measure of dispersion for each variable included in the study for the three organizations. Means and standard deviations of four societal values, four organizational values, and three outcome variables, viz. employee health (and its components physical, behavioural, and emotional health), turnover intention, and organizational commitment (and its components organizational identification, job involvement, and loyalty), were compared for the three organizations.
2. Inferential Statistics. At the bi-variate level, this included t-test and 1-way analysis of variance (ANOVA). Range test Significance of mean difference was computed for employees of three organizations, with regard to their perception of societal values, organizational values, and outcome variables. Further, the effect of personal variables on

organizational values and outcome variables was assessed by comparing groups of employees, using t-test (in case of two groups) and one-way analysis of variance (in case of more than two groups). ANOVA was followed by post hoc comparisons using Duncan Multiple Range test in order to find out which of the various subset means differ from other means.

3. Correlational Analysis (Pearson Product-Moment Method). In order to understand the relationships between the various independent variables and dependent variables, Pearson Product-Moment correlations were computed separately for the three organizations.
4. Step-wise Multiple Regression Analyses. Regression is the determination of a statistical relationship between two or more variables. In multiple regression, a number of independent variables are employed to predict a single dependent variable. Step-wise multiple regression analyses were undertaken to determine the predictors of the various dependent variables, that is, employee health (and its components), turnover intention, and organizational commitment (and its components) from among the various independent variables, viz. 4 societal values, 4 organizational values, and 9 personal variables. This was done separately for each of the three organizations.
5. Content Analysis of Interview Responses and Thematic Analysis of Organizational Stories. According to Van Maanen (1983), qualitative research is interpreted by "coming to terms with the meaning, not the frequency of events or phenomena." Accordingly, organizational stories were analyzed using themes, i.e. values and morals (if any) reflected in the prevalent stories (Gabriel, 1998). In addition, content analysis was used to analyze interview responses to study the espoused and practiced organizational values. Content analysis is a technique for making inferences by systematically and objectively identifying specified characteristics of messages (Holsti, 1968). Raw data was organized into conceptual categories on the basis of themes, and then quantified by counting the frequency of responses under each category.

# 8
# Findings

Over the past two decades, research literature has highlighted the role of societal values in shaping an organization's culture (Kanungo and Jaeger, 1990, Denison, 1990; Sinha, 1990a; Kanungo and Mendonca, 1994; Kao, Sinha and Hong, 1995; Biswas and Tripathi, 1998; Kao, Sinha and Wilpert, 1999). The socio-cultural environment of any society determines collective norms and values, and individual beliefs, attitudes, and action preferences. Since organizational functioning depends on the behaviour and attitudes of people working in the organization, work behaviour is profoundly influenced by the socio-cultural environment within which the organization operates. Hence, sensitivity to societal values is particularly important in multinational organizations for effective human resource management. This book addresses the impact of these cultural factors on individual outcomes in multinational organizations.

The main aim of the present study was to understand the extent to which Indian societal values influence the organizational culture of three multinational organizations (French, American, and Finnish) operating in India. Further, the study seeks to examine how Indian societal values and organizational values affect micro-level individual outcomes like employee's health, turnover intention, and organizational commitment. Six objectives were formulated to cover all these aspects. The findings have been reported and discussed in this chapter, in line with the objectives of the study.

## EMPLOYEE PERCEPTION OF SOCIETAL VALUES ACROSS 3 ORGANIZATIONS

The first objective was to assess employee's perception of the Indian societal values on 4 dimensions, viz. power distance, uncertainty avoidance, individualism/collectivism, and masculinity/femininity, in different MNCs.

**Table-8.1**
**Comparison of Employee Perception of Societal Values Across 3 Organizations**

| *Societal Values* | *Org 'A' (N=65)* | | *Org 'B' (N=71)* | | *Org 'C' (N=66)* | | *A Vs B* | *A Vs C* | *B Vs C* | *F-Ratio* |
|---|---|---|---|---|---|---|---|---|---|---|
| | *Mean* | *SD* | *Mean* | *SD* | *Mean* | *SD* | | | | |
| SPD | 2.56 | 0.58 | 2.41 | 0.65 | 2.43 | 0.42 | - | - | - | 1.40 |
| SUA | 3.12 | 0.54 | 3.01 | 0.72 | 2.96 | 0.61 | - | - | - | 1.05 |
| SID | 3.19 | 0.56 | 3.09 | 0.59 | 3.04 | 0.51 | - | - | - | 1.17 |
| SMAS | 2.80 | 0.27 | 2.77 | 0.41 | 2.73 | 0.40 | - | - | - | 0.59 |

*Note:* **$p<0.01$, *$p<0.05$.

Table 8.1 reveals that employees belonging to the three MNCs did not differ in their perceptions of Indian societal values. The F-ratios on the four societal values were non-significant, indicating that employees of the 3 organizations do not differ in their perception of societal values. This is in line with Laurent (1981), who reported that, "employees maintain or enhance their culturally specific ways of working when placed within a multinational or global organization."

All employees scored moderate on power distance, high on uncertainty avoidance, high on individualism, and moderate on masculinity. This implies that they emphasise power only to a moderate degree; have a high need for adherence to formal rules and a low tolerance for uncertainty and ambiguity; a great emphasis on individual and immediate family needs; construe the self independently; and a moderate emphasis on things, power, assertiveness, and quality of life and nurturance. These results are more or less in line with the findings of Hofstede (1980) on India, who reported scores of 77, 40, 48, 56 (out of 100) on PD, UA, IND, and MAS respectively, making it high on PD, low on UA, moderate on IND, and moderate on MAS. These results are also supported by the findings of Mathur, Aycan and Kanungo (1996), who found that public and private sector Indian managers did not differ in their perception of socio-cultural dimensions. They found all managers to be high on PD, paternalism, femininity, UA, and community loyalty. Further, they also found a significant preference for self-reliance (considered as a crucial component of Western individualism) among Indians, implying that the self is conceptualized as an independent and autonomous entity, which is responsible for actions and their consequences. Schwartz (1999) also found Indians to give the highest importance to hierarchy (cultural emphasis on the legitimacy of an unequal distribution of power, roles and resources), followed by conservatism (cultural emphasis on maintenance of the status-quo and propriety), and mastery (cultural emphasis on getting ahead through active self-assertion).

The findings of employees being high on individualism are contrary to the results of Sinha et al. (1994), who found a general factor of collectivism (familialism, hierarchy, and maintenance of relationships) common in the North, South, and Central India. Other investigators (Sinha and Verma, 1987; Triandis, 1994) have also substantiated that the Indian culture is collectivistic by nature. Roland (1987) observed that self in India is less individualistic than in the West. Naidoo (1999) commented that "dutiful deference to parental authority (vertical collectivism) with an extended family bonded by interdependence and sharing of resources (horizontal collectivism) is the accepted norm in the Indian community."

On the other hand, the findings of this study get support from Tripathi (1988), who after reviewing studies on individualism and collectivism, found that Indians, particularly in achievement situations, are just as competitive as individuals from any Western society. He further stated that, "in the Indian society, individualism and collectivism act like figure and ground. Depending on the situation, one rises from the figure and the other recedes to the background." Thus, both kinds of orientations seem to be present. Further Sinha and Tripathi (1994) observed that Indian culture is characterized by opposite values, including individualism and collectivism, which coexist in a balanced way. Triandis (1995) commented that Indians are characterized by "vertical collectivism," i.e. view their selves as being different from the selves of others. It has also been suggested that the degree of individualism in a society is associated with its degree of modernity (Tonnies, 1963; Blumberg and Winch, 1972). The trend towards modernization, at least in the Capital City of New Delhi, may have contributed to higher scores on individualism.

## SUMMARY

Employees belonging to the three MNCs do not differ in their perceptions of the Indian societal values. All employees are found to be moderate on PD, high on UA, high on IND, and moderate on MAS. Despite working for multinationals with different cultural values, the Indian employees working for them maintained their predominantly Indian socio-cultural preferences.

## EMPLOYEE PERCEPTION OF ORGANIZATIONAL VALUES ACROSS 3 ORGANIZATIONS

The second objective was to examine and compare the organizational values of different MNCs on 4 value dimensions, viz. PD, UA, IND/COLL, and MAS/FEM.

**Table-8.2**
**Comparison of Employee Perception of Organizational Values Across 3 Organizations**

| *Org. Values* | *Org 'A' (N=65)* | | *Org 'B' (N=71)* | | *Org 'C' (N=66)* | | *A Vs B* | *A Vs C* | *B Vs C* | *F-Ratio* |
|---|---|---|---|---|---|---|---|---|---|---|
| | *Mean* | *SD* | *Mean* | *SD* | *Mean* | *SD* | | | | |
| OPD | 3.09 | 0.52 | 2.57 | 0.60 | 2.33 | 0.69 | (*) | (*) | (*) | 26.94** |
| OUA | 3.36 | 0.52 | 3.13 | 0.55 | 2.67 | 0.49 | (*) | (*) | (*) | 30.43** |
| OID | 2.47 | 0.58 | 2.65 | 0.74 | 2.35 | 0.49 | - | - | (*) | 4.10* |
| OMAS | 2.35 | 0.81 | 2.34 | 0.63 | 2.48 | 0.80 | - | - | - | 0.80 |

*Note:* **p<0.01, *p<0.05.

(*) Denotes pairs of groups significantly different at the .05 level using Duncan's test.

Table 8.2 reveals that the employees of the three MNCs differed significantly in their perception of 3 organizational values namely PD, UA, and IND, but not MAS. Employees of the 3 organizations did not differ significantly on MAS, with a moderate position on MAS-FEM, owing to their emphasis on "masculine" values like achievement and competition, but at the same time valuing "feminine" traits like nurturance and caring for others. According to Hofstede (1998), expressions of masculinity in organizational life include: *(a)* job-centeredness: centrality of work and career, emphasis on visible achievements, and desire for tangible expressions of success; *(b)* performance-centeredness: challenge, excellence, "going the extra mile," and competition; and *(c)* results orientation: initiative, decisiveness, and efficiency. On the other hand, expressions of femininity in organizational life include: *(a)* employee-centeredness: centrality of personal and family life, emphasis on mutual help, social interaction, personal fulfillment and belonging; *(b)* relationship-centeredness: quality of relationships and work environment, competence, and collaboration; and *(c)* people orientation: solidarity, empathy, and consensus. A moderate position for all 3 organizations implies a balance between the above two sets of characteristics.

Significant differences existed among all three organizations on PD, with Organization 'A', the French MNC, being the highest, followed by Organization 'B' (American MNC) and lastly 'C' (Finnish MNC). High PD in organizations translates into significant differences in status, rewards, privileges, and opportunities between the various levels of the organization, deference, and lording behaviour (Kanungo, 1990). These results are in line with the findings of Hofstede (1980), who found France to be extremely high on PD (rank 15/16), followed by USA (rank 38), and then Finland (rank 46). Other researchers (Crozier, 1964; Marceau, 1977; Peabody, 1985; Hoppe, 1990; Mark, 1999) have also commented on preference for hierarchy in French Organizations. Moreover, low PD in Finland has also been observed by Bochner and Hesketh (1994) and Schwartz (1999).

Similar results have been obtained for UA, where significant differences existed among all three organizations, with Organization 'A' (French) being the highest, followed by Organization 'B' (American) and lastly 'C' (Finnish). High UA in organizations translates into highly rule driven bureaucratic systems, preference for directive styles of leadership, and salience of job security. These results are only partially validated by Hofstede's (1980) findings, who found France to be highest (rank 10/15), followed by Finland (rank 31/32), and then USA (rank 43). The results are, however, completely in line with Hoppe (1990), who in an extensive replication of Hofstede's work on 18 countries, found France to be higher on UA than both USA and Finland. These results have been supported by others like Leites (1969), who reported that French view change as a danger; similarly, Peabody (1985) commented on the tendency of French people to codify and classify, reflecting high UA. Moreover, Pages et al. (1979) observed a greater dependence on hierarchy and rules in an average French citizen as compared to an American, while the society of Finland was even less built on hierarchy and rules than U.S. Hofstede (1984), too, commented on low UA in Finland.

On individualism, however, a significant difference was found to exist only between Organization 'B' and 'C', with Organization 'B' being the most individualistic, and Organization 'C' being the least. Organization 'B', an American MNC, was found to be the highest on IND, followed by Organization 'A', a French MNC, and lastly Organization 'C', a Finnish MNC.. These results are in line with the findings of other researchers like Johnson (1985), Hoppe (1990), Triandis (1995), Mark (1999) who have all commented on the highly individualistic American culture. In fact, Hofstede (1980) found America to be the highest (among all 53 countries) on individualism, with a slight difference between France (rank 10/11) and Finland (rank 17), which support the results of the study.

The results of this study seem to suggest that organizational values of MNCs are strongly influenced by the organization's "home national cultures." Hofstede (1982) observed that, "In the multinational organizations, the values and beliefs of the home culture are taken for granted and serve as a frame of reference even for persons from other cultures who make a career in that organization." He emphasised that the presence of a dominant national culture is an asset rather than a liability for the functioning of a MNC and it should be fostered carefully.

Further, the sub-objectives of the study were to examine the effect of personal variables on organizational values.

### *(i) Effect of Gender on Perception of Organizational Values*

**Table–8.3**
**Comparison of Male and Female Employees of 3 Organizations on Perception of Organizational Values**

| *Org. Values* | *Female* | | *Male* | | *t-value* |
|---|---|---|---|---|---|
| | *Mean* | *SD* | *Mean* | *SD* | |
| **ORG. 'A'** | **N=24** | | **N=41** | | |
| OPD | 3.11 | 0.63 | 3.07 | 0.32 | 0.29 |
| OUA | 3.30 | 0.51 | 3.46 | 0.54 | 1.21 |
| OID | 2.60 | 0.62 | 2.27 | 0.46 | 2.33* |
| OMAS | 2.47 | 0.98 | 2.17 | 0.46 | 1.50 |
| **ORG.'B'** | **N=19** | | **N=52** | | |
| OPD | 2.45 | 0.60 | 2.61 | 0.60 | 0.99 |
| OUA | 3.15 | 0.45 | 3.12 | 0.59 | 0.23 |
| OID | 2.68 | 0.71 | 2.64 | 0.75 | 0.24 |
| OMAS | 2.17 | 0.49 | 2.40 | 0.67 | 1.37 |
| **ORG.'C'** | **N=20** | | **N=46** | | |
| OPD | 2.32 | 0.33 | 2.34 | 0.80 | 0.09 |
| OUA | 2.80 | 0.49 | 2.61 | 0.48 | 1.48 |
| OID | 2.29 | 0.27 | 2.38 | 0.56 | 0.73 |
| OMAS | 2.03 | 0.38 | 2.68 | 0.85 | 3.27** |

*Note:* **$p<0.01$, *$p<0.05$.

Table 8.3 reveals significant gender differences on perception of IND and MAS in Organization 'A' and 'C' respectively, with males perceiving the organization in less individualistic (Organization 'A') and more masculine terms (Organization 'C') than their female counterparts. These results imply that in Organization 'A', males are more emotionally dependent on the organization; they expect the organization to look after them like a family—and can become alienated if the organization does not satisfy them. Females, on the other hand, feel that they are expected to defend their personal interests, and organize work in such a way that their self-interest and the employer's interest become one.

In Organization 'C', men are more job-centered, performance-centered, and have a greater result orientation, while females are more employee-centered, relationship-centered, and have a people orientation. These results are in line with the findings of Manhardt (1972), Crowley et al. (1973), Bartol (1976), and McCann-Erickson (1977) who reported that women compared with men tend to rate the interpersonal aspects, rendering service, and the physical environment as more important, than advancement, independence, responsibility, and earnings.

***(ii) Effect of Promotion(s) Received on Perception of Organizational Values***

**Table–8.4**
**Comparison of Employees of 3 Organizations who Received/Not Received Promotion(s) on Perception of Organizational Values**

| *Org. Values* | *Promotion(s) Not Received* | | *Promotion (s) Received* | | *t-Value* |
|---|---|---|---|---|---|
| | *Mean* | *SD* | *Mean* | *SD* | |
| **ORG.'A'** | **N=48** | | **N=17** | | |
| **OPD** | 2.92 | 0.32 | 3.59 | 0.64 | 5.52** |
| **OUA** | 3.44 | 0.52 | 3.14 | 0.44 | 2.15* |
| **OID** | 2.30 | 0.46 | 2.94 | 0.60 | 4.52** |
| **OMAS** | 2.09 | 0.52 | 3.07 | 1.03 | 5.01** |
| **ORG.'B'** | **N=34** | | **N=37** | | |
| **OPD** | 2.67 | 0.59 | 2.46 | 0.58 | 1.45 |
| **OUA** | 3.30 | 0.49 | 2.96 | 0.55 | 2.71** |
| **OID** | 2.79 | 0.81 | 2.52 | 0.64 | 1.55 |
| **OMAS** | 2.38 | 0.66 | 2.30 | 0.61 | 0.56 |

*Contd...*

| *Org. Values* | *Promotion(s) Not Received* | | *Promotion (s) (s) Received* | | *t-Value* |
|---|---|---|---|---|---|
| | *Mean* | *SD* | *Mean* | *SD* | |
| **ORG.'C'** | N=22 | | N=44 | | |
| OPD | 2.39 | 0.53 | 2.30 | 0.75 | 0.50 |
| OUA | 2.74 | 0.40 | 2.62 | 0.52 | 0.89 |
| OID | 2.42 | 0.35 | 2.32 | 0.55 | 0.81 |
| OMAS | 2.77 | 0.68 | 2.34 | 0.81 | 2.13* |

*Note:* **p<0.01, *p<0.05.

Table 8.4 reveals that promotion(s) received has a very strong influence on perception of organizational values in Organization 'A', but a weak influence in Organization 'B' and 'C'. In Organization 'A' (French), those who have received promotion(s) perceive the organization to be more individualistic and more masculine. They also prefer greater PD and low UA in the organization. In Organization 'B' (American) also, those who have been promoted perceive low UA in the organization. However, in Organization 'C' (Finnish), those who have received promotion(s) perceive the organization in less "masculine" terms than those who have not received promotion(s). These results seem to imply that in all the 3 organizations, employees who conform to the organizational values are probably the ones who have received promotion(s) or those who received promotions have probably indoctrinated the organization's values along with its way of working.

### *(iii) Effect of Age on Perception of Organizational Values*

Age did not have any significant effect on perception of organizational values in Organization 'B' and 'C' (Table 8.5). However, in Organization 'A', a significant difference was observed on perception of UA. Expectedly, those employees aged above 35 years perceive greater UA in the organization as compared to those between 25+ and 35 years. These results are in line with Hofstede (1991), who found a strong association between UA index and average age, with older employees preferring greater rule orientation. Similar results were obtained by Mathur, Aycan, and Kanungo (1996), who found that compared to older managers, younger managers in India were more resourceful, and therefore, were more likely to perceive events to be controllable and manageable.

**Table–8.5**
**Comparison of Employees of 3 Different Age Groups from 3 Organizations on Perception of Organizational Values**

| *Org. Values* | *Group 1 (< 25 yrs)* | | *Group 2 (25-35 yrs)* | | *Group 3 (> 35 yrs)* | | *G1 Vs G3* | *G1 Vs G3* | *G2 Vs G3* | *F-Value* |
|---|---|---|---|---|---|---|---|---|---|---|
| | *Mean* | *SD* | *Mean* | *SD* | *Mean* | *SD* | | | | |
| **ORG 'A'** | **N=9** | | **N=42** | | **N=14** | | | | | |
| OPD | 2.74 | 0.34 | 3.15 | 0.53 | 3.18 | 0.40 | (*) | - | - | 2.50 |
| OUA | 3.64 | 0.63 | 3.28 | 0.47 | 3.71 | 0.55 | - | - | (*) | 3.25* |
| OID | 2.22 | 0.51 | 2.55 | 0.55 | 2.02 | 0.63 | - | - | - | 2.99 |
| OMAS | 1.98 | 0.60 | 2.43 | 0.84 | 2.20 | 0.64 | - | - | - | 1.27 |
| **ORG 'B'** | **N=13** | | **N=37** | | **N=21** | | | | | |
| OPD | 2.54 | 0.50 | 2.63 | 0.57 | 2.47 | 0.69 | - | - | - | 0.54 |
| OUA | 3.19 | 0.37 | 3.12 | 0.52 | 3.10 | 0.68 | - | - | - | 0.10 |
| OID | 2.70 | 0.57 | 2.71 | 0.72 | 2.51 | 0.85 | - | - | - | 0.53 |
| OMAS | 2.18 | 0.47 | 2.34 | 0.65 | 2.43 | 0.70 | - | - | - | 0.58 |
| **ORG 'C'** | **N=11** | | **N=43** | | **N=12** | | | | | |
| OPD | 2.30 | 0.34 | 2.37 | 0.67 | 2.18 | 0.80 | - | - | - | 0.37 |
| OUA | 2.85 | 0.34 | 2.67 | 0.48 | 2.55 | 0.57 | - | - | - | 0.80 |
| OID | 2.45 | 0.21 | 2.34 | 0.45 | 2.34 | 0.72 | - | - | - | 0.13 |
| OMAS | 2.33 | 0.37 | 2.54 | 0.78 | 2.35 | 1.01 | - | - | - | 0.38 |

*Note:* **p<0.01, *p<0.05.

**(*) Denotes pairs of groups significantly different at the .05 level using Duncan's test.**

Although overall F-value in case of PD was non-significant, post-hoc comparisons did yield a significant difference between those below 25 years and those between 25-35 years, with the former perceiving less PD in organization as compared to the latter. This means that younger employees do not emphasize hierarchy, they feel that bosses are accessible, and expect to be consulted before a decision is made that affects their work. These results are somewhat in line with Mathur, Aycan, and Kanungo (1996), who found that younger managers were less formal in their interpersonal relations, in emphasising mutual help and support.

### *(iv) Effect of Education on Perception of Organizational Values*

**Tablė–8.6**

**Comparison of Graduate, Engineers and Post-Graduate Employees of 3 Different Organizations on Perception of Organizational Values**

| *Org. Values* | *Group 1 (Grad.)* | | *Group 2 (Engineers)* | | *Group 3 (Post-Grad.)* | | *G1 Vs G3* | *G1 Vs G3* | *G2 Vs G3* | *F-Value* |
|---|---|---|---|---|---|---|---|---|---|---|
| | *Mean* | *SD* | *Mean* | *SD* | *Mean* | *SD* | | | | |
| **ORG 'A'** | **N=24** | | **N=31** | | **N=10** | | | | | |
| **OPD** | 2.90 | 0.31 | 3.05 | 0.43 | 3.68 | 0.75 | - | (*) | (*) | 10.45** |
| **OUA** | 3.64 | 0.48 | 3.26 | 0.45 | 3.01 | 0.50 | (*) | (*) | - | 7.67** |
| **OID** | 2.26 | 0.46 | 2.45 | 0.46 | 3.03 | 0.77 | - | (*) | (*) | 7.72** |
| **OMAS** | 1.88 | 0.32 | 2.39 | 0.59 | 3.34 | 1.25 | (*) | (*) | (*) | 17.23** |
| **ORG 'B'** | **N=13** | | **N=31** | | **N=27** | | | | | |
| **OPD** | 2.45 | 0.55 | 2.51 | 0.59 | 2.69 | 0.61 | - | - | - | 0.93 |
| **OUA** | 3.07 | 0.48 | 3.08 | 0.54 | 3.21 | 0.59 | - | - | - | 0.44 |
| **OID** | 2.65 | 0.83 | 2.54 | 0.67 | 2.77 | 0.77 | - | - | - | 0.69 |
| **OMAS** | 2.20 | 0.51 | 2.28 | 0.50 | 2.47 | 0.80 | - | - | - | 0.97 |
| **ORG 'C'** | **N=16** | | **N=22** | | **N=28** | | | | | |
| **OPD** | 2.45 | 0.33 | 2.55 | 0.94 | 2.09 | 0.52 | - | - | (*) | 3.33* |
| **OUA** | 2.89 | 0.45 | 2.61 | 0.51 | 2.58 | 0.46 | - | - | - | 2.45 |
| **OID** | 2.44 | 0.37 | 2.55 | 0.60 | 2.15 | 0.38 | - | - | (*) | 5.01** |
| **OMAS** | 2.53 | 0.73 | 2.80 | 0.85 | 2.21 | 0.70 | - | - | (*) | 3.62* |

*Note:* **p<0.01, *p<0.05.

(*) Denotes pairs of groups significantly different at the .05 level using Duncan's test.

Table 8.6 depicts that education has an influence on all 4 organizational values in Organization 'A', on 3 organizational values in Organization 'C', and none in Organization 'B'. In Organization 'A', post-graduates (mostly engineers with an additional degree like MBA/CA) perceive the organization to be more masculine, more individualistic, and to have greater PD than both engineers and graduates; engineers, in turn perceive the organization to be more masculine than graduates. Graduates, on the other hand, perceive higher UA in the organization than both engineers and post-graduates. However, engineers in Organization 'C' perceive the organization to be more individualistic, more masculine, and having greater PD than postgraduates.

These results imply a linear relation between education and MAS in Organization 'A': more educated employees perceive greater MAS in organizations. With greater education, probably employees become more competitive, assertive, emphasize visible achievements, and desire tangible expressions of success. At the same time, they also perceive greater PD in organizations, which implies preference for centralized decision-making, status symbols, and to initiate contact with subordinates (rather than the other way around).

### *(v) Effect of Tenure on Perception of Organizational Values*

**Table–8.7**
**Comparison of Employees with Varying Tenures from 3 Organizations on Perception of Organizational Values**

| *Org. Values* | *Group 1 (< 2 yrs)* | | *Group 2 (2.1-4 yrs)* | | *Group 3 (> 4 yrs)* | | *G1 Vs G3* | *G1 Vs G3* | *G2 Vs G3* | *F-Value* |
|---|---|---|---|---|---|---|---|---|---|---|
| | *Mean* | *SD* | *Mean* | *SD* | *Mean* | *SD* | | | | |
| **ORG 'A'** | **N=34** | | **N=14** | | **N=17** | | | | | |
| OPD | 2.89 | 0.33 | 3.20 | 0.49 | 3.50 | 0.64 | - | (*) | - | 11.11** |
| OUA | 3.33 | 0.47 | 3.48 | 0.34 | 3.37 | 0.69 | - | - | - | 0.31 |
| OID | 2.38 | 0.38 | 2.59 | 0.56 | 2.59 | 0.89 | - | - | - | 0.97 |
| OMAS | 2.11 | 0.49 | 2.53 | 0.80 | 2.79 | 1.18 | - | (*) | - | 4.90* |

*Contd...*

| *Org. Values* | *Group 1 (< 2 yrs)* | | *Group 2 (2.1-4 yrs)* | | *Group 3 (> 4 yrs)* | | *G1 Vs G3* | *G1 Vs G3* | *G2 Vs G3* | *F-Value* |
|---|---|---|---|---|---|---|---|---|---|---|
| | *Mean* | *SD* | *Mean* | *SD* | *Mean* | *SD* | | | | |
| **ORG 'B'** | **N=32** | | **N=21** | | **N=18** | | | | | |
| OPD | 2.60 | 0.55 | 2.47 | 0.66 | 2.62 | 0.60 | - | - | - | 0.39 |
| OUA | 3.30 | 0.46 | 2.95 | 0.62 | 3.02 | 0.55 | (*) | - | - | 3.22* |
| OID | 2.76 | 0.74 | 2.52 | 0.76 | 2.61 | 0.70 | - | - | - | 0.71 |
| OMAS | 2.29 | 0.56 | 2.18 | 0.66 | 2.61 | 0.66 | - | - | (*) | 2.51 |
| **ORG 'C'** | **N=24** | | **N=15** | | **N=27** | | | | | |
| OPD | 2.46 | 0.59 | 2.55 | 0.89 | 2.10 | 0.58 | - | - | - | 2.88 |
| OUA | 2.75 | 0.39 | 2.72 | 0.52 | 2.56 | 0.54 | - | - | - | 1.11 |
| OID | 2.44 | 0.35 | 2.41 | 0.58 | 2.24 | 0.53 | - | - | - | 1.15 |
| OMAS | 2.77 | 0.67 | 2.55 | 0.92 | 2.20 | 0.76 | - | (*) | - | 3.52* |

*Note:* **p<0.01, *p<0.05.

(*) Denotes pairs of groups significantly different at the .05 level using Duncan's test.

Tenure in the organization has a moderate effect on the perception of organizational values in the 3 MNCs (Table 8.7). In Organization 'A' (French), those with greater than 4 years tenure in the organization perceive greater PD (mean scores indicate high PD) and masculinity in the organization. In Organization 'B' (American), those with a tenure less than 2 years perceive less UA than those with a tenure of 2.1-4 years in the organization. Post-hoc comparisons indicate that the latter perceive the organization in less "masculine" terms than those with more than 4 years tenure, although overall F-value is insignificant. On the other hand, in Organization 'C' (Finnish), those who have spent more than 4 years in the organization perceive it to be less masculine than those with less than 2 years tenure.

These results seem to indicate that with increasing tenure, employees start perceiving the organizational values more in terms of the national cultural values of the respective organization. Members, who enter an organization with values that are not in tune with the organizational values, go through a systematic process of learning or socialisation. For instance, preference for greater PD is an organizational value for Organization 'A', the French MNC. With increase in tenure, employees perceive greater PD in the organization. Similarly, low masculinity is a Finnish cultural value. Those who have been with Organization 'C' for a longer period of time have probably indoctrinated the organization's feminine way of working, and hence perceive the organization in less "masculine" terms than those who have joined recently.

These results are in line with the findings of Chatman (1991), who found tenure to be positively correlated with person-organization fit. Katju (1986) also found an inverted U-shaped relationship between length of service and person-organization values discrepancy.

### *(vi) Effect of Number of Jobs Changed on Perception of Organizational Values*

**Table–8.8**

**Comparison of Employees with Varying Number of Jobs Changed from 3 Organizations on Perception of Organizational Values**

| *Org. Values* | *Group 1 (0-1 Job)* | | *Group 2 (2 Jobs)* | | *Group 3 (> 2 Jobs)* | | *G1 Vs G3* | *G1 Vs G3* | *G2 Vs G3* | *F-Value* |
|---|---|---|---|---|---|---|---|---|---|---|
| | *Mean* | *SD* | *Mean* | *SD* | *Mean* | *SD* | | | | |
| **ORG 'A'** | **N=18** | | **N=23** | | **N=24** | | | | | |
| OPD | 2.99 | 0.54 | 3.04 | 0.45 | 3.22 | 0.56 | - | - | - | 1.16 |
| OUA | 3.42 | 0.42 | 3.57 | 0.56 | 3.11 | 0.46 | - | (*) | (*) | 5.38** |
| OID | 2.66 | 0.46 | 2.09 | 0.52 | 2.68 | 0.53 | (*) | - | (*) | 9.42** |
| OMAS | 2.64 | 0.72 | 2.04 | 0.62 | 2.42 | 0.96 | (*) | - | - | 3.09 |
| **ORG 'B'** | **N=27** | | **N=24** | | **N=20** | | | | | |
| OPD | 2.50 | 0.61 | 2.74 | 0.64 | 2.44 | 0.49 | - | - | - | 1.62 |
| OUA | 3.05 | 0.55 | 3.20 | 0.59 | 3.13 | 0.51 | - | - | - | 0.47 |

*Contd...*

| *Org. Values* | *Group 1 (0-1 Job)* | | *Group 2 (2 Jobs)* | | *Group 3 (> 2 Jobs)* | | *G1 Vs G3* | *G1 Vs G3* | *G2 Vs G3* | *F-Value* |
|---|---|---|---|---|---|---|---|---|---|---|
| | *Mean* | *SD* | *Mean* | *SD* | *Mean* | *SD* | | | | |
| OID | 2.67 | 0.74 | 2.77 | 0.79 | 2.48 | 0.66 | - | - | - | 0.85 |
| OMAS | 2.27 | 0.50 | 2.49 | 0.72 | 2.25 | 0.68 | - | - | - | 1.06 |
| **ORG 'C'** | **N=25** | | **N=18** | | **N=23** | | | | | |
| OPD | 2.36 | 0.81 | 2.33 | 0.66 | 2.30 | 0.58 | - | - | - | 0.04 |
| OUA | 2.87 | 0.42 | 2.52 | 0.49 | 2.56 | 0.49 | (*) | (*) | - | 3.72* |
| OID | 2.28 | 0.52 | 2.51 | 0.49 | 2.31 | 0.44 | - | - | - | 1.26 |
| OMAS | 2.26 | 0.61 | 2.53 | 0.87 | 2.69 | 0.88 | - | - | - | 1.77 |

*Note:* **p<0.01, *p<0.05.

(*) Denotes pairs of groups significantly different at the .05 level using Duncan's test.

Number of jobs changed did not have a significant effect on perception of organizational values (Table 8.8). Only in the case of Organization 'A', those who have changed more than 2 jobs before joining the present one perceive less UA in the organization as compared to those who have changed either 0-1 or 2 jobs. The former also perceive the organization to be more individualistic than those who have changed 2 jobs, who, in turn perceive the organization to be less individualistic than those who have changed 0-1 job. Although, overall F-value in case of masculinity was non-significant, post-hoc comparisons did yield a significant difference between those who have changed 0/1 job and 2 jobs, with the former perceiving the organization to be more masculine than the latter. On the other hand, in Organization 'B', the perception of organizational values was not affected by number of jobs changed by employees. In Organization 'C', those who have changed 0-1 job perceive greater UA in the organization than those who have changed either 2 or more than 2 jobs.

These findings seem to suggest a link between changing jobs and perceiving uncertainty avoidance in organizations. Thus, people who change jobs more often feel that activities (like memos, reports, standard operating procedures) are not very structured, managers are more involved in strategy rather than detail, and employees prefer broad guidelines to detailed instructions. However, Downey et al.'s (1977) observation seems very apt here as they report that "uncertainty, complexity, and dynamics are dependent on the perception of organization members and thus, can vary in their incidence to the extent that individuals differ in their perceptions. Some individuals may have a very high tolerance for ambiguity and uncertainty so they may perceive situations as less uncertain than others with lesser tolerances." These findings suggest that employees who change more jobs probably have a high tolerance for uncertainty, and so perceive the organization as less uncertain than those who have changed fewer jobs.

## SUMMARY

Organizational values of the three MNCs as perceived by their employees differ significantly on 3 values-PD, UA, and IND, but not on MAS. The three organizations have moderate position on Masculinity-Femininity. Significant differences exist among all three organizations on PD and UA, with Organization 'A' (French) being the highest on both PD and UA, followed by Organization 'B' (American) and lastly 'C' (Finnish). For individualism, however, a significant difference exists only between Organization 'B' and 'C', with Organization 'B' (American) being the most individualistic, and Organization 'C' being the least. This implies that organizational values of MNCs are strongly influenced by the organization's "home national cultures."

Further, gender, age, and education had no effect on perception of organizational values in Organization 'B', implying that values in this organization are so clear and strong that they are perceived similarly by all organizational members irrespective of their gender, age, or education. In contrast, the effect of personal variables on the perception of organizational values was strongest in organization 'A', indicating that perception of organizational values is influenced to a large extent by an employee's demographic/personal characteristics and hence depicts a weak organizational culture.

## ORGANIZATIONAL VALUES (ESPOUSED AND PRACTICED) ACROSS 3 ORGANIZATIONS

The third objective was to understand the organizational values of the 3 MNCs (as exemplified in organizational stories), especially the espoused and practiced values as perceived by organizational members.

## Organizational Stories

Organizational stories are anecdotes about sequences of events in an organization's history. Current or past organizational members play the leading roles; and the stories always have morals that reflect important organizational beliefs, values, and basic assumptions (Martin and Siehl, 1983). Stories communicate their morals metaphorically; and the morals usually speak about core elements of an organization's culture, philosophies, policies, and/or practices. Selznick (1957) observed that organizational stories are "efforts to state, in the language of uplift and idealism, what is distinctive about the aims and methods of the enterprise."

Although an organizational story focuses on a single, unified sequence of events, apparently drawn from the institution's history, in some cases only some anecdotes are provided. The latter are however included, as they are also important in understanding important organizational beliefs and values.

### *(i) Popular Stories in Organization 'A'*

Only a few stories were narrated by employees, which are given below:

- One famous story is about a plant supervisor who dared to challenge the founder. The plant supervisor had planned a plant tour with the founder, who skipped the planned route and went straight to the production line. He leaned over one of the assembly line workers and asked him how things were going. The plant supervisor interrupted him abruptly and said firmly, "I'm sorry, but you can't enter here without your safety glasses." The founder, stopped in amazement, apologized, and went back to get his safety glasses, complimenting the supervisor. The moral seems to be: "Even the founder obeys the rules, so you certainly should." Another message is implied: "Uphold the rules, no matter who is disobeying."
- In 1999, the organization's office located in Oregan, USA, became the first underwater fiber optic cable facility to achieve ISO 14001 certification. Its innovative and patented

technology for telecom equipment power supply reduces energy consumption in large systems by 40 per cent, which is a good example of environmentally conscious engineering.

- The storms that hit France in December 1999 left behind total devastation in a number of regions. A foundation named "Reboison la France" was quickly formed to raise funds and begin to replant future generation of trees. Organization 'A' joined in this initiative, particularly in 4 public parks, showing its respect for the environment.
- To show solidarity with the Gujarat earthquake victims in 2001, employees of Organization 'A' collected relief material such as blankets, clothes, medicine, candles, etc. and themselves drove the supplies to the quake area. With the help of the *Sarpanch,* they distributed the relief materials.

*Conclusion*

The values reflected in the prevalent stories characterise the organization's concern for rules, environment and people.

***(ii) Popular Stories in Organization 'B'***

On asking questions regarding famous instances of the founder and/or CEO, which reflect their style of functioning and their philosophy, many stories came up. Some of them were repeated by an astonishing 80 per cent of the employees, which reflect how deeply ingrained the stories are in people's psyche. Some of the stories reflect instances of the organizational values being put into practice. Some stories are briefly enumerated below:

- The name 'B' came from a brand name for one of the company's first successful products- car radios. A story goes that in the 1930s, the founder Paul V. Galvin was travelling to Illinois, when he noticed people going for picnics carrying radios in their cars. A thought suddenly struck to him "Why not combine the two- motor and sound?" He coined the name 'B' for the company's new car radio, effectively linking the ideas of "motion" and "sound." At the time, he was ridiculed for the kind of product he was attempting to sell, but Galvin had the foresight and firmly believed in "inventing things for which there is a market."
- After producing the first reproducible car radio on earth,

Galvin's team put the first car radio on the moon. Astronaut Neil Armstrong's first words from the moon "One Small Step For Man, One Giant Leap for Mankind" were relayed to Earth via a transponder aboard the Apollo 11 lunar module designed and manufactured by Organization 'B'.

- One story depicts the trademark of the founder-a quiet graciousness with a thoughtful toughness. What was noteworthy about his first day at Motorola was his refusal to move to the front of the personnel line. Though others encouraged him to "pull name," he said, "I will wait my turn."
- It is reported that the founder once looked at an assembly line of women and thought, "These are all like my own mom- they have kids, homes to take care of, people who need them." It motivated him to work hard because he saw his mom in all of them. That's how it all begins – with fundamental respect and empathy.
- In 1969 in Latin America, to get one huge order amounting to about 10 per cent of the company's turnover, a kickback was demanded. The CEO turned the offer down and said that ethical values can never be compromised.
- A similar instance is talked about in Delhi. A contract was on the finalisation stage, when the other party asked for a cut. The Organization B's manager immediately pulled back his chair and said "The meeting stands terminated. We are withdrawing from this bid," leaving the other party shocked. Although 'B' lost a very big contact, but this manager was congratulated. He was actually rewarded for not giving a bribe at the cost of losing lucrative business.
- It is reported that when the Organization's employees travel to the U.S., emigration check is not required for them, keeping in mind the company's high ethical reputation. They only have to show their company's I-cards, and no questions with respect to what they are carrying are asked from them. This is the kind of reputation Organization 'B' commands in its home country.
- One instance reflects the company's humane concern for its employees. When a Senior Finance Manager in Singapore lost his vision while driving, CEO gave his own plane and got him to Australia. He was given full medical support on

company's expense. This man has not gained his vision, but is still working in the organization, and "for us he is just the same."

*Conclusion*

The values reflected in the prevalent stories characterise the organization's concern for ethical behaviour, fairness, pride in a high level of technological superiority, and a humane concern for employees.

***(iii) Popular Stories in Organization 'C'***

Some stories reflect the CEO's style of functioning and their philosophy, while some portray the organization's values and culture. Some stories are briefly narrated below:

- The company's history has shown that right decisions made at the right time breed success. Back in the fashion-conscious 1960s when one branch of the corporation was a major rubber manufacturer, it hit on the idea of making brightly-coloured rubber boots at a time when boots followed the Henry Ford principle: you could have any colour, so long as it was black! A similar vision of setting new trends was noticed in the 1990s when the organization introduced multi-coloured, clip-on facias that turned mobiles into a fashion item overnight.
- In 1995, the organization's stock plummeted by half, and calls for executive firings echoed from Wall Street to Helsinki. But the CEO resisted the pressure. He and his colleagues chopped up responsibility for inventory, logistics, and design, and divided them up by region. After a few months, they had the company back on track. This crisis is viewed as a precious lesson, vindicating the CEO's vision of gentle Finnish management. In his words, "In that situation, a typical American company would have fired 12 people."
- One famous story is about a board member, Neuvo, responsible for the company's mobile phone R&D worldwide. One of his babies is the sleek, silvery eye-catching mobile phone model, which is often compared to a Zippo lighter. Code-named Small Beauty when it was first conceived, the model was rushed through development and

introduced in 1998 in an effort to "surprise the market." It did surprise at least one rival company's executive who was seated besides Neuvo on a panel in Stockholm. When the moderator suggested the panelists show off their phones, Neuvo pulled out the new sleek model. The rival company's representative was so startled by the new model that he said, "I'm sorry. I don't have my phone with me," but at the same minute a phone started ringing in his pocket!

- The CEO is reported to be a man of extremes. A week after Easter, he drove to the family's lakeside cabin in Helsinki, when he was challenged by his kids to dive in the lake water, with ice still floating on it. Emerging from a hot sauna, he plunged into the icy lake. It is said that living by the plunge also characterizes the Organization's business philosophy.
- The CEO conjures up a sense of urgency by preparing the company for a metamorphosis. On July 1, 1998, he reached the company's headquarters, took the inner circle of four Finns who run the company's main divisions, and switched all their jobs. Every top person at the company was given a brand-new job – all in the name of "removing people from their comfort areas" – to position them for the first leg of the next century.

*Conclusion*

The values reflected in the prevalent stories are of innovation, variety, risk-taking, challenging tasks, and a gentle concern for employees.

The number and quality of stories drawn from the 3 organizations varies enormously. This variation is not a product of the methodology, but reflects, at least in part, the vitality and strength of folklore in different organizations. This appears to be linked to the tenure of those interviewed in their respective organizations, and also to the role of stories in inculcation of the culture of the organization. Organization 'A' had an ethos of factual precision and accountability that seemed to inhibit the making of unsubstantiated claims and the spinning of elaborate stories. Most narratives described events as purely facts, devoid of emotional or symbolic content. In Organization 'B', in contrast, many employees told stories to illustrate their knowledge and insight into how their organization works, and to show that they were loyal members of the team. They took pride in narrating stories about achievements or heroic exploits of the founder or other employees of the company. Some of the stories were repeated by an astonishing 80 per cent of the employees, which reflect how deeply ingrained the stories are in people's psyche. In Organization 'C', different stories were narrated by various people. However, most stories in Organization 'B' and 'C' focused either on achievement or on survival against the odds. Their chief emotional qualities exhibited were admiration, approval, and especially pride. In many cases the central character of these stories is a hero (never heroine), worthy of admiration.

Most stories were extremely helpful in expressing organizational morals and exemplifying core values symbolically. The values reflected in the prevalent stories of Organization 'A' characterise the organization's concern for rules, environment and people. The espoused values of the organization, on the other hand, are: 'customer focus, innovation, teamwork, and accountability'. In contrast, the values reflected in stories of Organization 'B' are ethics, fairness, pride in a high level of technological superiority, and a humane concern for employees. These values are in line with the organization's espoused values of 'uncompromising integrity' and 'constant respect for people'. As regards Organization 'C' the values reflected in the prevalent stories are of innovation, risk-taking, and a gentle concern for employees. These are somewhat in line with their espoused values of: 'customer satisfaction, respect for the individual, achievement, and continuous learning'.

Interestingly, the values reflected in organizational stories are in line with the 4 value dimensions, analysed by means of the quantitative measure on organizational values. For instance, Organization A's concern for rules is in line with its strong UA position. Organization B's 'fairness and a humane concern for employees' justifies its moderate position on Masculinity. Similarly, Organization C's value on innovation and risk-taking substantiates its weak UA position; its 'gentle concern for employees' underlines its moderate score on Masculinity.

Stories, as cultural manifestations, include rich detail and carry multiple interpretations. Stories are emotionally and symbolically charged narratives; they do not present information or facts about 'events', but they enrich, enhance and infuse facts with meaning.

This is both their strength and a potential weakness. Ultimately, the truth of a story lies not in its accuracy but in its meaning (Gabriel, 1998). The magic of stories in creating cultural focus, direction, and cohesion is well known among enlightened managers (Deal and Kennedy, 2000). Storytellers capture a dimension of the workplace that others usually overlook or ignore. They interpret what goes on and package reality to reveal its subtle secrets. The tales storytellers tell, like myths in a tribal setting, give meaning to the workaday world. As these stories are told and retold within an organization they create and reinforce cultural preferences for certain types of action. Their emotional appeal and vividness make them potentially powerful tools of management.

## ESPOUSED AND PRACTICED ORGANIZATIONAL VALUES

Interviews were conducted with a sample of employees in each organization to get some idea about values, as professed by the organization, and 'how things really are'. The responses obtained for specific interview questions were content analyzed. The data was pooled into four themes—each research question serving as a theme. Responses of the respondents were first categorized into five broad heads under each theme, frequencies of responses under each category was counted, and later converted into percentages. This is presented in 4 Tables (Tables 8.9-8.12) with respect to 4 main themes: *(i)* Espoused values of the organization; *(ii)* Culture of the organization; *(iii)* Qualities considered important for success; and *(iv)* Biggest mistake one can make in the organization.

### *(i) Espoused Values of the Organization*

**Table-8.9**
**Espoused Values:**
**A Comparison of 3 Organizations**

| *Espoused Values* | *Frequency* | *Percentage** |
|---|---|---|
| **ORGANIZATION 'A'** | | |
| Customer satisfaction | 12 | 60% |
| Quality excellence | 10 | 60% |
| Transparency of information | 9 | 45% |

*Contd...*

| *Espoused Values* | *Frequency* | *Percentage** |
|---|---|---|
| Commitment to the future | 6 | 30% |
| Respect for the environment | 5 | 25% |
| **ORGANIZATION 'B'** | | |
| Ethical value/Uncompromising integrity | 19 | 95% |
| Respect for people | 16 | 80% |
| Quality focus | 9 | 45% |
| Technological superiority | 5 | 25% |
| Achievement | 3 | 15% |
| **ORGANIZATION 'C'** | | |
| Innovation | 13 | 65% |
| Customer satisfaction | 10 | 50% |
| Achievement | 6 | 30% |
| Trust and respect for people | 6 | 30% |
| Equality | 5 | 25% |

*Note:* * The percentages do not add up to 100 as employees reported more than one value at a time.

Table 8.9 shows that when respondents were asked about values important in the organization, the clarity with which they answered differed across organizations. In Organization 'B', most of the respondents were clearly able to articulate the values important in the company with a great deal of consensus among them. In fact, the 2 core beliefs of the organization viz. 'uncompromising integrity' and 'constant respect for people' were paraphrased by an astonishing 95 per cent and 80 per cent of employees in statements like "integrity stands highest in 'B'," "immovable on ethics," "ethics very very fundamental to the company," "ethical business practice followed very very stringently," "a principles-based company where people and integrity always come first," "sensitive to people issues." Other values mentioned were quality success, technological superiority and achievement. In contrast, among the four core values of Organization 'A' viz. 'customer focus, innovation, teamwork, and accountability', 'customer satisfaction' was mentioned by 60 per cent respondents, and 'transparency of information' by 45 per cent. Other values mentioned were quality excellence, commitment to the future, and respect for the environment. This seems to suggest some amount of discrepancy between the professed values of the company and the desired values, particularly with regard to 'innovation' and 'teamwork'. In Organization 'C', among its four core values of 'customer satisfaction, respect for the individual, achievement, and continuous learning', 'customer satisfaction' was mentioned by 50 per cent respondents, 'achievement' by 30 per cent, again 'trust and respect for people' by 30 per cent, and 'equality' by 25 per cent. Although no respondent mentioned 'continuous learning', 65 per cent emphasised 'innovation' expressed in statements like "importance of original thinking," "out-of-the-box thinkers" (term used by 4 employees), "can embrace new ideas at great speed", "questioning of status-quo welcomed."

### *(ii) Cultural Characteristics of the Organization*

**Table–8.10**
**Culture of the Organization: A Comparison of 3 Organizations**

| *Cultural Characteristics* | *Frequency* | *Percentage** |
|---|---|---|
| **ORGANIZATION 'A'** | | |
| Low risk taking | 11 | 55% |
| Preference for formalized procedures | 10 | 50% |
| Accountability | 8 | 40% |
| "Caring" Organization | 6 | 30% |
| Formality | 5 | 25% |
| **ORGANIZATION 'B'** | | |
| Independence | 11 | 55% |
| Slow to respond/Traditional | 9 | 45% |
| Recognition for good work | 8 | 40% |
| Flat hierarchical arrangements | 5 | 25% |
| Family-orientation | 4 | 20% |

*Contd...*

| *Cultural Characteristics* | *Frequency* | *Percentage** |
|---|---|---|
| **ORGANIZATION 'C'** | | |
| Open channels of communication | 9 | 45% |
| Flat, non-hierarchical | 8 | 40% |
| Risk taking/flexibility | 6 | 30% |
| Nurturance | 6 | 30% |
| Humility and modesty | 5 | 25% |
| Emphasis on team work | 5 | 25% |

*Note:* * The percentages do not add up to 100 as employees used more than one cultural characteristic at a time.

Among the cultural characteristics of the organization as mentioned by respondents (Table 8.10), although some of these are at odds with the espoused core values, they are in line with the organizational value dimensions, as measured quantitatively by the questionnaire. For instance, 'low risk taking' (55% explained this as "a prudent/cautious approach to business," "decisions are well thought of, not quick, risky decisions," etc.), 'preference for formalized procedures'—attributes of Organization 'A' are against its espoused core value of 'innovation.' At the same time, however, these are in line with its strong UA position. 'Formality' (in speech, mannerisms, clothing, etc.) is in line with its strong PD position. Organization B's 'independence' is in line with its 'individualistic' position. The most commonly described characteristic was that of 'independence/individualism' (with 55% mentioning "respect for personal space of employees," "no babysitting/hand-holding of employees," "company expects the employee to learn himself," "typically American culture"), followed closely by 'slow to respond' (45% using phrases like "traditional," "low-ball lifters," "laid back," "lacks aggression," "lacks elasticity," etc.). A balance between 'recognition for good work' and 'family-orientation' explains its moderate position on Masculinity. 'Flat hierarchical arrangements' is in line with its moderate position on PD. The most striking cultural characteristic described in Organization 'C' was 'open channels of communication', with 45 per cent saying "absolutely no fear of bosses," "you can actually walk up to your boss and tell him what you think of him," "Even President has his mobile number printed on business cards and skims his mail himself,") followed by 'non-hierarchical' (40% describe the organization as "egalitarian," "decentralised," "flat," "levelled pyramids," "If you see 5 employees talking, you can never guess who is the seniormost," "There are absolutely zero power differentials in this organization"). This substantiates Organization C's weak PD position. 'Risk taking' and 'flexibility' is in line with its weak UA position; while 'nurturance,' 'humility and modesty' underlines its moderate Masculinity position. This was very articulately summed up by one respondent: "The working atmosphere is good natured, with a lot of freedom left to employees. Company rules are never absolute...One has to fit in with our culture. Fitting means avoiding conflicts, covering other's mistakes, loyalty, friendliness, modesty, and good-natured cooperation. One should not behave too conspicuously or flamboyantly in this organization. It is important to be a nice person. While the ends are important, the means are equally important."

### *(iii) Qualities Considered Important for Success*

**Table-8.11**
**Qualities Important for Success: A Comparison of 3 Organizations**

| *Qualities Important for Success* | *Frequency* | *Percentage** |
|---|---|---|
| **ORGANIZATION 'A'** | | |
| Good performance | 14 | 70% |
| Ability to get along with others | 11 | 55% |
| Prudent approach to business and decision-making | 9 | 45% |
| Honesty | 8 | 40% |
| **ORGANIZATION 'B'** | | |
| Technical competence | 15 | 75% |
| Hard work/task orientation | 10 | 50% |
| Commitment towards company values | 9 | 45% |
| Taking initiative | 8 | 40% |
| Loyalty | 6 | 30% |

*Contd...*

| *Qualities Important for Success* | *Frequency* | *Percentage** |
|---|---|---|
| **ORGANIZATION 'C'** | | |
| Original thinking | 15 | 75% |
| 'Can-do' attitude | 10 | 50% |
| High competence in subject matter | 8 | 40% |
| Down-to-earth | 6 | 30% |
| Interested in learning | 5 | 25% |

*Note:* * The percentages do not add up to 100 as employees reported more than one quality for success at a time.

As regards the qualities important for success (Table 8.11), there seems to be a high degree of consensus among respondents in each organization. The most important quality mentioned was 'good performance' in Organization 'A', 'technical competence' in Organization 'B', and 'original thinking' in Organization 'C'. In Organization 'A', importance of a 'prudent approach to business and decision making' is not surprising keeping into account its strong UA position. In sharp contrast in Organization 'C', the quality of 'original thinking' (mentioned by 75% respondents) which goes in line with its core value of 'innovation' as well as its low UA position. Other qualities considered important are 'can-do' attitude, high competence in subject matter, down-to-earth, and interested in learning. In Organization 'B', 'technical competence,' and 'taking initiative', mentioned by 75 per cent and 40 per cent of the respondents respectively, was in line with the organization's high emphasis on quality and constant renewal. Organization B, pioneers of 'six sigma' concept in quality, the highly coveted 'Malcolm Baldrige National Quality Award' have made 'B' "recognized quality leaders in the world" (Luthans, 1995). 30 per cent respondents also mentioned 'loyalty' implying 'long tenure with the company.' In fact, this is reflected in Organization 'B's' quasi-tenure employment system, which offers (or at least used to offer at the time data was collected) almost a job-for-life guarantee to "service club" employees-those who have performed well and been with the company for ten years.

***(iv) Biggest Mistake One Can Make in the Organization***

**Table-8.12**
**Biggest Mistake in the Organization:**
**A Comparison of 3 Organizations**

| *Biggest Mistake in the Organization* | *Frequency* | *Percentage** |
|---|---|---|
| **ORGANIZATION 'A'** | | |
| Spoiling relations with customers | 6 | 30% |
| Breaking rules/Not following procedures | 5 | 25% |
| Not meeting targets | 4 | 20% |
| Disregard for natural resources | 3 | 15% |
| Not behaving transparently | 2 | 10% |
| **ORGANIZATION 'B'** | | |
| Acting unethically/Unethical behaviour | 15 | 75% |
| Misuse of power | 3 | 15% |
| Not following rules and procedures | 2 | 10% |
| **ORGANIZATION 'C'** | | |
| Showing-Off/Being status conscious | 9 | 45% |
| Being aggressive | 4 | 20% |
| Indulging in office politics | 4 | 20% |
| Inability to work as a team member | 3 | 15% |

*Note:* * The percentages add up to 100 as employees were permitted only one response at a time.

Asking respondents about the biggest mistake one can make is an important clue to identify organizational values, as actually practiced, according to Hofstede et al. (1990). In Organization 'A' (Table 8.12), respondents gave many varied answers ranging from 'spoiling relations with customers,' 'breaking rules/not following procedures,' 'not meeting targets,' 'disregard for natural resources,' to 'not behaving transparently'. This seems to suggest some amount of conceptual confusion about what the company in reality values (maintaining the status quo) and what it thinks it should ideally value (innovation). In Organization 'B', there was a high degree of agreement, with a remarkable 75 per cent of respondents mentioning 'unethical behaviour' (included padding of travel or medical account, submitting wrong bills, accepting gifts from customers, giving/accepting bribes, etc.), and another 15 per cent reporting 'misuse of power,' followed by 'not following rules and procedures' (10%). This clearly shows that the company's high ethical stand is 'not just a slogan meant for walls' and it does practice what it preaches. As one respondent remarked, "our company is immovable on ethics, both in letter and in spirit." In fact, the company backs it up with its policies. Ethics workshops are conducted every two years; ethics surveys are conducted every quarter where employees are asked to report anonymously any unethical behaviour that they may have seen at the workplace.

In Organization 'C,' 'showing-off' was regarded as the most cardinal mistake by 45 per cent of respondents (expressed as "being status-conscious," "flashy," "pompous," "boastful," "being too conspicuous," "making exaggerated claims," etc.), followed by 'being aggressive' (20%), 'indulging in office politics' (20%), and finally 'inability to work as a team member' (15%). These are in line with Finnish values of femininity, humility, and harmony (Hofstede, 1980; Jones et al., 1986; Dunlap, Gallup and Gallup, 1993; Schwartz, 1999).

## SUMMARY

Organization 'B' has a strong culture as not only do stories communicate organizational values clearly, but the espoused core values of the organization are also perceived similarly by most of its members. In behavioural terms, a strong culture extracts more normative compliance than does a weak culture. The culture of Organization 'C' also seems to be quite strong as indicated by a fair amount of consensus among organizational members, while that of Organization 'A' appears to lack strength as indicated by absence of stories and a gap between espoused and practiced values. Research (Deal and Kennedy, 1982; Denison, 1990; Brown, 1998) suggests that strong, appropriate, adaptable cultures which value stakeholders and leadership, and which have a strong sense of mission, are likely to be associated with high performance over sustained periods of time.

## RELATIONSHIP BETWEEN SOCIETAL AND ORGANIZATIONAL VALUES ACROSS 3 ORGANIZATIONS

The fourth objective was to understand the extent to which Indian societal values have influenced organizational values of the 3 different MNCs.

### *(i) Extent of Relationship Between Societal and Organizational Values: A Comparison Across 3 Organizations*

**Table–8.13**
**Correlation Between Societal and Organizational Values Across 3 Organizations**

| *Value Dimensions* | *Organization 'A' (N=65)* | *Organization 'B' (N=71)* | *Organization 'C' (N=66)* |
|---|---|---|---|
| Power Distance | -0.24* | 0.21 | 0.23 |
| Uncertainty Avoidance | 0.28* | 0.34** | 0.24* |
| Individualism | 0.02 | 0.10 | 0.12 |
| Masculinity | 0.14 | 0.28* | -0.05 |

*Note:* **p<0.01, *p<0.05.

Table 8.13 reveals that values of Organization 'B' correlate most with the societal values, with significant positive correlations on two value dimensions: UA, and MAS. The correlation between SPD and OPD is also positive, although not significant. This was followed by Organization 'C', where one significant positive correlation was found between SUA and OUA. Similar to Organization 'B', the correlation between SPD and OPD is also positive, although not significant. For Organization 'A', the findings showed only one significant positive correlation between SUA and OUA, indicating good congruence on UA. Surprisingly, one significant negative correlation was observed between SPD and OPD, indicating lack of congruence on PD.

These results depict that in all three organizations, there is high congruence between SUA and OUA. Further, in Organization 'A', there is a lack of congruence on PD, while the other 2 organizations have a weak, but positive, relationship on PD. It should be recalled here that Organization 'A' was high on PD, while the other 2 organizations were moderate on PD. On the other hand, all employees were found to be moderate on power distance with regards to their perception of societal values. The results of the present study are in line with d'Iribarne (1989) who reported relationships between subordinates and superiors in a French multinational in France to be frequently loaded with emotion. According to him, "The often strongly emotional character of hierarchical relationships in France is intriguing. There is an extreme diversity of feelings towards superiors: they may be either adored or despised with equal intensity. This situation is not at all universal: we found it neither in the Netherlands nor in the USA."

### *(ii) Significant Predictors of Organizational Values: Comparison Across 3 Organizations*

*(a)* Determinants of Organizational Power Distance

**Table–8.14**
**Step-wise Multiple Regression: Determinants of OPD from Societal Values for 3 Organizations**

| *Indep. Variables* | *Dependent Variable: OPD* | | | | | |
|---|---|---|---|---|---|---|
| | *Multiple r* | *Simple r* | $R^2$ | $R^2$ *Change* | *Beta* | *t-Value* |
| **ORGANIZATION 'A'** | | | | | | |
| SID | 0.78 | -0.30* | 0.08 | - | -0.27** | 3.30 |
| **ORGANIZATION 'B'** | | | | | | |
| SMAS | 0.40 | 0.40** | 0.15 | - | 0.40** | 3.52 |
| **ORGANIZATION 'C'** | | | | | | |
| NO SIGNIFICANT PREDICTOR | | | | | | |

*Note:* **p<0.01, *p<0.05.

Table 8.14 reveals that among the societal values, "SID" and "SMAS" contributed 8 per cent and 15 per cent to the total variance of OPD in Organization 'A' and 'B' respectively. However, 92 per cent and 85 per cent of the variance for Organization 'A' and 'B' respectively is unaccounted for, implying that other factors besides societal values determine OPD. On the other hand, none of the societal values were found to predict OPD for Organization 'C'.

Normalized beta coefficients of these variables indicate that contributions made by SMAS were significant and positive, while SID contributed negatively to OPD. Thus, masculinity in society was found to predict OPD, i.e. a cultural emphasis on acquisition of money, status, material things and success influences deference and lording behaviour (Kanungo, 1990) in organizations. Further, greater collectivism in society was found to predict OPD, implying that preference for individualism in society translates itself to preferring lower PD in organizations. This is in line with Sinha et al. (1994) who found collectivism in Indian society to consist of hierarchy, as expressed in terms of caste and class differences.

*(b)* Determinants of Organizational Uncertainty Avoidance (OUA)

**Table–8.15**
**Step-wise Multiple Regression: Determinants of OUA from Societal Values for 3 Organizations**

| *Indep. Variables* | *Dependent Variable: OUA* | | | | | |
|---|---|---|---|---|---|---|
| | *Multiple r* | *Simple r* | $R^2$ | $R^2$ *Change* | *Beta* | *t-Value* |
| **ORGANIZATION 'A'** | | | | | | |
| SPD | 0.57 | 0.08 | 0.18 | - | 0.40** | 4.72 |
| **ORGANIZATION 'B'** | | | | | | |
| SUA | 0.35 | 0.35** | 0.17 | - | 0.33** | 3.24 |
| SPD | 0.45 | 0.31** | 0.28 | 0.11 | 0.29** | 2.89 |
| **ORGANIZATION 'C'** | | | | | | |
| SPD | 0.37 | 0.25* | 0.12 | - | 0.40** | 3.72 |
| SID | 0.44 | 0.06 | 0.18 | 0.06 | 0.38** | 3.04 |
| SUA | 0.51 | 0.24* | 0.25 | 0.07 | 0.32** | 2.73 |
| SMAS | 0.57 | -0.12 | 0.31 | 0.06 | -0.25* | 2.30 |

*Note:* **p<0.01, *p<0.05.

Table 8.15 depicts that among the societal values, in Organization 'A', "SPD" accounted for 18 per cent of the total variance in OUA. In Organization 'B', two societal values namely "SUA" (17%) and "SPD" (11%) contributed 28 per cent of the variance in OPD. However 72 per cent of the variance is unaccounted for. In Organization 'C', interestingly, all four societal values, viz. "SPD" (12%), "SID" (6%), "SUA" (7%), and "SMAS" (6%) contribute 31 per cent to the total variance in OUA. However, 74 per cent of the total variance still remains unaccounted.

Normalized beta coefficients of these variables indicate that SPD, SUA, and SID contributed positively to OUA, while SMAS contributed negatively to OUA. SPD contributed positively to OUA in all 3 organizations, implying that greater the PD in society, higher the perception of UA in all 3 organizations. This is in line with Pareek (1988), according to whom, people in high power distance societies faithfully carry out procedures and systems laid down by seniors. Such cultures are usually ritualistic, following the traditions more faithfully. Similarly, SID and SUA predicted OUA, implying that rigid codes of social conduct, sex role clarity, worship characterized by appeasement of externalities, and highly developed systems of prognostication, including astrology and horoscopes-all features of Indian high UA-get translated into uncertainty avoiding rituals in organizations, i.e. preference for clear requirements and instructions, less risk taking, and even suspicion towards foreigners as managers (Hofstede, 1980). Finally, femininity at the societal level, i.e. a concern for social welfare, relationships, and issues such as quality of life, protection of the environment, etc. would result in preference for rules, avoiding change, and salience of job security.

*(c)* Determinants of Organizational Individualism (OID)

**Table–8.16**
**Step-wise Multiple Regression: Determinants of Organizational Individualism from Societal Values for 3 Organizations**

| *Indep. Variables* | *Dependent Variable: Organizational Individualism* | | | | | |
|---|---|---|---|---|---|---|
| | *Multiple r* | *Simple r* | $R^2$ | $R^2$ *Change* | *Beta* | *t-Value* |
| **ORGANIZATION 'A'** | | | | | | |
| SMAS | 0.67 | 0.28* | 0.10 | - | 0.39** | 4.58 |
| SID | 0.78 | 0.02 | 0.18 | 0.08 | 0.21* | 2.31 |

*Contd...*

| *Indep Variables* | *Dependent Variable: Organizational Individualism* | | | | | |
|---|---|---|---|---|---|---|
| | *Multiple r* | *Simple r* | $R^2$ | $R^2$ *Change* | *Beta* | *t-Value* |
| **ORGANIZATION 'B'** | | | | | | |
| SMAS | 0.43 | 0.43** | 0.18 | - | 0.42** | 3.92 |
| SUA | 0.49 | 0.25* | 0.24 | 0.06 | 0.23* | 2.20 |
| **ORGANIZATION 'C'** | | | | | | |
| SUA | 0.32 | -0.32** | 0.11 | - | -0.40** | 3.68 |
| SPD | 0.56 | 0.17 | 0.16 | 0.05 | 0.23* | 2.13 |

*Note:* **p<0.01, *p<0.05.

Table 8.16 reveals that in Organization 'A', "SMAS" (10%), and "SID" (8%) together explain 18 per cent of the variance of OID. 72 per cent of the variance is unaccounted for. In Organization 'B', two societal values namely "SMAS" (18%) and "SUA" (6%) together contribute 24 per cent of the variance. However 76 per cent of the variance is unaccounted for. In Organization 'C', "SUA" (11%) and "SPD" (5%) contribute 16 per cent towards the variance of OID, the rest 84 per cent being contributed by other unknown factors.

Normalized beta coefficients indicate that contributions made by SMAS, and SID were significant and positive, while SPD contributed negatively to OID. SUA, interestingly, had a selective effect: it contributed positively in Organization 'B', but negatively in Organization 'C'. These results can be explained by Hofstede's (1980) observation that the degree of individualism in organizations will depend on the societal norms in addition to the employees' educational level, and the organization's own history and subculture.

Expectedly, SMAS was found to predict OID in two MNCs, implying that masculinity at the societal level, i.e. valuing things, power, assertiveness, and distinct gender roles were related to individualism in organizations. Further, in one MNC, SID was found to predict OID, implying that the way we conceive of ourselves-independent versus interdependent self-construct—will influence our behaviour in organizations, for e.g. preference for equity rather than equality based distribution of rewards (Gudykunst et al., 1996).

Finally, SPD as contributing to OID in one MNC indicates that accepting that power and rewards are distributed unequally in society would result in individualism in organizations, i.e. acting according to one's own personal needs and self-interests.

*(d)* Determinants of Organizational Masculinity

**Table–8.17**
**Step-wise Multiple Regression: Determinants of Organizational Masculinity from Societal Values for 3 Organizations**

| *Indep. Variables* | *Dependent Variable: Organizational Masculinity* | | | | | |
|---|---|---|---|---|---|---|
| | *Multiple r* | *Simple r* | $R^2$ | $R^2$ *Change* | *Beta* | *t-Value* |
| ORGANIZATION 'A' | | | | | | |
| SMAS | 0.79 | 0.14 | 0.09 | - | 0.27** | 3.62 |
| ORGANIZATION 'B' | | | | | | |
| SMAS | 0.29 | 0.29* | 0.11 | - | 0.33** | 3.44 |
| ORGANIZATION 'C' | | | | | | |
| SUA | 0.57 | -0.23 | 0.05 | - | -0.23* | 2.06 |

*Note:* **p<0.01, *p<0.05.

Table 8.17 indicates that when the societal values were entered in the regression model with organizational masculinity, only one value each was found to be a significant determinant. For Organization 'A' and 'B', "SMAS" contributed 9 per cent and 11 per cent respectively to the total variance. However, 91 per cent and 89 per cent of the variance for Organization 'A' and 'B' respectively is unaccounted for. With regard to Organization 'C', "SUA" contributed 5 per cent towards the variance observed in organizational masculinity, with the rest 95 per cent being contributed by other unknown factors.

Normalized beta coefficients of these variables indicate that contributions made by SMAS were significant and positive, whereas SUA contributed negatively to OMAS. Thus, societal preference for UA was related to greater femininity in one organization, i.e. an emphasis on employee-centeredness, relationship-centeredness, and people orientation. Further, SMAS was found to predict OMAS, implying that masculinity at the societal level, i.e. valuing things, material success, and assertiveness was related to job-centeredness, performance-centeredness, and results orientation in organizations (Hofstede, 1998).

## SUMMARY

The degree of relationship between the societal and organizational values was strongest for Organization 'B', followed by Organization 'C', and lastly Organization 'A'. Furthermore, societal values explained a higher percentage of the variance in all the organizational values for Organization 'B' as compared to the other two organizations, especially Organization 'A'. These results seem to suggest that organizational values of Organization 'B' and 'C' (to a lower extent) are influenced by the contextual societal culture more than those of Organization 'A'. Results revealed many societal values as predictors of organizational values. Not only did SUA predict OUA, SID predict OID, and SMAS predict OMAS, but other societal values, too were important determinants of some organizational values (for e.g., SMAS predicted OPD). Thus, Indian societal values were found to influence organizational values, although varying in different degrees in the three MNCs.

## OUTCOME VARIABLES ACROSS 3 ORGANIZATIONS

The fifth objective was to examine and compare the various outcome variables: employee health, turnover intention, and organizational commitment of employees of 3 different MNCs.

**Table-8.18**
**Comparison of Outcome Variables Across 3 Organizations**

| *Outcome Variables* | *Org 'A' (N=65)* | | *Org 'B' (N=71)* | | *Org 'C' (N=66)* | | *A Vs B* | *A Vs C* | *B Vs C* | *F-Ratio* |
|---|---|---|---|---|---|---|---|---|---|---|
| | *Mean* | *SD* | *Mean* | *SD* | *Mean* | *SD* | | | | |
| EH(O) | 13.49 | 5.77 | 16.18 | 7.76 | 18.07 | 6.31 | (*) | (*) | - | 5.87** |
| PH | 4.37 | 2.97 | 4.52 | 3.04 | 4.59 | 2.17 | - | - | - | 0.09 |
| BH | 4.94 | 2.33 | 4.93 | 3.05 | 6.38 | 2.95 | - | (*) | (*) | 4.78** |

*Contd...*

| *Outcome Variables* | *Org 'A' (N=65)* | | *Org 'B' (N=71)* | | *Org 'C' (N=66)* | | *A Vs B* | *A Vs C* | *B Vs C* | *F-Ratio* |
|---|---|---|---|---|---|---|---|---|---|---|
| | *Mean* | *SD* | *Mean* | *SD* | *Mean* | *SD* | | | | |
| EH | 4.52 | 3.30 | 6.85 | 3.36 | 7.12 | 4.04 | (*) | (*) | - | 8.64** |
| TI | 2.38 | 0.90 | 2.44 | 0.84 | 2.31 | 0.73 | - | - | - | 1.11 |
| OC | 4.65 | 0.86 | 5.11 | 0.73 | 4.92 | 0.89 | (*) | - | - | 5.11** |
| OCI | 5.07 | 1.05 | 5.50 | 0.88 | 5.21 | 1.11 | (*) | - | - | 3.19* |
| OCJI | 4.88 | 1.18 | 4.99 | 1.00 | 5.11 | 0.97 | - | - | - | 0.77 |
| OCL | 4.30 | 0.87 | 4.65 | 0.83 | 4.96 | 1.07 | (*) | (*) | - | 8.44** |

*Note:* **p<0.01, *p<0.05.

(*) Denotes pairs of groups significantly different at the .05 level using Duncan's test.

Table 8.18 reveals that out of the 3 outcome variables, organizations differed significantly on 2, viz. employee health, and organizational commitment. No significant differences were, however, found on turnover intention. Mean scores imply good physical health, "rare" intention of quitting, and moderate job involvement for all employees.

Employees of the three organizations differed significantly on organizational commitment, with employees from Organization 'B' being high on commitment as depicted by their mean scores, followed by employees of Organization 'C', and lastly Organization 'A', being moderately committed. As regards the dimensions of commitment, the same pattern also holds true for organizational identification. On loyalty, significant differences have been found between employees of Organization 'A' and 'C', with the latter being high on loyalty, and the former being moderately loyal. These results are at odds with many skeptics who believe that dramatic changes at the workplace (increased global competition, the impact of IT, and the like) have reduced motivation and commitment, and "left loyalty dead" (Worrall, Cooper, and Campbell, 2000). There are, however, no significant differences among employees of the three organizations on job involvement, i.e. "psychological immersion or absorption in the activities of their work roles" (Buchanan, 1974), with all employees moderately identifying with their jobs (Kanungo, 1979). Since the work culture of multinationals is very professional, with rewards being linked to one's performance, it seems that inspite of differences of values, employees have remained involved with their jobs.

The findings of the present study suggest that strength of an organization's culture and its congruence with societal values is related to increased commitment among organizational members, since employees of Organization 'B' (organizational culture being most strong and having the highest congruence with Indian societal values) are most committed. This is in line with findings by Cheng (1995) who found that organizational commitment was influenced by internal integration and external adaptation of organizational cultures. These results are also in line with Posner, Kouzes and Schmidt (1985), who found that clearly articulated organizational cultures to be related to organizational commitment. Maeher (1987), Meglino, Ravlin and Adkins (1989), and Khatib (1997) also found evidence for relationships between shared values and organizational commitment. Studies by Harris and Mossholder (1996), Garr (1998), O' Driscoll et al. (1998), Pool (2000) have also identified the potent role of an organization's culture in fostering commitment. Denison (1990) and Brown (1998) have suggested two reasons why a strong culture leads to high levels of employee motivation and commitment. First, there is something intrinsically appealing about strong cultures that encourage people to identify with them, i.e. people like to be part of an organization with a distinctive style and ethos with its own peculiarities and idiosyncrasies, and with those who share their view on how an organization should work. Second, strong culture organizations incorporate practices that make working for them rewarding, leading to higher commitment.

Further, the results indicate significant differences on employee health (overall) between employees of Organizations 'A' and 'B', and Organization 'A' and 'C', but not between Organization 'B' and 'C'. Employees of Organization 'A' were healthier as compared to 'B' and 'C', although mean scores indicate a proficient level of health functioning for all employees. As regards the dimensions of health, the same pattern also holds true for emotional health. For behavioural health, significant differences are found between employees of Organization 'A' and 'C', and Organization 'B' and 'C', with former having better behavioural health than the latter, but not between Organization 'A' and 'B'. On the other hand, no significant differences were found among employees of the three organizations on physical health.

The findings of the present study suggest that factors other than the congruence between societal and organizational values lead to employee health, since employees of Organization 'A' have better behavioural and overall health than employees from the other two organizations. These results are contrary to the findings of Furnham and Schaeffer (1984), who examined the consequences of person-environment congruence at work and found that employees who experienced low person-environment congruence had higher level of mental distress.

Lastly, the three organizations did not differ significantly on turnover intention of employees, with all employing reporting a "rare" intention of quitting as indicated by their mean scores. There could be three reasons for this unexpected finding: (1) present recession in the Indian economy (as well as the world over) and the gloomy job market may have led to a fear of losing one's livelihood; (2) since the compensation structures of all the MNCs is very competitive, and the employees' material needs are well-taken care of, they may not mind working for the organization, even if the organizational values are sometimes at odds with their cultural values; and (3) due to the sensitive nature of the issue, even after assurances of confidentiality, respondents may not have been honest about their turnover intentions.

These results, thus, imply that irrespective of the kind of organizational cultures, employees have a low turnover intention. These results are in line with Carsten and Spector (1987), who found turnover to be much higher in times of low unemployment and expanding opportunities than in times of high unemployment and limited opportunities. Further, according to Deal and Kennedy (2000), the recent effects of economic forces (globalisation and technology) and management trends (downsizing, outsourcing, short-termism, and mergers and acquisitions) have decimated traditional corporate cultures, replacing joy, commitment, and loyalty with fear, alienation, and self-interest. Continuing waves of downsizing have led to widespread fear that jobs are constantly up for grabs. This 'fear psychosis' could have led employees to banish all thoughts about quitting, and rather holding on to one's job. These results are, however, contrary to the findings of Sheridan (1992), and Ellett (2000) who pointed the significant role of an organization's culture in explaining employee turnover.

Further, the sub-objectives of the study were to examine the effect of personal variables on outcome variables.

***(i) Effect of Gender on Employee Health, Turnover Intention, and Organizational Commitment***

**Table–8.19**
**Comparison of Male and Female Employees of 3 Organizations on Outcome Variables**

| *Outcome Variables* | *Female* | | *Male* | | *t-Value* |
|---|---|---|---|---|---|
| | *Mean* | *SD* | *Mean* | *SD* | |
| **ORG 'A'** | **N=24** | | **N=41** | | |
| EH(O) | 13.66 | 5.12 | 13.26 | 5.36 | 0.23 |
| PH | 4.63 | 2.02 | 4.00 | 2.92 | 0.84 |
| BH | 5.03 | 3.79 | 4.81 | 2.63 | 0.25 |
| EH | 4.58 | 2.77 | 4.44 | 2.56 | 0.16 |
| TI | 2.26 | 1.06 | 2.55 | 0.58 | 1.30 |
| OC | 4.45 | 0.97 | 4.93 | 0.59 | 2.27* |
| OCI | 4.93 | 1.19 | 5.27 | 0.78 | 1.28 |
| OCJI | 4.58 | 1.36 | 5.30 | 0.69 | 2.54* |
| OCL | 4.13 | 0.96 | 4.55 | 0.66 | 2.07* |
| **ORG 'B'** | **N=19** | | **N=52** | | |
| EH(O) | 16.79 | 6.57 | 15.96 | 7.90 | 0.35 |
| PH | 4.68 | 2.62 | 4.46 | 3.20 | 0.27 |
| BH | 5.26 | 2.92 | 4.81 | 3.11 | 0.55 |

*Contd...*

| *Outcome Variables* | *Female* | | *Male* | | *t-Value* |
|---|---|---|---|---|---|
| | *Mean* | *SD* | *Mean* | *SD* | |
| EH | 7.05 | 4.72 | 6.77 | 4.27 | 0.24 |
| TI | 2.10 | 0.87 | 2.17 | 0.83 | 0.30 |
| OC | 5.02 | 0.52 | 5.14 | 0.79 | 0.61 |
| OCI | 5.54 | 0.55 | 5.48 | 0.98 | 0.27 |
| OCJI | 4.72 | 1.01 | 5.08 | 0.99 | 1.36 |
| OCL | 4.89 | 0.74 | 4.98 | 0.87 | 0.38 |
| ORG 'C' | N=20 | | N=46 | | |
| EH(O) | 19.20 | 7.13 | 17.59 | 5.42 | 0.82 |
| PH | 5.20 | 3.87 | 4.33 | 2.81 | 1.03 |
| BH | 6.40 | 3.08 | 6.37 | 2.93 | 0.04 |
| EH | 7.60 | 3.95 | 6.91 | 4.10 | 0.63 |
| TI | 2.25 | 0.64 | 2.35 | 0.77 | 0.50 |
| OC | 4.99 | 0.65 | 4.88 | 0.97 | 0.44 |
| OCI | 5.36 | 0.80 | 5.14 | 1.22 | 0.73 |
| OCJI | 5.34 | 0.83 | 5.01 | 1.02 | 1.29 |
| OCL | 4.59 | 0.85 | 4.68 | 1.16 | 0.28 |

*Note:* **p<0.01, *p<0.05.

Table 8.19 reveals significant differences between male and female respondents in Organization 'A' on organizational commitment, job involvement and loyalty, with males being more committed, more loyal, and more involved in their jobs than their female counterparts. No significant gender differences, however, were found to exist in Organization 'B' and 'C'.

These results are in line with Marsden, Kalleberg and Cook (1993) who found employed men to be more committed than women. On the other hand, Grusky (1966), Hrebiniak and Alutto (1972), Gould (1979) found women, as a group, to be more committed than men. Wahn (1998) reported women to have higher, levels of continuance commitment than men. In contrast, Bruning and Snyder (1983), Al-Ajmi (2006) did not find any gender differences on commitment.

No gender differences have been found on turnover intention in any organization. These findings are in line with trends from current research on turnover of women (Mattis, 2002), which suggests that women who voluntarily leave their employers are pursuing better career opportunities (just like men). They are not choosing family over a career as companies often erroneously conclude. These results contradict the finding of Hofstede (1980), who found that men, on an average, intended to stay longer than women in the same countries and occupations. Fletcher (1999), too, found a positive association between gender and the hazard of turnover. It appears that women no longer want (or have) to leave their jobs any more than men.

Further, gender differences have not been found on both overall employee health and all components of employee health, indicating that men and women are equally healthy in all the 3 organizations. These results are in line with Agervold (1985), who did not find any relationship between health problems and gender. Sekaran (1986) reported that career orientation rather than gender more strongly influenced mental health. Greenhaus et al. (1989) found no difference between men and women on their measure of strain-based conflict; Similarly, Fontana and Abouserie (1993), Soyibo (1994) found no gender differences in the degree of stress experienced at work. O'Driscoll (2001) concluded that the relationship between interrole conflict (job and off-job roles) and psychological well-being does not vary among men and women. The results of this study, however, are not in line with the observations made by Cooper and Davidson (1982), Davidson and Cooper (1984), Jick and Mitz (1985) who suggested that women experience higher stress than men which is manifested in symptoms like headaches, increased cigarette smoking and use of drugs.

***(ii) Effect of Marital Status on Employee Health, Turnover Intention, and Organizational Commitment.***

Table 8.20 depicts a significant difference between married and unmarried employees in Organization 'B', but not in 'C', on

**Table–8.20**
**Comparison of Married and Unmarried Employees of 3 Organizations on Outcome Variables**

| *Outcome Variables* | *Unmarried* | | *Married* | | *t-Value* |
|---|---|---|---|---|---|
| | *Mean* | *SD* | *Mean* | *SD* | |
| **ORG 'A'** | **N=21** | | **N=44** | | |
| EH(O) | 13.48 | 6.17 | 13.50 | 5.09 | 0.01 |
| PH | 3.43 | 2.50 | 4.81 | 3.09 | 1.79 |
| BH | 5.76 | 2.54 | 4.54 | 2.54 | 1.69 |
| EH | 4.38 | 2.68 | 4.59 | 2.65 | 0.24 |
| TI | 2.48 | 1.12 | 2.34 | 0.77 | 0.57 |
| OC | 4.45 | 1.12 | 4.75 | 0.70 | 1.28 |
| OCI | 4.96 | 1.42 | 5.12 | 0.83 | 0.58 |
| OCJI | 5.11 | 1.04 | 4.77 | 1.24 | 1.09 |
| OCL | 3.82 | 1.12 | 4.53 | 0.60 | 3.31** |
| **ORG 'B'** | **N=16** | | **N=55** | | |
| EH(O) | 16.50 | 7.39 | 16.09 | 8.65 | 0.16 |
| PH | 3.87 | 2.60 | 4.71 | 3.15 | 0.96 |
| BH | 5.56 | 2.89 | 4.74 | 2.97 | 0.94 |
| EH | 7.31 | 4.21 | 6.71 | 4.13 | 0.48 |
| TI | 1.94 | 0.85 | 2.22 | 0.83 | 1.18 |
| OC | 4.62 | 0.50 | 5.24 | 0.72 | 3.24** |
| OCI | 5.04 | 0.94 | 5.63 | 0.82 | 2.44* |
| OCJI | 4.56 | 1.14 | 5.11 | 0.93 | 1.96 |
| OCL | 4.41 | 0.70 | 5.11 | 0.80 | 3.14** |

*Contd...*

| *Outcome Variables* | *Unmarried* | | *Married* | | *t-Value* |
|---|---|---|---|---|---|
| | *Mean* | *SD* | *Mean* | *SD* | |
| **ORG 'C'** | **N=17** | | **N=49** | | |
| EH(O) | 20.12 | 9.54 | 17.36 | 6.32 | 1.34 |
| PH | 4.76 | 2.94 | 4.53 | 2.89 | 0.26 |
| BH | 7.18 | 2.87 | 6.10 | 2.96 | 1.30 |
| EH | 8.18 | 3.33 | 6.75 | 3.90 | 1.26 |
| TI | 2.29 | 0.68 | 2.32 | 0.74 | 0.16 |
| OC | 4.84 | 0.49 | 4.94 | 0.98 | 0.41 |
| OCI | 5.27 | 0.83 | 5.18 | 1.19 | 0.29 |
| OCJI | 5.04 | 0.66 | 5.13 | 1.06 | 0.34 |
| OCL | 4.49 | 0.72 | 4.71 | 1.16 | 0.71 |

*Note:* **$p<0.01$, *$p<0.05$.

organizational commitment and two of its dimensions, identification and loyalty, with the former being more committed, more loyal, and identified more with their organization than their unmarried counterparts. Similar results were found in Organization 'A', with married respondents being more loyal than unmarried ones.

These results thus imply that being married is related to greater commitment and loyalty with the organization. This finding seems contrary to that of Blau (1985), who found commitment to be negatively related with marital status. The reason could be that since marriage increases responsibility of one's family, off-the-job commitment and loyalty (to one's spouse and children) finds itself translated in on-the-job commitment and loyalty. Research has documented a spill-over effect between what happens at work and at home (Zedeck and Mosier, 1990), and that quality of one's life in general can rub off on a person's work life (Katzell, 1998). It is possible that such an effect operates in case of organizational commitment as well.

*(iii) Effect of Family Structure on Employee Health, Turnover Intention, and Organizational Commitment*

**Table–8.21**
**Comparison of Employees of 3 Organizations from Nuclear and Joint Families on Outcome Variables**

| *Outcome Variables* | *Nuclear* | | *Joint* | | *t-Value* |
|---|---|---|---|---|---|
| | *Mean* | *SD* | *Mean* | *SD* | |
| ORG 'A' | N=51 | | N=14 | | |
| EH(O) | 12.86 | 5.62 | 15.78 | 6.02 | 1.44 |
| PH | 4.33 | 2.69 | 4.50 | 2.06 | 0.18 |
| BH | 4.53 | 2.97 | 6.43 | 4.20 | 1.93 |
| EH | 4.43 | 2.63 | 4.86 | 2.65 | 0.40 |
| TI | 2.43 | 0.94 | 2.21 | 0.69 | 0.80 |
| OC | 4.60 | 0.90 | 4.84 | 0.65 | 0.91 |
| OCI | 5.00 | 1.11 | 5.31 | 0.72 | 0.97 |
| OCJI | 4.76 | 1.25 | 4.31 | 0.74 | 1.56 |
| OCL | 4.29 | 0.89 | 4.32 | 0.81 | 0.11 |
| ORG 'B' | N=45 | | N=26 | | |
| EH(O) | 17.78 | 7.51 | 13.42 | 5.58 | 2.06* |
| PH | 4.89 | 2.60 | 3.88 | 2.45 | 1.35 |
| BH | 5.13 | 3.15 | 4.58 | 2.88 | 0.74 |
| EH | 7.93 | 3.74 | 4.96 | 2.50 | 2.91** |
| TI | 2.16 | 0.82 | 2.15 | 0.88 | 0.01 |
| OC | 4.98 | 0.76 | 5.33 | 0.61 | 2.01* |
| OCI | 5.38 | 0.96 | 5.69 | 0.69 | 1.43 |
| OCJI | 4.89 | 0.99 | 5.15 | 1.01 | 1.07 |
| OCL | 4.80 | 0.85 | 5.23 | 0.73 | 2.14* |

*Contd...*

| *Outcome Variables* | *Nuclear* | | *Joint* | | *t-Value* |
|---|---|---|---|---|---|
| | *Mean* | *SD* | *Mean* | *SD* | |
| **ORG 'C'** | **N=54** | | **N=12** | | |
| EH(O) | 17.96 | 6.82 | 18.58 | 4.50 | 0.26 |
| PH | 4.46 | 3.21 | 5.17 | 3.01 | 0.69 |
| BH | 6.52 | 2.95 | 5.75 | 2.98 | 0.81 |
| EH | 7.00 | 3.96 | 7.67 | 3.47 | 0.51 |
| TI | 2.26 | 0.58 | 2.58 | 1.16 | 1.14 |
| OC | 4.95 | 0.90 | 4.76 | 0.81 | 0.68 |
| OCI | 5.33 | 1.03 | 4.65 | 1.31 | 1.95 |
| OCJI | 5.06 | 1.00 | 5.32 | 0.82 | 0.83 |
| OCL | 4.68 | 1.06 | 4.51 | 1.15 | 0.51 |

*Note:* **p<0.01, *p<0.05.

Table 8.21 shows that family structure did not influence any outcome variable in Organization 'A' and 'C'. However, in Organization 'B', significant differences were found on employee health (overall) and one of its dimensions viz. emotional health, organizational commitment and its dimension loyalty, between those who belong to nuclear and joint families. Those belonging to nuclear families have poorer employee health (overall) and emotional health. The mean scores, however, as per the norms indicate a proficient level of health functioning for both. These findings indicate the role of the joint family system as a buffer in reducing stress, thereby leading to better health. These results are in line with the findings of Chaturvedi (1983), who found persons belonging to nuclear families having significantly more psychiatric problems than those from joint families. Sharma (1999), in his review on the role of family structure on stress and health, concluded that, "What matters more than nuclearity or jointness as a structural phenomenon is the nature and quality of social interactions and consequently the efficacy of social support emanating from it." The importance of social support in coping with stress and improving health and well-being is well documented (Rosen, 1984; Kasl and Cooper, 1987; Leiter,

1991; Heaney, Price and Rafferty, 1995; Wilkinson, 1997). According to Pareek (1988), social and emotional support available to the person helps him to cope effectively with stress. Sandhu (1993), too, reported a positive correlation between career commitment and social support from family.

Further, results indicate that employees coming from joint families are significantly more committed and more loyal than those coming from nuclear families. This interesting finding suggests a link between loyalty as fostered by a joint family system and loyalty towards the organization. It is possible that the values of collectivism, dependence, and importance of long-term relationships fostered in a joint family structure lead to employees' being loyal and committed to their organizations.

### *(iv) Effect of Promotion(s) Received on Employee Health, Turnover Intention, and Organizational Commitment*

**Table–8.22**
**Comparison of Employees of 3 Organizations Who Received/did not Receive Promotion(s) on Outcome Variables**

| *Outcome Variables* | *Promotion (s) Not Received* | | *Promotion (s) Received* | | *t-Value* |
|---|---|---|---|---|---|
| | *Mean* | *SD* | *Mean* | *SD* | |
| **ORG 'A'** | **N=48** | | **N=17** | | |
| EH(O) | 14.06 | 6.04 | 11.88 | 4.98 | 1.14 |
| PH | 4.52 | 2.84 | 3.94 | 2.36 | 0.69 |
| BH | 5.04 | 3.55 | 4.64 | 2.69 | 0.42 |
| EH | 4.75 | 2.25 | 3.88 | 2.44 | 1.08 |
| TI | 2.29 | 0.68 | 2.65 | 1.32 | 1.42 |
| OC | 4.08 | 0.67 | 4.85 | 1.09 | 3.44** |
| OCI | 4.46 | 0.84 | 5.28 | 1.33 | 2.94** |
| OCJI | 4.09 | 0.85 | 5.16 | 1.58 | 3.49** |
| OCL | 3.87 | 0.74 | 4.45 | 1.06 | 2.47* |

*Contd...*

| *Outcome Variables* | *Promotion (s) Not Received* | | *Promotion (s) Received* | | *t-Value* |
|---|---|---|---|---|---|
| | *Mean* | *SD* | *Mean* | *SD* | |
| **ORG 'B'** | **N=34** | | **N=37** | | |
| EH(O) | 16.32 | 7.38 | 16.05 | 7.21 | 0.13 |
| PH | 4.35 | 2.79 | 4.67 | 2.94 | 0.78 |
| BH | 4.97 | 2.86 | 4.89 | 2.11 | 0.19 |
| EH | 7.12 | 3.35 | 6.59 | 3.42 | 0.50 |
| TI | 2.08 | 0.89 | 2.23 | 0.79 | 0.77 |
| OC | 4.95 | 0.68 | 5.25 | 0.74 | 1.71 |
| OCI | 5.33 | 0.96 | 5.64 | 0.77 | 1.52 |
| OCJI | 4.75 | 1.01 | 5.19 | 0.95 | 1.90 |
| OCL | 4.85 | 0.79 | 5.05 | 0.86 | 1.01 |
| **ORG 'C'** | **N=22** | | **N=44** | | |
| EH(O) | 16.95 | 7.30 | 18.63 | 7.33 | 0.88 |
| PH | 4.95 | 2.52 | 4.41 | 2.96 | 1.08 |
| BH | 5.64 | 3.06 | 6.75 | 2.86 | 1.46 |
| EH | 6.36 | 3.95 | 7.50 | 3.49 | 1.08 |
| TI | 2.45 | 0.91 | 2.25 | 0.61 | 1.08 |
| OC | 4.50 | 1.22 | 5.12 | 0.56 | 2.85** |
| OCI | 4.67 | 1.32 | 5.48 | 0.88 | 2.96** |
| OCJI | 4.70 | 1.22 | 5.31 | 0.74 | 2.54* |
| OCL | 4.30 | 1.50 | 4.83 | 0.73 | 1.94 |

*Note:* **$p<0.01$, *$p<0.05$.

Table 8.22 depicts that promotion(s) received influenced outcome variable in Organization 'A' and 'C', but not in 'B'. In Organization 'A', those who have received promotion(s) are significantly more committed, more loyal, identify more with the organization, and are more involved with their jobs than those who have not received promotions(s). Similar results are found for Organization 'C', with those who have received promotion(s) being more committed, more involved in their jobs, and identifying more with their organization than those who have not received promotion(s).

These findings suggest that promotions play an important role in fostering commitment, identification, and loyalty among employees. This finding is supported with the growing body of research which recognises the motivational potential of rewards (Kanungo and Mendonca, 1994; Misra and Kanungo, 1994), and hails performance management as a culture-building tool. Similarly, Whitener and Waltz (1993) found that commitment tends to be greater when people have ample opportunities for promotion.

### *(v) Effect of Education on Employee Health, Turnover Intention, and Organizational Commitment*

**Table-8.23**

**Comparison of Graduate, Engineers and Post-Graduate Employees of 3 Different Organizations on Outcome Variables**

| *Outcome Variables* | *Group 1 (Graduates)* | | *Group 2 (Engineers)* | | *Group 3 (Post-Grad.)* | | *G1 Vs G2* | *G1 Vs G3* | *G2 Vs G3* | *F-value* |
|---|---|---|---|---|---|---|---|---|---|---|
| | *Mean* | *SD* | *Mean* | *SD* | *Mean* | *SD* | | | | |
| **ORG 'A'** | **N=24** | | **N=31** | | **N=10** | | | | | |
| EH(O) | 11.12 | 4.92 | 15.35 | 5.66 | 13.40 | 3.59 | (*) | - | - | 2.79 |
| PH | 4.21 | 2.82 | 4.58 | 2.83 | 4.10 | 2.96 | - | - | - | 0.15 |
| BH | 4.04 | 2.89 | 5.42 | 3.76 | 5.60 | 1.83 | - | - | - | 1.40 |
| EH | 2.96 | 1.68 | 5.68 | 3.25 | 4.70 | 3.02 | (*) | - | - | 5.21** |
| TI | 2.04 | 0.69 | 2.39 | 0.66 | 3.20 | 1.39 | - | (*) | (*) | 7.01** |
| OC | 4.75 | 0.45 | 4.88 | 0.81 | 3.73 | 1.18 | - | (*) | (*) | 8.54** |
| OCI | 5.26 | 0.71 | 5.26 | 0.92 | 4.02 | 1.48 | - | (*) | (*) | 7.08** |
| OCJI | 5.29 | 0.44 | 5.02 | 1.20 | 3.45 | 1.32 | - | (*) | (*) | 12.17** |
| OCL | 4.17 | 0.66 | 4.59 | 0.76 | 3.73 | 1.26 | - | - | (*) | 4.58* |

*Contd...*

| *Outcome Variables* | *Group 1 (Graduates)* | | *Group 2 (Engineers)* | | *Group 3 (Post-Grad.)* | | *G1 Vs G2* | *G1 Vs G3* | *G2 Vs G3* | *F-Value* |
|---|---|---|---|---|---|---|---|---|---|---|
| | *Mean* | *SD* | *Mean* | *SD* | *Mean* | *SD* | | | | |
| **ORG 'B'** | **N=13** | | **N=31** | | **N=27** | | | | | |
| EH(O) | 19.46 | 8.68 | 14.87 | 7.38 | 16.11 | 6.37 | - | - | - | 1.27 |
| PH | 5.69 | 2.42 | 3.74 | 2.19 | 4.85 | 2.98 | - | - | - | 2.21 |
| BH | 5.31 | 3.42 | 4.87 | 2.93 | 4.81 | 2.98 | - | - | - | 0.12 |
| EH | 8.46 | 4.25 | 6.26 | 3.58 | 6.74 | 3.55 | - | - | - | 1.19 |
| TI | 1.85 | 0.89 | 2.16 | 0.82 | 2.30 | 0.82 | - | - | - | 1.27 |
| OC | 5.12 | 0.52 | 5.16 | 0.79 | 5.03 | 0.75 | - | - | - | 0.23 |
| OCI | 5.65 | 0.80 | 5.52 | 0.96 | 5.39 | 0.82 | - | - | - | 0.39 |
| OCJI | 4.68 | 0.81 | 5.20 | 0.95 | 4.88 | 1.11 | - | - | - | 1.51 |
| OCL | 5.08 | 0.49 | 4.94 | 0.93 | 4.92 | 0.85 | - | - | - | 0.17 |
| **ORG 'C'** | **N=16** | | **N=22** | | **N=28** | | | | | |
| EH(O) | 19.00 | 7.35 | 19.23 | 6.47 | 16.64 | 6.89 | - | - | - | 0.94 |
| PH | 4.56 | 2.52 | 4.36 | 2.46 | 4.78 | 3.21 | - | - | - | 0.11 |
| BH | 6.50 | 2.82 | 6.86 | 3.19 | 5.93 | 2.86 | - | - | - | 0.63 |
| EH | 7.94 | 4.91 | 8.00 | 3.59 | 5.96 | 3.64 | - | - | - | 2.06 |
| TI | 2.56 | 0.81 | 2.59 | 0.67 | 1.96 | 0.57 | - | (*) | (*) | 6.81** |
| OC | 4.53 | 0.71 | 4.81 | 1.18 | 5.22 | 0.56 | - | (*) | - | 3.62* |
| OCI | 4.75 | 1.19 | 5.03 | 1.27 | 5.61 | 0.76 | - | (*) | - | 3.74* |
| OCJI | 5.11 | 0.78 | 4.86 | 1.24 | 5.30 | 0.79 | - | - | - | 1.24 |
| OCL | 4.09 | 0.93 | 4.66 | 1.34 | 4.97 | 0.75 | - | (*) | - | 3.74* |

*Note:* **p<0.01, *p<0.05.

(*) Denotes pairs of groups significantly different at the .05 level using Duncan's test.

Table 8.23 indicates significant differences among graduates, engineers, and post-graduates on emotional health, turnover intention, organizational commitment and all its dimensions viz. organizational identification, job involvement, and loyalty in Organization 'A'. Engineers had poorer overall health and emotional health than graduates; post-graduates had greater turnover intention than both graduates and engineers, were less committed, identified less with the organization, and were less involved with their jobs than both graduates and engineers, and were also less loyal than engineers. In Organization 'C', a reverse trend was observed, with post-graduates having lesser turnover intention than both graduates and engineers, and being more committed, loyal, and identifying more with the organization as compared to graduates. On the other hand, education did not influence any outcome variable in Organization 'B'.

These results imply that the effect of education on both turnover intention and organizational commitment cannot be generalized across organizations. While in Organization 'A', education seemed to increase turnover intention and decrease commitment, in Organization 'C', the reverse was found. It is probable that the cultural values of employees with higher education in Organization 'C' are more congruent with the organizational values, leading to higher commitment. In Organization 'C', PD was found to be quite low, which may be compatible with increased education (Hofstede, 1991). Its corollary that Organization 'A', found to be the highest on PD, is associated with lower levels of commitment with increased education, is also in line with this explanation. The results of the present study thus suggest that organizational factors moderate the relationship between education and commitment and turnover intention.

There is support for both positions in research literature. Research has generally found education to be inversely related to commitment (Steers, 1977; Morris and Steers, 1980; Angle and Perry, 1981; Morris and Sherman, 1981). The inverse relation is attributed to the difficulty faced by organizations in providing sufficient rewards (as perceived by employees) to equalize the exchange, when employees have higher levels of education. And highly educated employees can be more clear about their long-range interests, with the result that they are ready to quit the organization for better prospects elsewhere. Further, these employees are likely to be less committed to their organization, but more committed to their profession. In a meta-analysis of turnover research, Cotton and Tuttle (1986) found turnover to be positively related to level of education. At the other extreme, researchers like Anantharaman and John (1983), Sharma and Sharma (1987) found education to be positively correlated with job involvement. In contrast, Sommer, Bae and Luthans (1996) found education to be unrelated to commitment.

Mottaz (1988) studied the effects of education on commitment and found that when demographic variables like sex, marital status, job tenure, and family income are included in the analysis, the effect of education on commitment is positive. But when "work values" such as task autonomy, task significance, task involvement, supervisory assistance, co-worker assistance, working conditions, salary, promotional opportunity and fringe benefits are entered, the effect becomes negative. One probable explanation of this finding can be that education may have a positive effect on commitment by increasing the availability of both intrinsic and extrinsic rewards, but a negative effect when rewards are held constant.

***(vi) Effect of Age on Employee Health, Turnover Intention, and Organizational Commitment***

**Table -8.24**
**Comparison of Employees of 3 Different Age Groups from 3 Organizations on Outcome Variables**

| *Outcome Variables* | *Group 1 (< 25 yrs.)* | | *Group 2 (25-35 yrs.)* | | *Group 3 (> 35 yrs.)* | | *G1 Vs G2* | *G1 Vs G3* | *G2 Vs G3* | *F-Value* |
|---|---|---|---|---|---|---|---|---|---|---|
| | *Mean* | *SD* | *Mean* | *SD* | *Mean* | *SD* | | | | |
| **ORG 'A'** | **N=9** | | **N=42** | | **N=14** | | | | | |
| EH(O) | 17.00 | 8.51 | 12.53 | 5.26 | 17.00 | 10.24 | - | - | - | 2.51 |
| PH | 6.11 | 3.82 | 3.88 | 2.50 | 6.20 | 4.43 | (*) | - | - | 3.42* |
| BH | 6.89 | 4.85 | 4.47 | 2.74 | 6.20 | 4.81 | - | - | - | 2.51 |
| EH | 4.22 | 2.73 | 4.57 | 3.10 | 4.60 | 2.74 | - | - | - | 0.04 |
| TI | 2.11 | 0.60 | 2.39 | 0.93 | 2.80 | 0.83 | - | - | - | 0.96 |

*Contd...*

| *Outcome Variables* | *Group 1 (< 25 yrs.)* | | *Group 2 (25-35 yrs.)* | | *Group 3 (> 35 yrs.)* | | *G1 Vs G2* | *G1 Vs G3* | *G2 Vs G3* | *F-Value* |
|---|---|---|---|---|---|---|---|---|---|---|
| | *Mean* | *SD* | *Mean* | *SD* | *Mean* | *SD* | | | | |
| OC | 4.89 | 0.65 | 4.52 | 0.85 | 5.56 | 0.75 | - | - | (*) | 4.12* |
| OCI | 5.67 | 0.64 | 4.88 | 1.04 | 5.93 | 1.03 | (*) | - | (*) | 4.42* |
| OCJI | 5.13 | 0.39 | 4.74 | 1.22 | 5.83 | 1.29 | - | - | - | 2.27 |
| OCL | 4.34 | 0.91 | 4.20 | 0.85 | 5.21 | 0.34 | - | - | (*) | 3.34* |
| **ORG 'B'** | **N=13** | | **N=37** | | **N=21** | | | | | |
| EH(O) | 17.61 | 8.01 | 16.68 | 8.19 | 14.43 | 6.91 | - | - | - | 0.65 |
| PH | 4.00 | 2.41 | 4.70 | 2.64 | 4.52 | 2.86 | - | - | - | 0.55 |
| BH | 5.92 | 2.92 | 5.11 | 2.94 | 4.00 | 2.79 | - | - | - | 1.77 |
| EH | 8.00 | 4.74 | 6.86 | 3.55 | 6.09 | 3.78 | - | - | - | 0.94 |
| TI | 1.77 | 0.83 | 2.30 | 0.81 | 2.14 | 0.85 | - | - | - | 1.96 |
| OC | 4.59 | 0.41 | 5.15 | 0.72 | 5.35 | 0.76 | (*) | (*) | - | 4.97** |
| OCI | 5.04 | 0.80 | 5.53 | 0.93 | 5.72 | 0.74 | - | (*) | - | 2.59 |
| OCJI | 4.29 | 1.02 | 5.16 | 0.81 | 5.10 | 1.14 | (*) | (*) | - | 4.15* |
| OCL | 4.51 | 0.67 | 4.93 | 0.86 | 5.28 | 0.74 | - | (*) | - | 3.76* |
| **ORG 'C'** | **N=11** | | **N=43** | | **N=12** | | | | | |
| EH(O) | 23.17 | 7.57 | 16.89 | 7.42 | 20.25 | 5.37 | - | - | - | 2.75 |
| PH | 5.00 | 2.09 | 4.50 | 3.42 | 4.75 | 2.63 | - | - | - | 0.08 |
| BH | 8.33 | 1.86 | 5.77 | 2.06 | 7.83 | 1.95 | - | - | (*) | 4.14* |
| EH | 9.83 | 3.99 | 6.62 | 3.91 | 7.75 | 3.74 | - | - | - | 1.91 |
| TI | 2.33 | 0.52 | 2.29 | 0.77 | 2.42 | 0.66 | - | - | - | 0.14 |
| OC | 4.91 | 0.75 | 4.83 | 0.95 | 5.24 | 0.60 | - | - | - | 1.02 |
| OCI | 5.31 | 0.92 | 5.00 | 1.13 | 5.97 | 0.76 | - | - | (*) | 4.02* |
| OCJI | 4.89 | 0.87 | 5.13 | 1.07 | 5.12 | 0.51 | - | - | - | 0.16 |
| OCL | 4.71 | 0.83 | 4.58 | 1.14 | 4.91 | 0.87 | - | - | - | 0.46 |

*Note:* **p<0.01, *p<0.05.

(*) Denotes pairs of groups significantly different at the .05 level using Duncan's test.

Age influenced outcome variables moderately in all three organizations (Table 8.24). Although no age-differences were found on overall employee health in any of the three organizations, in Organization 'A', surprisingly, those aged less than 25 years had poorer physical health than those aged between 25-35 years. In all 3 organizations, age had a strong influence on commitment. In Organization 'A', those aged more than 35 years were more committed, loyal, and also identified more with the organization than those aged between 25-35 years; who, in turn, identified even less with the organization as compared to those below 25 years. Similar results were found for Organization 'B' and 'C'. Further, in Organization 'C', those above 35 years had poorer behavioural health than those between 25-35 years.

These results suggest a positive relation between age and commitment (and its components identification and loyalty). This is consistent with earlier research, which has found age to be positively related to commitment (Hall, Schneider, and Nygren, 1970; Sheldon, 1971; Lee, 1971; Hrebiniak and Alutto, 1972; Morris and Sherman, 1981; Luthans, McCaul and Dodd, 1985; Sommer, Bae and Luthans, 1996). It has been suggested that as age of employees increases, employees' opportunities for alternative employment elsewhere diminish, with the result that they may become more attached to their organization.

No significant differences have emerged between various age groups and turnover intention. This is in line with Michaels and Spector (1982) and Sarker et al. (2003) who found age to be unrelated to turnover. However, this contradicts the findings of Miller, Katerberg, and Hulin (1979), Hofstede (1991), Krecker (1994), who found age to be negatively correlated with turnover.

### *(vii) Effect of Tenure on Employee Health, Turnover Intention, and Organizational Commitment*

Tenure affected employees of the three organizations differently (Table 8.25). In Organization 'A', significant differences were found on turnover intention, with those with more than 4 years tenure having higher turnover intention than both the other two groups: those with less than 2 years, and those with 2.1-4 years tenure. The mean scores indicate that while the former, on an average "sometimes" think about quitting, the other two groups "rarely" do

**Table–8.25**
**Comparison of Employees with Varying Tenures from 3 Organizations on Outcome Variables**

| *Outcome Variables* | *Group 1 (< 2 yrs.)* | | *Group 2 (2.1-4 yrs.)* | | *Group 3 (> 4 yrs.)* | | *G1 Vs G2* | *G1 Vs G3* | *G2 Vs G3* | *F-Value* |
|---|---|---|---|---|---|---|---|---|---|---|
| | *Mean* | *SD* | *Mean* | *SD* | *Mean* | *SD* | | | | |
| **ORG 'A'** | **N=34** | | **N=14** | | **N=17** | | | | | |
| EH(O) | 13.56 | 5.79 | 13.55 | 3.74 | 13.29 | 5.14 | - | - | - | 0.01 |
| PH | 4.21 | 2.40 | 5.44 | 2.82 | 4.18 | 2.82 | - | - | - | 0.98 |
| BH | 4.74 | 2.92 | 4.68 | 2.34 | 5.53 | 3.04 | - | - | - | 0.36 |
| EH | 4.67 | 2.79 | 5.67 | 3.36 | 3.59 | 2.85 | - | - | - | 1.27 |
| TI | 2.13 | 0.61 | 2.11 | 0.78 | 3.12 | 1.11 | - | (*) | (*) | 9.83** |
| OC | 4.84 | 0.59 | 4.34 | 0.67 | 4.40 | 1.30 | - | - | - | 2.31 |
| OCI | 5.26 | 0.80 | 4.96 | 0.61 | 4.69 | 1.56 | - | - | - | 1.88 |
| OCJI | 5.07 | 0.61 | 4.42 | 1.95 | 4.69 | 1.58 | - | - | - | 1.41 |
| OCL | 4.48 | 0.71 | 3.96 | 0.50 | 4.08 | 1.22 | - | - | - | 2.13 |
| **ORG 'B'** | **N=32** | | **N=21** | | **N=18** | | | | | |
| EH(O) | 16.56 | 7.07 | 16.28 | 8.57 | 15.39 | 7.04 | - | - | - | 0.10 |
| PH | 4.22 | 2.83 | 4.48 | 2.31 | 5.11 | 3.16 | - | - | - | 0.69 |
| BH | 5.12 | 2.72 | 4.71 | 2.73 | 4.83 | 2.87 | - | - | - | 0.21 |
| EH | 7.34 | 4.17 | 7.09 | 4.55 | 5.67 | 4.48 | - | - | - | 0.90 |
| TI | 2.06 | 0.84 | 2.52 | 0.75 | 1.89 | 0.83 | (*) | - | (*) | 3.34* |
| OC | 5.06 | 0.65 | 4.90 | 0.82 | 5.43 | 0.67 | - | - | (*) | 2.77 |
| OCI | 5.45 | 0.89 | 5.38 | 0.86 | 5.71 | 0.87 | - | - | - | 0.76 |
| OCJI | 4.97 | 1.07 | 4.67 | 0.95 | 5.37 | 0.84 | - | - | (*) | 2.44 |
| OCL | 4.89 | 0.80 | 4.77 | 0.92 | 5.30 | 0.68 | - | - | - | 2.31 |

*Contd...*

| *Outcome Variables* | *Group 1 (< 2 yrs.)* | | *Group 2 (2.1-4 yrs.)* | | *Group 3 (> 4 yrs.)* | | *G1 Vs G2* | *G1 Vs G3* | *G2 Vs G3* | *F-Value* |
|---|---|---|---|---|---|---|---|---|---|---|
| | *Mean* | *SD* | *Mean* | *SD* | *Mean* | *SD* | | | | |
| **ORG 'C'** | **N=24** | | **N=15** | | **N=27** | | | | | |
| EH(O) | 17.83 | 6.56 | 15.47 | 4.89 | 19.74 | 8.70 | - | - | - | 1.70 |
| PH | 5.04 | 3.21 | 3.07 | 1.43 | 5.04 | 3.62 | - | - | - | 2.34 |
| BH | 5.88 | 3.13 | 5.67 | 2.09 | 7.22 | 3.08 | - | - | - | 1.94 |
| EH | 6.92 | 3.54 | 6.73 | 3.19 | 7.51 | 4.07 | - | - | - | 0.42 |
| TI | 2.54 | 0.83 | 2.53 | 0.74 | 2.00 | 0.48 | - | (*) | (*) | 4.91* |
| OC | 4.47 | 1.15 | 4.96 | 0.58 | 5.29 | 0.51 | - | (*) | - | 6.37** |
| OCI | 4.62 | 1.23 | 5.13 | 1.07 | 5.76 | 0.69 | - | (*) | - | 8.25** |
| OCJI | 4.74 | 1.20 | 5.11 | 0.88 | 5.44 | 0.64 | - | (*) | - | 3.59* |
| OCL | 4.24 | 1.41 | 4.77 | 0.42 | 4.95 | 0.86 | - | (*) | - | 3.11 |

*Note:* **$p<0.01$, *$p<0.05$.

(*) Denotes pairs of groups significantly different at the .05 level using Duncan's test.

so. Contrary results were found for Organization 'B', with those with more than 4 years tenure having a lower turnover intention than those with 2.1-4 years tenure; however, those with less than 2 years tenure have a lower turnover intention than those with 2.1-4 years tenure. In keeping with this, those with more than 4 years tenure are more committed and also more involved in their jobs than those with 2.1-4 years tenure. Somewhat similar results are found for Organization 'C', with those with more than 4 years tenure being more committed, loyal, identifying more with the organization, and also being more involved with their jobs than those with less than 2 years tenure. The former also have a lower turnover intention than those with 2-4 years tenure and less than 2 years tenure. No significant differences were found among employees with different tenures on job involvement. This contradicts findings of Anantharaman and Kalippan (1982), Anantharaman and John (1983), Sharma and Sharma (1987), who found length of service to be correlated with job involvement. A possible reason could be that since the culture of MNCs is very work-oriented and professional, all employees work hard and are almost equally involved.

The findings of the present study imply that while in Organization 'A', tenure was positively related to turnover intention, the reverse was true for the other two organizations, where tenure seemed to be negatively related to turnover intention. In Organization 'C', tenure was also related to increased commitment, loyalty, and identification with the organization. This is in line with researches by Hall, Scheider, and Nygren (1970), Sheldon (1971), Lee (1971), Hrebiniak (1974), Stevens, Beyer and Trice (1978), Luthans, McCaul and Dodd (1985), Cain and Bruce (1987), Gregersen and Black, (1992), Sommer, Bae and Luthans (1996), who found tenure to be positively related to organizational commitment. This follows from the side-bets approach in so far as the longer one has been working for an organization, the more he is likely to have invested in it. In contrast, Al-Qarioti and Al-Enezi (2004) found commitment to be negatively related to length of service.

However, the relation between tenure and turnover intention is not as straightforward, as indicated by our results. Research has found a negative relation between tenure and turnover intention. Mobley et al. (1978) found that intentions to search for an alternative job are stronger when the employee is younger and less tenured. Werbel and Gould (1984), similarly, found that the more tenured employees were less likely to quit than the newly hired. Cotton and Tuttle (1986) demonstrated that younger and less-tenured employees who were less psychologically committed to the organization were more likely to quit. In contrast, Miller, Katerberg, and Hulin (1979) did not find a significant correlation between tenure and withdrawal cognitions.

These results thus suggest that organizational factors moderate the relationship between tenure and turnover intention. When employees' cultural values are incompatible with those of the organization (as in Organization 'A'), greater time spent in the organization only compounds these differences, probably leading to greater intention to quit. These results are in line with Mark (1999), who in his model of cultural adaptation, commented on an initial "honeymoon phase," where all encounters in the new place are seen as exciting, positive, and stimulating. "Culture shock," the experience of foreignness with a creeping awareness of disorientation, sets in only a little later. However, when organizational values are more in tune with societal values (as in Organization 'B' and also 'C', to some extent), employees get to realize this only after a longer tenure, leaving them more committed and with a lower intention to leave.

***(viii) Effect of Number of jobs Changed on Employee Health, Turnover Intention, and Organizational Commitment***

**Table–8.26**
**Comparison of Employees with Varying Number of Jobs Changed from 3 Organizations on Outcome Variables**

| *Outcome Variables* | *Group 1 (0-1 Job)* | | *Group 2 (2 Job)* | | *Group 3 (> 2 Job)* | | *G1 Vs G2* | *G1 Vs G3* | *G2 Vs G3* | *F-Value* |
|---|---|---|---|---|---|---|---|---|---|---|
| | *Mean* | *SD* | *Mean* | *SD* | *Mean* | *SD* | | | | |
| **ORG 'A'** | **N=18** | | **N=23** | | **N=24** | | | | | |
| EH(O) | 16.22 | 7.07 | 12.83 | 5.45 | 12.08 | 5.56 | - | - | - | 2.17 |
| PH | 4.67 | 3.02 | 4.35 | 2.87 | 4.17 | 2.53 | - | - | - | 0.19 |
| BH | 5.89 | 3.57 | 4.61 | 2.72 | 4.54 | 2.71 | - | - | - | 1.11 |
| EH | 6.89 | 3.08 | 3.87 | 2.49 | 3.37 | 2.42 | (*) | (*) | - | 7.93** |
| TI | 2.28 | 0.66 | 2.43 | 0.78 | 2.42 | 1.13 | - | - | - | 0.17 |
| OC | 4.74 | 0.55 | 4.93 | 0.70 | 4.18 | 1.05 | - | (*) | (*) | 4.39* |
| OCI | 5.00 | 0.74 | 5.35 | 0.90 | 4.81 | 1.32 | - | - | - | 1.45 |
| OCJI | 5.33 | 1.49 | 4.41 | 0.73 | 4.80 | 1.14 | (*) | - | - | 3.44* |
| OCL | 4.56 | 0.47 | 4.47 | 0.75 | 3.72 | 1.01 | (*) | (*) | - | 6.61** |
| **ORG 'B'** | **N=27** | | **N=24** | | **N=20** | | | | | |
| EH(O) | 13.96 | 7.31 | 18.79 | 8.38 | 16.05 | 6.48 | - | - | - | 1.99 |
| PH | 3.56 | 2.77 | 5.58 | 3.20 | 4.55 | 2.89 | (*) | - | - | 2.98 |
| BH | 4.63 | 2.10 | 5.67 | 3.40 | 4.45 | 3.01 | - | - | - | 1.08 |
| EH | 5.93 | 3.44 | 7.54 | 4.33 | 7.25 | 2.59 | - | - | - | 1.11 |

*Contd...*

| Outcome Variables | Group 1 (0-1 Job) | | Group 2 (2 Job) | | Group 3 (> 2 Job) | | G1 Vs G2 | G1 Vs G3 | G2 Vs G3 | F-Value |
|---|---|---|---|---|---|---|---|---|---|---|
| | Mean | SD | Mean | SD | Mean | SD | | | | |
| TI | 1.70 | 0.72 | 2.37 | 0.76 | 2.50 | 0.82 | (*) | (*) | - | 7.64** |
| OC | 5.17 | 0.73 | 5.03 | 0.68 | 5.11 | 0.80 | - | - | - | 0.23 |
| OCI | 5.51 | 0.99 | 5.41 | 0.85 | 5.58 | 0.76 | - | - | - | 0.21 |
| OCJI | 4.90 | 1.01 | 5.15 | 0.80 | 4.90 | 1.21 | - | - | - | 0.50 |
| OCL | 5.13 | 0.84 | 4.75 | 0.76 | 4.97 | 0.88 | - | - | - | 1.30 |
| ORG 'C' | N=25 | | N=18 | | N=23 | | | | | |
| EH(O) | 17.56 | 5.94 | 20.33 | 6.98 | 16.87 | 6.07 | - | - | - | 1.24 |
| PH | 3.96 | 2.33 | 6.67 | 3.55 | 3.65 | 2.32 | (*) | - | (*) | 6.24** |
| BH | 6.36 | 3.14 | 6.22 | 3.33 | 6.52 | 2.52 | - | - | - | 0.05 |
| EH | 7.24 | 3.80 | 7.50 | 3.60 | 6.69 | 3.69 | - | - | - | 0.21 |
| TI | 2.20 | 0.76 | 2.22 | 0.73 | 2.52 | 0.66 | - | - | - | 1.41 |
| OC | 5.30 | 0.44 | 4.86 | 0.50 | 4.54 | 1.25 | - | (*) | - | 5.12** |
| OCI | 5.46 | 0.75 | 5.18 | 0.83 | 4.95 | 1.52 | - | - | - | 1.28 |
| OCJI | 5.32 | 0.77 | 5.14 | 0.73 | 4.85 | 1.26 | - | - | - | 1.40 |
| OCL | 5.21 | 0.55 | 4.53 | 0.79 | 4.14 | 1.38 | (*) | (*) | - | 7.34** |

*Note:* **p<0.01, *p<0.05.

(*) Denotes pairs of groups significantly different at the .05 level using Duncan's test.

Table 8.26 indicates that expectedly, those who have changed fewer jobs are more committed and loyal (in Organization 'A' and 'C') than those who have changed more jobs. The former also have lower turnover intention than the latter (in Organization 'B'). However, those who have changed fewer jobs have poorer emotional health (in Organization 'A'), but better physical health (in Organization 'B' and 'C') than those who have changed more jobs.

These results can be explained if one takes into account the severe emotional stress and sometimes physical discomfort of people who change jobs frequently. Leong, Furnham, and Cooper (1996) found stress to be a significant predictor of ill-health (both physical and mental), and intention to quit. It can thus be inferred that people who change jobs more often face greater stress, which may translate into poorer physical health. Further, increased stress may also have contributed to greater turnover intention. This is supported by Porter and Steers (1973), Steers and Rhodes (1978), Mobley et al. (1979), who have pointed to a relation between stress and increases in such withdrawal behaviour as absenteeism and turnover. Spector and Jex (1991) found a positive correlation between turnover intention and number of doctor visits.

## SUMMARY

On the 3 outcome variables, employees of the 3 organizations differed significantly on 2, viz. employee health, and organizational commitment. No significant differences were, however, found on turnover intention, with all respondents reporting a "rare" intention of quitting. As regards employee health, all respondents are found to have a proficient level of health functioning, on an average. Employees of organization 'A' emerge to be healthier as compared to 'B' and 'C'. Further, employees of Organization 'B' are most committed (high mean commitment), followed by employees of Organization 'C', and lastly Organization 'A' (moderate commitment).

Gender differences are found only in Organization 'A' on organizational commitment, but not in Organization 'B' and 'C' on any of the outcome variable. Married employees are found to be more loyal than unmarried ones in two organizations. Family structure does not affect any outcome variables in two organizations; in Organization 'B', however, those belonging to joint families have better health and are more committed and loyal than their counterparts belonging to nuclear families. Employees who have received promotion(s) are significantly more committed, loyal, involved with their jobs, and identify more with the organization than those who have not received promotion(s) (in two organizations). Older employees are more committed, loyal, and also identify more with the organization than younger employees across all organizations. Those who have changed fewer jobs are significantly more committed and loyal (in Organization 'C'), have lower turnover intention (in Organization 'B'), have better physical health (in both Organization 'B' and 'C') than those who have changed more jobs. On the other hand, education and tenure did not have a consistent effect across organizations, suggesting that organizational factors may moderate the relationship between tenure and turnover intention, and education and commitment.

CORRELATES OF OUTCOME VARIABLES ACROSS 3 ORGANIZATIONS

The sixth objective was to investigate the relationships between all the independent variables (Indian societal values, organizational values, and demographic variables) and the dependent variables (employee health, turnover intention, and organizational commitment), in each of the 3 MNCs.

**Table-8.27**
**Correlation Between Independent Variables and Dependent Variables in Organization 'A' (N=65)**

| *Indep. Vars.* | *Outcome Variables* | | | | | | | | |
|---|---|---|---|---|---|---|---|---|---|
| | *EH(O)* | *PH* | *BH* | *EH* | *TI* | *OC* | *OCI* | *OCJI* | *OCL* |
| **Personal Variables** | | | | | | | | | |
| SEX | -0.02 | -0.10 | -0.03 | -0.02 | 0.16 | 0.27* | 0.15 | 0.30* | 0.24 |
| AGE | -0.06 | -0.07 | -0.11 | 0.03 | 0.17 | 0.09 | -0.03 | 0.07 | 0.16 |
| EDU | 0.18 | 0.00 | 0.18 | 0.26* | 0.41** | -0.30* | -0.32** | -0.46** | -0.06 |
| MS | 0.00 | 0.22 | -0.17 | 0.03 | -0.07 | 0.15 | 0.07 | -0.13 | 0.38** |
| FS | 0.17 | 0.02 | 0.23 | 0.05 | -0.10 | 0.11 | 0.12 | 0.19 | 0.01 |
| PRO | -0.14 | -0.08 | -0.05 | -0.11 | -0.17 | 0.39** | 0.34** | 0.40** | 0.29* |
| TEN | -0.01 | 0.01 | 0.09 | -0.11 | 0.44** | -0.24* | -0.23 | -0.16 | -0.21 |
| EXP | -0.28* | -0.09 | -0.25* | -0.27* | 0.25* | 0.12 | -0.08 | 0.05 | 0.25* |
| NOJ | -0.24* | -0.06 | -0.15 | -0.41** | 0.05 | -0.23 | -0.05 | -0.10 | -0.37** |
| **Societal Values** | | | | | | | | | |
| SPD | -0.07 | -0.25* | -0.12 | 0.14 | -0.36** | 0.08 | 0.10 | 0.25* | -0.07 |
| SUA | -0.16 | -0.07 | -0.15 | -0.15 | 0.07 | -0.05 | 0.04 | -0.01 | -0.15 |

*Contd...*

| *Indep. Vars.* | *Outcome Variables* | | | | | | | | |
|---|---|---|---|---|---|---|---|---|---|
| | *EH(O)* | *PH* | *BH* | *EH* | *TI* | *OC* | *OCI* | *OCJI* | *OCL* |
| SID | 0.27* | -0.13 | 0.33** | 0.32** | 0.03 | 0.09 | 0.06 | 0.15 | 0.04 |
| SMAS | 0.35** | 0.26* | 0.42** | 0.08 | 0.29* | 0.00 | 0.02 | -0.03 | 0.00 |
| **Organizational Values** | | | | | | | | | |
| OPD | -0.15 | -0.05 | -0.13 | -0.01 | 0.52** | -0.61** | -0.64** | -0.63** | -0.37** |
| OUA | -0.02 | 0.25* | -0.17 | -0.06 | -0.05 | 0.23 | 0.18 | 0.21 | 0.20 |
| OID | 0.09 | -0.12 | 0.26* | 0.15 | 0.34** | -0.67** | -0.61** | -0.66** | -0.50** |
| OMAS | 0.13 | -0.17 | 0.26* | 0.30* | 0.52** | -0.76** | -0.70** | -0.74** | -0.57** |

*Note:*$^{**}p<0.01$, $^{*}p<0.05$.

In Organization 'A' (Table 8.27), employee health (and its components) was positively related to SMAS and SID. This implies that masculinity in society, i.e. a cultural emphasis on achievement, assertiveness, competition, and rigid gender roles is related to poorer health (as high scores on health depict poor health). Similarly, individualism in society, i.e. being separate and less emotionally attached to one's in-group, is related to poorer health of employees. Turnover intention is positively related to education, prior work experience, and tenure, which implies that higher the education, more the job opportunities, and greater the turnover intention. Turnover intention is also positively related to SMAS, OPD, OID, OMAS, and negatively related to SPD. This implies that societal emphasis on achievement and competition is associated with a greater turnover intention. Further, an organization with a high emphasis on visible achievements, performance-centeredness, results orientation, and an emphasis on hierarchy would result in a greater intention to quit. Organizational commitment is positively related to sex and promotion, implying that males, and those who have received promotions are more committed. Organizational commitment is negatively related to education and tenure, implying that more educated employees, who have more job opportunities are more committed. This is in line with Sharma (1998), who reported a negative correlation between education and commitment. Organizational commitment was negatively related to OPD, OID, and OMAS. Similar pattern of correlations can be seen for the dimensions of commitment, viz. organizational identification, job involvement, and loyalty. In addition, loyalty is also found to be positively related to marital status, experience prior to joining, and number of jobs changed. This implies that married respondents are more loyal. Further, surprisingly those who have changed more jobs and consequently have a greater prior work experience are actually more loyal with their present employer. Probably, after changing many jobs they have chosen this job and organization because it suits their interests, skills, and temperaments. This is line with the positive view of job-hoppers held today. According to Muchinsky (1997), the meaning attached to a chronic job hopper has changed over the years. Twenty years ago, they were viewed with some suspicion at the management level as they seemed unstable and unable to hold a job for long. Today, however, job-hoppers are regarded much more positively in that exposure to different jobs is taken to mean that they have more breadth of experience, which may have even resulted in greater loyalty.

**Table–8.28**
**Correlation Between Independent Variables and Dependent Variables in Organization 'B' (N=71)**

| *Indep. Vars.* | *Outcome Variables* | | | | | | | | |
|---|---|---|---|---|---|---|---|---|---|
| | *EH(O)* | *PH* | *BH* | *EH* | *TI* | *OC* | *OCI* | *OCJI* | *OCL* |
| **Personal Variables** | | | | | | | | | |
| SEX | -0.04 | -0.03 | -0.06 | -0.03 | 0.04 | 0.07 | -0.03 | 0.16 | 0.04 |
| AGE | -0.13 | 0.04 | -0.22 | -0.14 | 0.12 | 0.33** | 0.25* | 0.24* | 0.31** |
| EDU | -0.10 | -0.04 | -0.05 | -0.10 | 0.18 | -0.05 | -0.10 | 0.02 | -0.06 |
| MS | -0.02 | 0.11 | -0.11 | -0.06 | 0.14 | 0.36** | 0.28 | 0.22 | 0.35** |
| FS | -0.24* | 0.16 | -0.08 | -0.33** | 0.00 | 0.23 | 0.16 | 0.12 | 0.25* |
| PRO | -0.01 | 0.05 | -0.01 | -0.06 | -0.09 | 0.20 | 0.18 | 0.22 | 0.12 |
| TEN | -0.05 | 0.11 | -0.04 | -0.14 | -0.04 | 0.17 | 0.10 | 0.12 | 0.17 |
| EXP | 0.04 | 0.12 | -0.02 | 0.01 | 0.34** | 0.16 | 0.12 | 0.24* | 0.06 |
| NOJ | 0.11 | 0.15 | 0.00 | 0.13 | 0.40** | -0.04 | 0.03 | 0.01 | -0.09 |

*Contd...*

| *Indep. Vars.* | *Outcome Variables* | | | | | | | | |
|---|---|---|---|---|---|---|---|---|---|
| | *EH(O)* | *PH* | *BH* | *EH* | *TI* | *OC* | *OCI* | *OCJI* | *OCL* |
| **Societal Values** | | | | | | | | | |
| SPD | 0.06 | 0.15 | 0.02 | 0.00 | -0.27* | 0.00 | 0.09 | -0.18 | 0.06 |
| SUA | 0.04 | 0.07 | 0.11 | -0.03 | 0.01 | 0.18 | 0.15 | 0.11 | 0.18 |
| SID | 0.06 | 0.24* | -0.02 | -0.02 | -0.23 | -0.06 | -0.02 | -0.12 | -0.02 |
| SMAS | 0.08 | 0.14 | 0.04 | 0.05 | 0.04 | -0.20 | -0.24* | -0.07 | -0.19 |
| **Organizational Values** | | | | | | | | | |
| OPD | 0.33** | 0.42** | 0.20 | 0.21 | 0.06 | -0.24* | -0.34** | 0.00 | -0.25* |
| OUA | 0.37** | 0.32** | 0.41** | 0.20 | -0.04 | -0.15 | -0.15 | -0.13 | -0.10 |
| OID | 0.31** | 0.31** | 0.25* | 0.23 | 0.07 | -0.16 | -0.33** | 0.01 | -0.12 |
| OMAS | 0.24* | 0.29* | 0.15 | 0.16 | 0.07 | -0.03 | -0.24* | 0.13 | 0.00 |

*Note:* **$p<0.01$, *$p<0.05$.

In Organization 'B' (Table 8.28), total employee health (and one of its components emotional health) is negatively related to family structure, implying that employees belonging to joint families have better health. Employee health is positively related to all organizational values, i.e. OPD, OMAS, OUA, and OID, implying that in this organization greater the emphasis on hierarchy, competitiveness and achievement, greater the structuring of activities, and lesser emotional dependence of employees on the company, poorer the health of employees. Physical health is positively related to SID in addition to all the 4 organizational values. This is similar to the results obtained from Organization 'A'. Turnover intention is found to have a negative, significant relationship with SPD, similar to Organization 'A'. Turnover intention is positively related to experience prior to joining and number of jobs changed. These results are in contrast to those obtained for Organization 'A', implying that in this organization, those who have changed more jobs and have a greater prior work experience also have a higher intention to quit. Organizational commitment and all its components, viz. identification, job involvement, and loyalty, are positively related to age, implying that in this organization, greater the age of employee, greater the commitment, loyalty, involvement, and identification with the organization. This is consistent with earlier research, which has found age to be positively related to commitment (Hall, Schneider and Nygren, 1970; Sheldon, 1971; Hrebiniak and Alutto, 1972; Morris and Sherman, 1981; Luthans, McCaul and Dodd, 1985; Sommer, Bae and Luthans, 1996). It has been suggested that as age of employees increases, employees' opportunities for alternative employment elsewhere diminish, with the result that they may become more attached to their organization. Interestingly, while organizational commitment, identification, and loyalty are positively related to marital status, job involvement is unrelated to marital status. This implies that although married employees may be more committed and loyal, they are not more involved with their jobs. Organizational commitment and its components, identification, and loyalty are negatively related to OPD, implying that an emphasis on hierarchy, inaccessibility of superiors leads to lower commitment, loyalty, and identification with the organization. In addition, identification is negatively related to SMAS, OID, and OMAS, further suggesting that employees whose societal preferences emphasise people-orientation over money and things-orientation, who "work to live" rather than "live to work" may be a misfit in the organization because of its high performance and achievement-orientation, and thus identify less with the organization.

**Table–8.29**
**Correlation Between Independent Variables and Dependent Variables for Organization 'C' (N=66)**

| *Indep. Vars.* | *Outcome Variables* | | | | | | | | |
|---|---|---|---|---|---|---|---|---|---|
| | *EH(O)* | *PH* | *BH* | *EH* | *TI* | *OC* | *OCI* | *OCJI* | *OCL* |
| **Personal Variables** | | | | | | | | | |
| SEX | -0.10 | -0.13 | 0.00 | -0.08 | 0.06 | -0.05 | -0.09 | -0.16 | 0.03 |
| AGE | -0.02 | 0.00 | 0.06 | -0.06 | 0.04 | 0.13 | 0.23 | 0.05 | 0.07 |
| EDU | -0.14 | 0.03 | -0.09 | -0.22 | -0.36** | 0.32** | 0.32** | 0.10 | 0.32** |
| MS | -0.16 | -0.03 | -0.16 | -0.15 | 0.02 | 0.05 | -0.04 | 0.04 | 0.09 |
| FS | 0.03 | 0.09 | -0.10 | 0.06 | 0.17 | -0.08 | 0.23 | 0.10 | -0.06 |

*Contd...*

| *Indep. Vars.* | *Outcome Variables* | | | | | | | | |
|---|---|---|---|---|---|---|---|---|---|
| | *EH(O)* | *PH* | *BH* | *EH* | *TI* | *OC* | *OCI* | *OCJI* | *OCL* |
| PRO | 0.11 | -0.08 | 0.18 | 0.13 | -0.13 | 0.33** | 0.35** | 0.30* | 0.23 |
| TEN | 0.12 | 0.01 | 0.20 | 0.06 | -0.33** | 0.41** | 0.46** | 0.32** | 0.29* |
| EXP | 0.15 | 0.12 | 0.07 | 0.13 | 0.28* | 0.04 | 0.05 | 0.05 | 0.03 |
| NOJ | -0.04 | -0.03 | -0.02 | -0.06 | 0.19 | -0.37** | -0.19 | -0.20 | -0.43** |
| **Societal Values** | | | | | | | | | |
| SPD | -0.17 | -0.06 | -0.05 | -0.23 | -0.18 | 0.17 | 0.09 | 0.13 | 0.18 |
| SUA | -0.10 | 0.15 | -0.25* | -0.13 | -0.06 | 0.05 | 0.24* | -0.26* | 0.07 |
| SID | 0.07 | 0.06 | -0.01 | 0.08 | 0.18 | -0.20 | -0.19 | -0.09 | -0.19 |
| SMAS | -0.41** | 0.00 | -0.38** | -0.46** | 0.40** | -0.19 | -0.03 | -0.20 | -0.04 |
| **Organizational Values** | | | | | | | | | |
| OPD | -0.18 | -0.25* | -0.08 | -0.08 | 0.39** | -0.36** | -0.38** | -0.16 | -0.33** |
| OUA | 0.12 | 0.15 | 0.01 | 0.08 | -0.06 | 0.09 | 0.22 | 0.04 | 0.02 |
| OID | 0.05 | -0.04 | 0.04 | 0.09 | 0.22 | -0.24* | -0.35** | 0.03 | -0.23 |
| OMAS | -0.08 | -0.10 | -0.08 | -0.01 | 0.29* | -0.53** | -0.58** | -0.30* | -0.44** |

*Note:* **$p<0.01$, *$p<0.05$.

In Organization 'C' (Table 8.29), employee health and its components were not significantly related to any personal variable. Employee health, and its components, behavioural health and emotional health are negatively related to SMAS. These results, opposite to that of Organization 'A', imply that femininity in society, i.e. an emphasis on nurturance, caring for others, and quality of life is related to poorer health. Turnover intention is negatively related to education and tenure, implying that higher the education level of employees, lower their turnover intention. It is possible that this organization, which highly emphasizes competence in subject matter, rewards those with higher education leading to a longer intention to stay with the company. Having a greater tenure with the organization is also linked to lower turnover intention. Turnover intention is positively related to SMAS, OPD, and OMAS. This implies that, similar to Organization 'A', a socio-cultural emphasis on assertiveness and achievement, and an organizational emphasis on hierarchy, visible achievements, challenge, performance-centeredness, and results orientation is linked with greater intention to quit. Organizational commitment is positively related to education, promotion, and tenure, and negatively related to number of jobs changed. Similar results are obtained for components of commitment viz. identification, job involvement, and loyalty. This implies that higher educational levels are linked with greater commitment, identification, loyalty, and job involvement. Organizational commitment is negatively related to OPD, OID, and OMAS. These results are similar to those obtained for Organization 'A', implying that greater the emphasis on hierarchy, competitiveness and achievement, and lesser the emotional dependence of employees on the company, lower the commitment of employees. Further, job involvement and behavioural health is negatively related to SUA. This interesting finding suggests that lower the societal preference on avoiding uncertainty and seeking change, which is also in line with the organizational values of innovation, risk taking, and flexibility, greater the involvement, but poorer the behavioural health of employees. This is supported by the results obtained by Stoetzel (1983), who found a strong negative correlation between a country's level of UA and its citizens' level of subjective well-being.

## SUMMARY

Employee health is positively related to SMAS in Organization 'A', but negatively in Organization 'C'. Employee health is positively related to SID in Organization 'A' and 'B', implying that individualism in society is related to poorer health of employees. Organizational commitment is negatively related to OPD OID, and OMAS in Organization 'A' and 'C'. Further, organizational commitment (and its components) are negatively related to education and tenure (in Organization 'A'), but positively related to education, promotion, and tenure (in Organization 'C'), and age and marital status (in Organization 'B'). Turnover intention is negatively related to SPD in Organization 'A' and 'B', positively with SMAS in Organization 'A', and positively with OPD and OMAS in both Organization 'A' and 'C'. Thus, an undue emphasis on achievement, competition, performance-orientation, and status-differences according to hierarchy in organizations is associated with employees' lower levels of commitment and higher levels of turnover intention. Turnover intention is positively related to education, prior work experience, and tenure (in Organization 'A'), positively with experience prior to joining and number of jobs changed (in Organization 'B'), and negatively to education and tenure (in Organization 'C'), indicating that probably organizational factors moderate the relationship between tenure and turnover intention.

## SIGNIFICANT PREDICTORS OF OUTCOME VARIABLES ACROSS 3 ORGANIZATIONS

The seventh objective was to examine how Indian societal values, organizational values, and personal variables, determine the outcome variables of employee health, turnover intention, and organizational commitment, in each of the 3 MNCs.

### *(i) Determinants of Employee Health (Overall)*

**Table–8.30**
**Step-wise Multiple Regression: Determinants of Employee Health from Among Societal, Organizational and Personal Variables for 3 Organizations**

| *Indep. Variables* | *Dependent Variable: Employee Health* | | | | | |
|---|---|---|---|---|---|---|
| | *Multiple r* | *Simple r* | $R^2$ | $R^2$ *Change* | *Beta* | *t-Value* |
| **ORGANIZATION 'A'** | | | | | | |
| SMAS | 0.36 | 0.35** | 0.18 | - | 0.62** | 6.47 |
| EXP | 0.53 | -0.28* | 0.32 | 0.14 | -0.55** | 5.72 |
| SID | 0.65 | 0.27* | 0.43 | 0.11 | 0.37** | 3.98 |
| EDU | 0.71 | 0.18 | 0.50 | 0.07 | 0.38** | 3.73 |
| OUA | 0.74 | -0.02 | 0.54 | 0.04 | 0.21* | 2.17 |
| **ORGANIZATION 'B'** | | | | | | |
| OUA | 0.37 | 0.37** | 0.14 | - | 0.36** | 3.30 |
| FS | 0.43 | -0.24* | 0.19 | 0.05 | -0.23* | 2.08 |
| **ORGANIZATION 'C'** | | | | | | |
| SMAS | 0.41 | -0.41** | 0.17 | - | -0.41** | 3.58 |

*Note:* **p<0.01, *p<0.05

Table 8.30 clearly indicates that among the societal, organizational and personal variables, in Organization 'A', SMA (18%), experience prior to joining (16%), SID (14%), education (7%), and OUA (4%) explained 54 per cent of variance in employee health. Rest 46 per cent of the variance is unaccounted for. In Organization 'B', OUA (14%), and family structure (5%) accounted for 19 per cent of the total variance in employee health. However, 81 per cent of the variance is unaccounted for. In Organization 'C', SMAS alone emerged as a determinant of employee health, accounting for 17 per cent of the total variance. Rest 83 per cent of the variance is contributed by other unknown factors.

Normalized beta coefficients of these variables indicate that contributions made by SID, education, and OUA were significant and positive, while those made by experience prior to joining, and family structure were significant and negative. An interesting finding is that SMAS contributes positively to employee health in Organization 'A' (French), but negatively in Organization 'C' (Finnish), implying that greater the SMAS, poorer the health of employees in Organization 'A', but greater the SMAS, better the health of employees in Organization 'C'. Thus, the results seem to suggest that organizational culture seems to moderate the influence of societal factors in predicting health of employees. These results are somewhat in line with Arrindell et al. (1997) who found MAS to correlate positively with subjective well-being for poorer countries, whereas in the richer countries, the opposite was found, implying that countries that had both a feminine culture and were rich had the highest levels of subjective well-being.

Further, SID contributed positively to employee health implying that a society where individuals are expected to take care of their self-interests pays the price in terms of poorer health of members. This can be explained in terms of the effect of loss of social support of the in-group resulting in a feeling of alienation that probably in turn affects health. In highly collectivist cultures, members expect the in-group to take care of them in exchange for loyalty, which probably in turn contributes to better health.

A significant positive beta-coefficient between OUA and employee health implies that employees of organizations that are highly rule driven and bureaucratic, with directive styles of leadership, have more health problems and hence have poor health. According to Hofstede (1980), UA expresses itself in higher levels of anxiety and energy release, possibly having consequences for employee health. These results are in line with researchers (Cox, 1991; Sutherland and Davidson, 1993; Lindstrom, 1994; Warren, 1997; Peterson and John, 1998; Dick, 2000), who have identified the potent role of organizational culture in producing stress in organizational members, which in turn is associated with reduced mental health.

Experience prior to joining was negatively related to employee health, implying that individuals with prior work experience have already gone through anticipatory socialization and are better equipped to deal with work and organizational stressors, possibly leading to better health.

Family structure also contributed negatively to employee health, implying that people coming from joint families are healthier. These findings indicate the role of support of the joint family system acting as a buffer in reducing stress, thereby leading to better health.

Finally, the results show that higher education is linked to poorer employee health in Organization 'A'. This implies that higher the educational level of employees, greater may be the expectations of the organization from them, with increased responsibility for people as against responsibility for things, resulting in poorer health. This is contrary to findings by Agervold (1985), who suggested a strong link between low educational level and health problems, due to the often monotonous nature of the work of low-level employees.

An overview of these results indicates that 2 societal values-SMAS (for Organization 'A' and 'C') and SID (for Organization 'A') were predictors of employee health. OUA was the only organizational value which emerged as determinant of employee health (for Organization 'A' and 'B'). This implies that societal values were more significant in predicting employee health for Organizations 'A' and 'C', while organizational value was stronger only in Organization 'B'. Among personal variables, those found to predict employee health were experience prior to joining, education, and family structure.

***(ii) Determinants of Physical Health, a Dimension of Employee Health***

**Table–8.31**
**Step-wise Multiple Regression: Determinants of Physical Health from Among Societal, Organizational and Personal Variables for 3 Organizations**

| *Indep. Variables* | *Dependent Variable: Physical Health* | | | | | |
|---|---|---|---|---|---|---|
| | *Multiple r* | *Simple r* | $R^2$ | $R^2$ *Change* | *Beta* | *t-Value* |
| **ORGANIZATION 'A'** | | | | | | |
| SMAS | 0.26 | 0.26* | 0.07 | - | 0.36** | 3.11 |
| SPD | 0.39 | -0.25* | 0.16 | 0.09 | -0.36** | 3.15 |
| OMAS | 0.49 | -0.17 | 0.24 | 0.08 | -0.30* | 2.62 |
| **ORGANIZATION 'B'** | | | | | | |
| OPD | 0.42 | 0.42** | 0.18 | - | 0.42** | 3.89 |
| **ORGANIZATION 'C'** | | | | | | |
| OPD | 0.25 | -0.25* | 0.06 | - | -0.25* | 2.04 |

*Note:* **p<0.01, *p<0.05.

Table 8.31 indicates that in Organization 'A', SMAS (7%), SPD (9%), and OMAS (8%) explained 24 per cent of the variance of physical health. In Organization 'B' and 'C', only OPD contributed 18 per cent and 6 per cent respectively towards the total variance of physical health.

Normalized beta coefficients of these variables indicate that contributions made by SMAS and OUA were significant and positive, while those made by SPD were significant and negative. This implies that greater the SMAS, poorer the physical health. Thus, a cultural emphasis on achievement, success, assertiveness, competition, acquisition of money and status, 'fast life', 'live in order to work' as opposed to 'work in order to live etc. probably leads to stress and hence to ill-health. An interesting finding is that CPD contributes positively to physical health in Organization 'B', but negatively in Organization 'C', implying that greater the OPD, poorer the physical health of employees in Organization 'B', but lower the OPD, poorer the physical health of employees in Organization 'C'. Organization

'B' which is higher on OPD, possibly unduly emphasises hierarchy and inaccessibility of superiors which contributes to ill health, whereas Organization 'C', with its low emphasis on OPD (Table 8.2), also leads to poorer physical health, since employees may feel directionless in absence of hierarchy and bosses. Thus, these results seem to suggest that too little or too much OPD can both result in stress possibly leading to poor physical health of employees.

However, a large proportion of the variance in all the 3 organizations is left unaccounted. This seems to suggest that since health is a product of complex biophysical interactions, the work situation is only one of the many influential factors that contribute to ill-health (Frese, 1982). Other factors, such as stress outside work, personal habitat, biological factors, genetic predispositions, and so forth, also contribute to physical ill-health.

An overview of these results indicates that neither societal nor organizational values had a very strong impact on physical health. While organizational values were stronger in predicting physical health in Organizations 'B' and 'C', societal values were stronger in Organization 'A'. No personal variable was found to predict physical health in any organization.

### *(iii) Determinants of Behavioural Health, a Dimension of Employee Health*

**Table–8.32**

**Step-wise Multiple Regression: Determinants of Behavioural Health from Among Societal, Organizational and Personal Variables for 3 Organizations**

| *Indep. Variables* | *Dependent Variable: Behavioural Health* | | | | | |
|---|---|---|---|---|---|---|
| | *Multiple r* | *Simple r* | $R^2$ | $R^2$ *Change* | *Beta* | *t-Value* |
| **ORGANIZATION 'A'** | | | | | | |
| SMAS | 0.42 | 0.42** | 0.18 | - | 0.69** | 8.89 |
| SID | 0.59 | 0.33** | 0.35 | 0.17 | 0.36** | 4.13 |
| EXP | 0.74 | -0.25* | 0.54 | 0.19 | -0.56** | 6.77 |
| EDU | 0.78 | 0.18 | 0.62 | 0.08 | 0.38** | 4.11 |

*Contd...*

| *Indep. Variables* | *Dependent Variable: Behavioural Health* | | | | | |
|---|---|---|---|---|---|---|
| | *Multiple r* | *Simple r* | $R^2$ | $R^2$ *Change* | *Beta* | *t-Value* |
| TEN | 0.82 | 0.09 | 0.67 | 0.05 | 0.34** | 3.87 |
| OPD | 0.84 | -0.13 | 0.70 | 0.03 | -0.25* | 2.30 |
| **ORGANIZATION 'B'** | | | | | | |
| OUA | 0.41 | 0.41** | 0.17 | - | 0.41** | 3.78 |
| **ORGANIZATION 'C'** | | | | | | |
| SMAS | 0.38 | -0.38** | 0.14 | - | -0.38** | 3.24 |

*Note:* **p<0.01, *p<0.05.

Table 8.32 depicts that among all the independent variables, in Organization 'A', SMAS (18%), SID (17%), experience prior to joining (19%), education (8%), tenure (5%), and OPD (3%), together explained 70 per cent of the variance of behavioural health. Only 30 per cent of the variance is unaccounted for. On the other hand, in Organization 'B', OUA was the only determinant of behavioural health, accounting for 17 per cent of the total variance. In Organization 'C', only SMAS accounted for 14 per cent of the total variance. Remaining 83 per cent and 86 per cent of the variance for Organization 'B' and 'C' respectively is contributed by other unknown factors.

Normalized beta coefficients of these variables indicate that contributions made by SID, education, tenure, and OUA were significant and positive, while those made by experience prior to joining and OPD were negative. An interesting finding, similar to employee health (total) is that SMAS contributes positively to behavioural health in Organization 'A', but negatively in Organization 'C', implying that organizational factors seem to moderate the influence of societal factors in predicting behavioural health of employees.

An overview of these results indicates that all three sets of predictor variables had an equally strong impact on behavioural health. Societal values were stronger in Organization 'A' and 'C', while organizational value was stronger in Organization 'B'. Two societal values—SMAS (for Organization 'A' and 'C'), and SID (for

Organization 'A') were predictors of behavioural health. Similarly, two organizational values, viz. OPD (for Organization 'A'), and OUA (for Organization 'B') emerged as determinants of behavioural health. Among personal variables, those found to predict behavioural health were experience prior to joining, education, and tenure.

### *(iv) Determinants of Emotional Health, a Dimension of Employee Health*

**Table–8.33**
**Step-wise Multiple Regression: Determinants of Emotional Health from Among Societal, Organizational and Personal Variables for 3 Organizations**

| *Indep. Variables* | *Dependent Variable: Emotional Health* | | | | | |
|---|---|---|---|---|---|---|
| | *Multiple r* | *Simple r* | *$R^2$* | *$R^2$ Change* | *Beta* | *t-Value* |
| **ORGANIZATION 'A'** | | | | | | |
| NOJ | 0.41 | -0.41** | 0.17 | - | -0.39** | 3.69 |
| EDU | 0.53 | 0.26* | 0.28 | 0.11 | 0.49** | 4.57 |
| SPD | 0.61 | 0.14 | 0.38 | 0.10 | 0.31** | 2.95 |
| SMAS | 0.65 | 0.08 | 0.42 | 0.04 | 0.26** | 2.70 |
| SID | 0.69 | 0.32** | 0.48 | 0.06 | 0.30** | 3.23 |
| EXP | 0.72 | -0.27* | 0.52 | 0.04 | -0.31** | 2.75 |
| MS | 0.75 | 0.03 | 0.56 | 0.04 | 0.23* | 2.29 |
| **ORGANIZATION 'B'** | | | | | | |
| FS | 0.33 | -0.33** | 0.11 | - | -0.33** | 2.91 |
| **ORGANIZATION 'C'** | | | | | | |
| SMAS | 0.46 | -0.46** | 0.21 | - | -0.46** | 4.17 |

*Note:* **p<0.01, *p<0.05.

Table 8.33 depicts that in Organization 'A', number of jobs changed (17%), education (11%), SPD (10%), SMAS (4%), SID (6%), experience prior to joining (4%), and marital status (4%), together explained 56 per cent of the variance of emotional health. Rest 44 per cent of the variance is unaccounted for. In Organization 'B', however, family structure was the only determinant of emotional health, accounting for 11 per cent of the total variance. In Organization 'C', SMAS emerged as the only determinant of emotional health, accounting for 21 per cent of the total variance. However, 89 per cent and 79 per cent of the variance for Organization 'B' and 'C' respectively is unaccounted for.

Normalized beta coefficients of these variables indicate that contributions made by education, SPD, SID, and marital status were significant and positive, while those made by number of jobs changed, experience prior to joining and family structure were significant and negative. These results imply that greater the SPD and SID, poorer the emotional health. Higher education was also found to be related to poorer emotional health, possibly because of the need to make quick decisions, 'responsibility for people' as against 'responsibility for things.' Being married was associated with poorer emotional health. This is in line with Marshall and Cooper (1979) who suggested a link between marriage patterns and managerial stress. Greater prior work experience and more number of jobs changed were associated with better emotional health (in Organization 'A'). This suggests that people who have changed more jobs and have a greater prior work experience at the time of joining the organization, are better prepared to handle the work pressures of working in an MNC, and consequently may have fewer emotional health problems. Further, employees coming from joint families also have fewer emotional health problems than those coming from nuclear families. This further accentuates the role of the joint family system in providing social support and acting as a buffer in reducing stress, thereby leading to better health. Further, similar to employee health (total): SMAS contributes positively to emotional health in Organization 'A', but negatively in Organization 'C', suggesting that organizational factors seem to moderate the influence of SMAS in predicting emotional health of employees.

An overview of these results indicates that personal variables, followed closely by societal values were potent in predicting emotional health. Among personal variables, those found to predict emotional health were number of jobs changed, education, experience prior to joining, marital status, and family structure. Three societal values—SMAS (for Organization 'A' and 'C'), SID and SPD (for Organization 'A') were predictors of emotional health. Surprisingly, no organizational value was found to predict emotional health.

### *(v) Determinants of Turnover Intention*

**Table-8.34**

**Step-wise Multiple Regression: Determinants of Turnover Intention from Among Societal, Organizational and Personal Variables for the 3 Organizations**

| *Indep. Variables* | *Dependent Variable: Turnover Intention* | | | | | |
|---|---|---|---|---|---|---|
| | *Multiple r* | *Simple r* | $R^2$ | $R^2$ *Change* | *Beta* | *t-Value* |
| **ORGANIZATION 'A'** | | | | | | |
| OMAS | 0.53 | 0.52** | 0.28 | - | 0.51** | 4.86 |
| EXP | 0.59 | 0.44** | 0.35 | 0.07 | 0.54** | 4.47 |
| PRO | 0.70 | -0.17 | 0.49 | 0.14 | -0.49** | 3.72 |
| SMAS | 0.73 | 0.29* | 0.53 | 0.04 | 0.24** | 2.69 |
| SPD | 0.75 | -0.36** | 0.57 | 0.04 | -0.21* | 2.27 |
| **ORGANIZATION 'B'** | | | | | | |
| NOJ | 0.40 | 0.40** | 0.16 | - | 0.44** | 4.23 |
| SPD | 0.46 | -0.27* | 0.22 | 0.06 | -0.38** | 3.40 |
| PRO | 0.56 | -0.09 | 0.31 | 0.09 | -0.35** | 3.10 |
| **ORGANIZATION 'C'** | | | | | | |
| SMAS | 0.40 | 0.40** | 0.16 | - | 0.33** | 3.34 |
| OPD | 0.55 | 0.39** | 0.30 | 0.14 | 0.37** | 3.71 |
| TEN | 0.62 | -0.33** | 0.38 | 0.08 | -0.29** | 2.96 |
| SPD | 0.66 | -0.18 | 0.43 | 0.05 | -0.24* | 2.48 |
| EXP | 0.69 | 0.28* | 0.47 | 0.04 | 0.20* | 2.11 |

*Note:* **p<0.01, *p<0.05.

Table 8.34 depicts that in Organization 'A', OMAS (28%), experience prior to joining (7%), promotion (14%), SMAS (4%), and

SPD (4%), together explained 57 per cent of the variance of turnover intention. In Organization 'B', three variables namely number of jobs changed (16%), SPD (6%), and promotion (9%) were found to be the determinants of turnover intention, in all accounting for 31 per cent of the total variance. In Organization 'C', SMAS (16%), OPD (14%), tenure (8%), SPD (5%), and experience prior to joining (4%), together explained 47 per cent of the variance of turnover intention. Rest 53 per cent of the variance is unaccounted for.

Normalized beta coefficients of these variables indicate that contributions made by experience prior to joining, number of jobs changed, SMAS, OPD, and OMAS were significant and positive, while those made by promotion, tenure, and SPD were significant and negative. A socio-cultural emphasis on assertiveness, achievement, and 'live in order to work' philosophy predicts greater turnover intention in two organizations. Greater power distance in society predicted lower turnover intention in all 3 organizations. According to Hofstede (1991), high power distance fosters dependence on authority, which may translate into dependence on the organization, possibly leading to lower intention to quit the job. Further, greater prior work experience and more number of jobs changed was associated with a higher turnover intention. This may be explained by the demonstrated relation between thoughts of quitting and number of jobs already changed (Mobley et al., 1978). Thus, employees who have changed more jobs are more prone to thinking about quitting in the present job. This is further supported by findings of Miller, Katreberg, and Hulin (1979), who found that career mobility influenced turnover through withdrawal cognitions. Expectedly, tenure in the present organization was linked with lower turnover intention. These results are supported by the findings of Motowidlo (1983), who found a negative correlation between tenure and turnover. Further, promotion(s) received was also linked with lower turnover intention. This is supported by findings of Wells and Muchinsky (1985), who found that the performance of promoted employees was significantly superior to those employees who quit. Finally, two organizational values viz. OPD (in Organization 'C') and OMAS (in Organization 'A') were found to predict turnover intention, implying that masculinity in organizations, i.e. an undue emphasis on performance, meeting targets, achievement (as in Organization 'A') is related to greater turnover intention. Giving emphasis to hierarchical relationships, centralised decision-making is also found to predict turnover intention.

An overview of these results indicates that personal variables, followed closely by societal values were potent in predicting turnover intention. In Organization 'A', organizational value of OMAS is more significant in predicting turnover intention than societal values, while the reverse is found to be true for Organization 'B' and 'C'. Among personal variables, those found to predict turnover intention were number of jobs changed, experience prior to joining, tenure, and promotion.

### *(vi) Determinants of Organizational Commitment (Overall)*

**Table-8.35**
**Step-wise Multiple Regression: Determinants of Organizational Commitment from Among Societal, Organizational and Personal Variables for 3 Organizations**

| *Indep. Variables* | *Dependent Variable: Organizational Commitment* | | | | | |
|---|---|---|---|---|---|---|
| | *Multiple r* | *Simple r* | $R^2$ | $R^2$ *Change* | *Beta* | *t-Value* |
| **ORGANIZATION 'A'** | | | | | | |
| OMAS | 0.77 | -0.76** | 0.59 | - | -0.44** | 2.78 |
| EDU | 0.79 | -0.30* | 0.62 | 0.03 | -0.27** | 2.86 |
| SMAS | 0.80 | 0.00 | 0.65 | 0.03 | 0.21** | 2.72 |
| OID | 0.82 | -0.67** | 0.67 | 0.02 | -0.41** | 3.47 |
| OPD | 0.83 | -0.61** | 0.69 | 0.02 | -0.39** | 3.67 |
| NOJ | 0.85 | -0.23 | 0.72 | 0.03 | -0.19* | 2.39 |
| PRO | 0.86 | 0.39** | 0.74 | 0.02 | 0.19* | 2.08 |
| SEX | 0.87 | 0.27* | 0.75 | 0.01 | 0.18* | 2.02 |
| **ORGANIZATION 'B'** | | | | | | |
| MS | 0.36 | 0.36** | 0.13 | - | 0.48** | 4.15 |
| OPD | 0.46 | -0.24* | 0.21 | 0.08 | -0.29** | 2.74 |
| NOJ | 0.51 | -0.04 | 0.26 | 0.05 | -0.23* | 2.03 |

*Contd...*

| *Indep. Variables* | *Dependent Variable: Organizational Commitment* | | | | | |
|---|---|---|---|---|---|---|
| | *Multiple r* | *Simple r* | $R^2$ | $R^2$ *Change* | *Beta* | *t-Value* |
| **ORGANIZATION 'C'** | | | | | | |
| OMAS | 0.53 | -0.53** | 0.28 | - | -0.70** | 5.43 |
| OID | 0.59 | -0.24* | 0.35 | 0.07 | -0.31** | 2.43 |
| EDU | 0.65 | 0.32** | 0.42 | 0.07 | 0.37** | 4.54 |
| NOJ | 0.69 | -0.37** | 0.47 | 0.05 | -0.46** | 4.90 |
| EXP | 0.74 | 0.04 | 0.55 | 0.08 | 0.35** | 3.82 |
| SPD | 0.77 | 0.17 | 0.59 | 0.04 | 0.25** | 3.10 |
| SMAS | 0.79 | -0.09 | 0.63 | 0.04 | -0.22* | 2.65 |
| TEN | 0.81 | 0.41** | 0.65 | 0.02 | 0.21* | 2.45 |
| SEX | 0.81 | 0.05 | 0.66 | 0.01 | 0.21* | 2.24 |

*Note:* **$p<0.01$, *$p<0.05$.

Table 8.35 depicts that among the societal, organizational, and personal variables in Organization 'A', OMAS (59%), education (3%), SMAS (3%), OID (2%), OPD (2%), number of jobs changed (3%), promotion (2%), and sex (1%) together explained 75 per cent of the variance of organizational commitment. In Organization 'B', marital status (13%), OPD (8%), and number of jobs changed (5%) were found to be determinants of organizational commitment, in all accounting for 26 per cent of the total variance. In Organization 'C', OMAS (28%), OID (7%), education (7%), number of jobs changed (5%), and experience prior to joining (11%), SPD (4%), SMAS (4%), tenure (2%), and sex (1%) together explained 66 per cent towards the variance of organizational commitment. Only 34 per cent of the variance is unaccounted for.

Normalized beta coefficients of these variables indicate that contributions made by promotion, marital status, experience prior to joining, tenure, SPD, and sex were significant and positive, while those made by OMAS, OID, OPD, and number of jobs changed were significant and negative. These results imply that being promoted; having greater prior work experience and more tenure in the present organization was associated with higher commitment levels of employees. These results are supported by findings of Hall, Scheider, and Nygren (1970), Sheldon (1971), Hrebiniak (1974), Stevens, Beyer and Trice (1978), Luthans, McCaul and Dodd (1985), Cain and Bruce (1987), Gregersen and Black (1992), and Sommer, Bae and Luthans (1996), who found tenure to be positively related to organizational commitment. Promotions emerging as a significant determinant of commitment is in line with findings of Chinnappan (1996), who found number of promotions to be the most significant predictor of employee commitment, among all background variables. When employees receive many promotions in the course of their organizational life, they are likely to develop positive attitudes towards their higher responsibility and authority. They tend to have a sense of achievement and nurture a feeling of belongingness to the organization. They may also perceive fairness in organizational practices. Consequently, they are likely to perceive a high level of commitment (Konavsky, et al., 1987; Lind and Tyler, 1988; McFarlin and Sweeney, 1992). Further, more the number of jobs changed, lower the commitment in all 3 organizations. Finally, being married and being a male also predicted organizational commitment. Hrebiniak and Alutto (1972), Chinnappan (1996) found married persons to show higher commitment than unmarried ones. Sharma (1998) found age, tenure, family responsibility, and marital status to be positively correlated with commitment. The results of the present study are in line with findings of Marsden, Kalleberg and Cook (1993) who found men to be more committed than women. On the other hand, these contradict findings by Grusky (1966), Hrebiniak and Alutto (1972), Gould (1975), Wahn (1998), who found women, as a group, to be more committed than men. In contrast, Sekaran (1983), Bruning and Snyder (1983) and Al-Ajmi (2006) did not find any gender differences on commitment.

Greater power distance in society was also found to be related to higher levels of organizational commitment. According to Hofstede (1991), high power distance fosters dependence on authority, which may translate into dependence on the organization, possibly leading to high levels of commitment. With regards to the organizational variables, it was found that greater OMAS, OID, and OPD—were all related to low organizational commitment. This suggests that paradoxically, organizations that put an undue emphasis on achievement, competition, high concern for production and high work centrality may actually result in lowering commitment of employees. Further, significant differences in status, rewards, privileges, and opportunities between various levels of the organization also lowers commitment. Finally, having a primarily "business transaction" relation with employees, the importance of task over any personal relationships also lowers commitment of employees. These results are in line with the findings of Parkes, Bochner, and Schneider (2001), who found collectivists to be more committed to their organizations and having longer tenure than individualists in Asian, as compared to Australian organizations.

SMAS and education had a selective effect: SMAS contributed positively in Organization 'A', but negatively in Organization 'C'; education contributed negatively in Organization 'A', but positively in 'C'. This suggests that organizational factors moderate the influence of SMAS and education in predicting organizational commitment. It is possible that since educated employees are more rewarded/promoted in Organization 'C' than 'A' (with its high emphasis on competence in subject matter), they are more committed in the former, while in Organization 'A', promotions are strongly correlated with tenure but unrelated with education, possibly leading to lower commitment of educated employees. Dornstein and Matalon (1989) found that age and education in addition to several other variables like interesting work, co-worker attitudes towards the organization, organizational dependency, employment alternatives, attitudes of family/friends, and importance to organization explain as much as 65 per cent of the variance in organizational commitment. Glisson and Durick (1988) also found education to be a significant predictor of commitment.

An overview of these results indicates that a large amount of variance in organizational commitment was explained by a combination of all the independent variables taken in the present study. For all 3 organizations, organizational values were much more stronger in predicting organizational commitment than either societal values or personal variables. Two societal values—SMAS and SPD were predictors of organizational commitment, while three organizational values viz. OMAS, OID, and OPD were found to predict commitment. This is in line with Gunter and Furnham (1996), who found climate factors to be more significant than biographical factors as predictors of pride in the organization, a construct similar to organizational commitment. Garr (1998), too, found organizational culture as a predictor of organizational commitment. Among personal variables, those found to predict organizational commitment were number of jobs changed, education, experience prior to joining, marital status, tenure, promotion and sex.

### *(vii) Determinants of Organizational Identification, a Dimension of Organizational Commitment*

**Table-8.36**
**Step-wise Multiple Regression: Determinants of Organizational Identification from Among Societal, Organizational and Personal Variables for 3 Organizations**

| *Indep. Variables* | *Dependent Variable: Organizational Identification* | | | | | |
|---|---|---|---|---|---|---|
| | *Multiple r* | *Simple r* | $R^2$ | $R^2$ *Change* | *Beta* | *t-Value* |
| **ORGANIZATION 'A'** | | | | | | |
| OMAS | 0.70 | -0.70** | 0.49 | - | -0.49** | 4.16 |
| OPD | 0.74 | -0.64** | 0.54 | 0.05 | -0.30* | 2.55 |
| **ORGANIZATION 'B'** | | | | | | |
| OPD | 0.34 | -0.34** | 0.12 | - | -0.34** | 3.06 |
| MS | 0.46 | 0.28* | 0.21 | 0.09 | 0.38** | 3.63 |
| SPD | 0.52 | 0.09 | 0.27 | 0.06 | 0.32** | 2.82 |
| SMAS | 0.56 | -0.24* | 0.31 | 0.04 | -0.25* | 2.14 |
| **ORGANIZATION 'C'** | | | | | | |
| OMAS | 0.58 | -0.58** | 0.33 | - | -0.70** | 5.31 |
| TEN | 0.64 | 0.46** | 0.41 | 0.08 | 0.34** | 3.65 |
| OUA | 0.70 | 0.22 | 0.49 | 0.08 | 0.32** | 3.81 |
| EXP | 0.74 | 0.05 | 0.54 | 0.05 | 0.24** | 2.95 |
| EDU | 0.76 | 0.32** | 0.58 | 0.04 | 0.26** | 2.90 |
| OID | 0.78 | -0.35** | 0.61 | 0.03 | -0.37** | 2.79 |
| SUA | 0.81 | 0.24* | 0.65 | 0.04 | 0.23* | 2.60 |

*Note:* **p<0.01, *p<0.05.

Table 8.36 depicts that in Organization 'A', OMAS (49%) and OPD (5%), accounted for 54 per cent of the variance in organizational identification. However, 46 per cent of the variance is unaccounted for. In Organization 'B', four variables namely OPD (12%), marital status (9%), SPD (6%), and SMAS (4%) were found to be the determinants of organizational identification, in all accounting for 31 per cent of the total variance. In Organization 'C', OMAS (33%), tenure (8%), OUA (8%), experience prior to joining (5%), education (4%), OID (3%), and SUA (4%) together explained 65 per cent towards the variance of organizational identification. Only 35 per cent of the variance is unaccounted for.

Normalized beta coefficients of these variables indicate that contributions made by marital status, experience prior to joining, tenure, education, SPD, SUA, and OUA were significant and positive, while those made by OMAS, OID, and OPD were significant and negative. These results imply that having greater tenure in the present organization, greater prior work experience, and higher education was associated with greater identification with the organization. Being married also predicted identification. Interestingly, greater UA, both at the level of the society and the organization were found to enhance identification. According to Hofstede (1991), greater UA is expressed in a need for predictability. This need possibly translates into greater identification by organizational members with the organization. Further, greater PD in society increased employee's identification with the organization. This can be understood by taking into account the psychological connotations of PD (Hofstede, 1980), viz. dependency. In a high PD environment, the superego may be personified in the form of a powerful person -the father, the leader, the boss — and possibly even the organization, resulting in greater identification. Finally, as regards organizational variables, similar to the results for commitment, organizaticnal emphasis on achievement, competition, hierarchy, and independence of employees was associated with lower identification with the organization.

An overview of these results indicates that all three sets of predictors were effective in explaining variance in organizational identification. However, in all 3 organizations, organizational values were stronger in predicting identification than both societal and personal variables. Among personal variables, those found to predict identification were marital status, tenure, education, and experience prior to joining.

*(viii) Determinants of Job Involvement, a Dimension of Organizational Commitment*

**Table-8.37**
**Step-wise Multiple Regression: Determinants of Job Involvement from among Societal, Organizational and Personal Variables for 3 Organizations**

| *Indep. Variables* | *Dependent Variable: Job Involvement* | | | | | |
|---|---|---|---|---|---|---|
| | *Multiple r* | *Simple r* | $R^2$ | $R^2$ *Change* | *Beta* | *t-Value* |
| **ORGANIZATION 'A'** | | | | | | |
| OMAS | 0.74 | -0.74** | 0.55 | - | -0.71** | 9.54 |
| MS | 0.77 | -0.13 | 0.59 | 0.04 | -0.34** | 4.12 |
| SEX | 0.81 | 0.30* | 0.65 | 0.06 | 0.32** | 3.90 |
| AGE | 0.82 | 0.07 | 0.67 | 0.02 | 0.29** | 2.73 |
| **ORGANIZATION 'B'** | | | | | | |
| EXP | 0.24 | 0.24* | 0.06 | - | 0.24* | 2.06 |
| **ORGANIZATION 'C'** | | | | | | |
| TEN | 0.32 | 0.32** | 0.10 | - | 0.32** | 2.70 |

*Note:* **$p<0.01$, *$p<0.05$.

In predicting job involvement (Table 8.37), for Organization 'A', 4 variables, viz. OMAS (55%), marital status (4%), sex (6%), and age (2%) contributed 67 per cent towards the variance of job involvement in Organization 'A'. Rest 33 per cent of the variance is contributed by unknown factors. In Organization 'B' and 'C', only one predictor emerged as a determinant of job involvement, viz. experience prior to joining and tenure, accounting for 6 per cent and 10 per cent of the total variance in job involvement, for the 2 organizations respectively. However, 94 per cent and 90 per cent of the variance for Organization 'B' and 'C' respectively is contributed by other unknown factors.

Normalized beta coefficients of these variables indicate that contributions made by sex, age, experience prior to joining, and tenure were significant and positive, while those made by marital status and OMAS were significant and negative. These results imply that being promoted, having greater prior work experience, and more tenure in the present organization was associated with greater job involvement. These results are in line with Anantharaman and Kalippan (1982), who found length of service to be positively related to job involvement. Males were found to be higher on job involvement. Age of employees also contributed positively to job involvement. This is supported by findings of Anantharaman and John (1983), who found age to be positively correlated with job involvement. Sharma and Sharma (1987) also found high job involvement to be positively related to age and tenure of service. In Organization 'A', unmarried and male respondents were more involved with their jobs. Finally, greater MAS in Organization 'A' was found to be associated with lower levels of job involvement, indicating that putting an undue emphasis on achievement, competition, performance-orientation, and competency may result in lower job involvement.

An overview of these results indicates that personal variables were the strongest in explaining variance in job involvement. However, in Organization 'A', OMAS was stronger than personal variables in predicting job involvement. Surprisingly, no societal value emerged as significant in explaining job involvement. Among personal variables, those found to predict job involvement were sex, marital status, age, experience prior to joining, and tenure.

### *(ix) Determinants of Loyalty, a Dimension of Organizational Commitment*

**Table-8.38**

**Step-wise Multiple Regression: Determinants of Loyalty from Among Societal, Organizational and Personal Variables for 3 Organizations**

| *Indep. Variables* | *Dependent Variable: Loyalty* | | | | | |
|---|---|---|---|---|---|---|
| | *Multiple r* | *Simple r* | $R^2$ | $R^2$ *Change* | *Beta* | *t-Value* |
| **ORGANIZATION 'A'** | | | | | | |
| OMAS | 0.58 | -0.57** | 0.33 | - | -0.71** | 6.60 |
| MS | 0.67 | 0.38** | 0.45 | 0.12 | 0.25** | 2.81 |

*Contd...*

| *Indep. Variables* | *Dependent Variable: Loyalty* | | | | | |
|---|---|---|---|---|---|---|
| | *Multiple r* | *Simple r* | $R^2$ | $R^2$ *Change* | *Beta* | *t-Value* |
| EDU | 0.73 | -0.06 | 0.53 | 0.08 | -0.30** | 2.75 |
| NOJ | 0.75 | -0.37** | 0.56 | 0.03 | -0.20* | 2.15 |
| **ORGANIZATION 'B'** | | | | | | |
| MS | 0.35 | 0.35** | 0.13 | - | 0.49** | 4.35 |
| OPD | 0.45 | -0.19 | 0.21 | 0.08 | -0.30** | 2.90 |
| NOJ | 0.53 | -0.09 | 0.28 | 0.07 | -0.29* | 2.59 |
| **ORGANIZATION 'C'** | | | | | | |
| OMAS | 0.44 | -0.44** | 0.19 | - | -0.34** | 3.88 |
| NOJ | 0.56 | -0.43** | 0.31 | 0.12 | -0.59** | 5.99 |
| EXP | 0.65 | 0.03 | 0.42 | 0.11 | 0.37** | 3.70 |
| EDU | 0.71 | 0.32** | 0.50 | 0.08 | 0.36** | 4.10 |
| SPD | 0.75 | 0.18 | 0.56 | 0.06 | 0.28** | 3.26 |
| SMAS | 0.77 | -0.04 | 0.59 | 0.03 | -0.19* | 2.16 |

*Note:* **p<0.01, *p<0.05.

In predicting loyalty (Table 8.38), for Organization 'A', OMAS (33%), marital status (12%), education (8%), and number of jobs changed (3%) together accounted for 56 per cent towards the total variance, while the rest 44 per cent is unaccounted for. In Organization 'B', marital status (13%), OPD (8%), and number of jobs changed (7%), together accounted for 28 per cent towards the total variance of loyalty. In Organization 'C', OMAS (19%), number of jobs changed (12%), experience prior to joining (11%), education (8%), SPD (6%) and SMAS (3%) contributed with 59 per cent of the variance of loyalty. Rest 41 per cent of the variance is unaccounted for.

Normalized beta coefficients of these variables indicate that contributions made by marital status, experience prior to joining, number of jobs changed and SPD were significant and positive, while those made by SMAS, OMAS and OPD were significant and negative. These results imply that having greater prior work experience contributed to greater loyalty. Being married, male and having changed fewer jobs also predicted loyalty. These results are in line with those obtained for organizational commitment. Greater power distance in society was also found to be related to greater loyalty. On the other hand, greater masculinity, both at the level of the society and the organization, and OPD were related to lesser loyalty. This suggests that high concern for production high work centrality lowers loyalty. Further, significant differences in status, rewards, privileges, and opportunities between various levels of the organization also lower loyalty. Finally, education was found to contribute negatively in Organization 'A', but positively in Organization 'C' (as was the case with organizational commitment), suggesting that organizational factors may moderate the influence of education in predicting loyalty.

An overview of these results indicates that all the three sets of predictor variables were potent in determining loyalty. However, in all 3 organizations, organizational values were stronger in predicting loyalty than both societal values and personal variables. Two societal values emerged as significant in explaining loyalty, viz. SPD and SMAS. Two organizational values, viz. OMAS and OPD were found to be determinants of loyalty. Among personal variables, those found to predict loyalty were education, marital status, experience prior to joining, and number of jobs changed.

## SUMMARY

All the three sets of predictor variables had an extremely strong impact on the outcome variables. Personal variables like education, marital status, experience prior to joining, and number of jobs changed emerged to be very potent in predicting outcome variables. While the effect of some personal variables remained constant across all three organizations, there were some personal variables whose contribution was selective. For e.g., number of jobs changed contributed negatively to commitment in all 3 organizations, promotion(s) received contributed negatively to turnover intention in 2 organizations; while education contributed negatively to commitment in Organization 'A', but positively in 'C'. These results suggest that organizational culture seems to moderate the influence of some personal variables in predicting outcome variables.

Among the societal values, SMAS emerged as the strongest in determining outcome variables, contributing negatively to turnover intention, organizational commitment, identification, and loyalty, followed by SPD, SID, and SUA. Similar to the effect of personal variables, the contribution of some societal values remained constant across 3 organizations, while the effect of some varied across organizations. For e.g, SPD contributed negatively to turnover intention in all 3 organizations; while SMAS contributed positively to emotional, behavioural, and overall employee health in Organization 'A', but negatively in Organization 'C', implying that organizational culture seems to moderate the influence of societal factors in predicting health of employees.

Among the organizational values, OMAS emerged as most potent in predicting outcome variables, contributing negatively to organizational commitment (in all 3 organizations), identification, loyalty, and even physical health; and negatively to turnover intention. OID and OPD contributed negatively to commitment (in 2 organizations), identification and loyalty.

Interestingly, although organizational values were not very significant in predicting employee health, they were quite potent in predicting organizational commitment, and organizational identification, especially in Organization 'A' and 'C'. However, since a large proportion of the variance in employee health is left unaccounted (especially in Organizations 'B' and 'C'), some other factors, perhaps job stress, coping, strain, etc. kept out of research focus in the present book predict health at the workplace. Turnover intention was equally predicted by personal variables and societal values, followed by organizational values (for Organization 'A' and 'C'). For Organization 'B', on the other hand, no organizational value predicted turnover intention. Promotion(s) given to employees as a determinant of organizational commitment and turnover intention has practical implications for using performance management as a culture-building tool in fostering commitment and reducing turnover intention of employees.

# 9

# Where Does this Leave Us?

## CONCLUSIONS

Since employees belonging to the three multinationals do not differ in their perception of the Indian societal values, it can be concluded that employees uphold their Indian socio-cultural values even when placed within different multinational organizations. One does not have to search for "Indian-ness" too far. The measures used in the present study may not be perfect and the findings are indeed not always unequivocal. The term "Indian societal values" is used in a broad general way, although these values may be restricted to societal values as perceived by employees working in multinationals located in and around New Delhi, and may not be generalized to other parts of India. Turnover intention rather than actual turnover was studied. Longitudinal research could be carried out in order to reach conclusive results regarding the role of societal values and organizational values as predictors of actual turnover. Two limitation of story-based research must also be mentioned. First, the selective use of organizational narratives may amplify and reinforce the researcher's preconceived ideas or assumptions. In the present study, although I have tried to acquire an insider's point of view, while maintaining the analytical distance of an outsider, it is possible that it might be contaminated by my personal biases. A second danger is the risk of regarding stories as facts, since in many stories, the idea that something 'actually happened' is itself a part of poetic elaboration by respondents.

Despite the above mentioned limitations, at the end of this exploration, it seems reasonable to conclude that although organizational values of the MNCs were influenced by their respective "home national cultures," the Indian employees working for them maintained their socio-cultural preferences and culturally specific ways of working. It is preposterous to assume that when employees arrive to work they can or should leave at the point of entry their cultural baggage, and pick it up at the end of the workday for use in their non-work life and activities. I am reminded of the famous phrase, *"You can take a man away from India, but not India away from a man."*

Indian societal values do influence organizational values, although their influence varies in different degrees in different MNCs. Organizational culture, being a microcosm of the encompassing culture, reflects the dominant values and norms of the societal culture. Cultural values provide elaborate and generalized norms both for appropriate behaviour for the members and for activities and functions of the system (Enz, 1988; Chatman, 1991). These results are in keeping with Schein's (1985) statement that, "organizational culture paradigms are adapted versions of broader cultural paradigms." Similarly, Hofstede (1980) concluded that, "Organizations are (host) culture-bound." Sinha (1990), too, conceived an organization as fully embedded in its socio-cultural milieu, and viewed organizational culture as a sub-culture of the larger engulfing societal culture.

On the other hand, it also seems plausible that organizational values take precedence over employees' societal values in determining some outcomes, if the corporate culture is strong (like Organization 'B'). Members who enter an organization go through a systematic process of organizational socialization, through which organizations transmit its culture, instilling in new members the values and norms of the organization, transforming an outsider into an insider. This socialization process apparently has a strong impact in determining an employee's commitment and identification with the organization. Furthermore, since the relationship between organizational values and the Indian societal values is strong in Organization 'B', it is likely that this results in greater commitment, loyalty, and identification of employees with the organization. At the same time, however, congruence of organizational values with societal values may only influence some outcome variables like commitment, but not others like health of employees. While the importance of strong organizational cultures has been emphasized time and again by research, the present investigation suggests that the culture has to be strong (at least in certain respects), as well as congruent with the contextual societal culture, in order for an organization to be effective in various cultural contexts and maintain loyalty of its employees.

In todays's times of downsizing, "right-sizing", mergers and reengineering, employees are confused as to their purpose at work, distrustful of almost everyone, and motivated to pursue self-interests, as do their bosses (Deal and Kennedy, 2000). They are detached, disillusioned, and prone to gather in underground subsultures. In what appears to be the world's largest bankruptcy in history, Leman Brothers, the leading US-Based investment bank filed for bankruptcy (September 15, 2008), leaving employees in a rule shock, with accompanying feelings of isloation, fear and panic, Layoffs have been reported in companies like Merrill-Lynch, CitiGroup. Detroit, Daimler, Ebay, Hewlett-Packard, and many others owing to recession. The employer-employee relationship is moving away from long-term and stable in the diection of short-term and contingent. This confusion will be further aggravated for multinationals if their organization values are at odds with the socio-cultural values are at odds with the socio-cultural values of their employees. The main focus of organizations is growth, expansion, and increased profitability. Thus, if shared organizational values are to support competitive advantage across national borders, management must determine the degree to which these value 'fit' with the larger socio-cultural context, and then integrate members into the general organizational culture.

## EMERGING PARADIGM

It is clear that a macro perspective is required to transcend the limitations of the organization-bound model of organizational culture by looking across organizational boundaries. The concept of organizational culture, as currently used, focuses on the inside of the organization and treats the organization as if it were separate from the societal environment in which it is embedded. However, in an era of increasing global competition and the presence of MNCs, societal culture can no longer be ignored. As asserted by Adler and Jelinek (1986), the role of societal culture must be incorporated within the organizational culture paradigm to make it more relevant for the MNC.

A theoretical paradigm (Figure 9.1) may be proposed, rather tentatively, in which societal values and personal characteristics influence the perception of organizational values, which in turn shapes work behaviour and has consequences for employees. Societal values not only influence organizational values, but also employee outcomes like turnover intention, employee health and even organizational commitment. Further, organizational values may moderate the influence of both societal values and personal variables of employees in determining work behaviour. In fact, further research could test the soundness of this paradigm by adding other outcomes, both organizational like perhaps organizational citizenship behaviour, or even personal ones like life satisfaction.

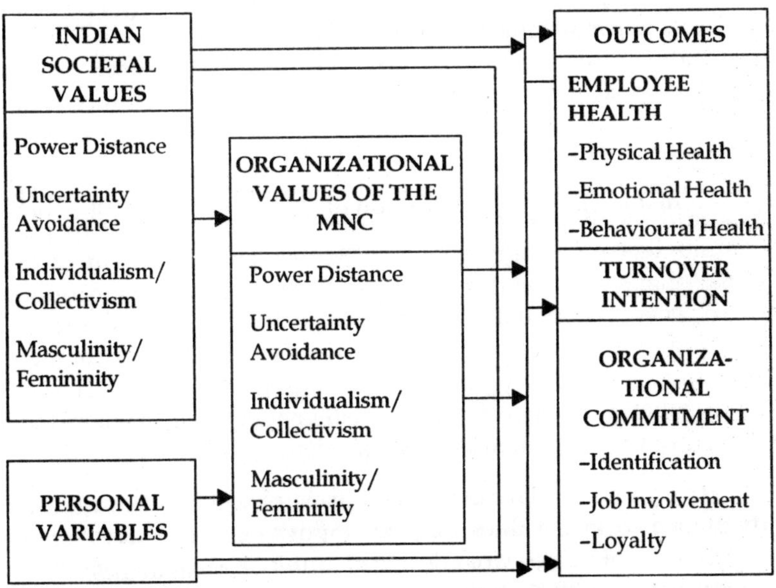


**Fig. 9.1: Emerging Paradigm: Interplay Among Societal Values, Organizational Values, and Personal Variables of Employees and Consequences for Work Behaviour**

## IMPLICATIONS FOR MANAGERS OF MULTINATIONALS

Multinational organizations in developing countries like India have invested considerable resources, time, and effort to adopt the state-of-the-art human resource management practices developed in Europe and North America, based on Western thought and value systems. The effectiveness of this approach, however, is open to serious question based on the experience of employees working in these organizations and the findings of this study. Thus, organizations should consider the critical features of their organizational cultures that are likely to facilitate or hinder the effective adoption of these practices and techniques and, based on these considerations, design organizational interventions or strategies that are necessary to ensure their 'cultural fit.' As suggested by Hofstede (1991), "culturally a manager is the follower of his followers: he has to meet the subordinates on these subordinates' cultural ground."

Managing organizations across national borders can be made easier by first matching organizational context with the larger socio-cultural context and then integrating members into the general organizational culture. The belief that organizational culture erases the influence of national societal culture is a myth. The practice of subsidiaries of multinationals to overlook the host country's culture, particularly that of third-world countries like India on the assumption that they are dysfunctional, may result in poor commitment and loyalty of their workforce. These results are in line with Adler's (1997) statement that, "The myth that 'organizations can be beyond nationality in their design and operations' remains, in reality, a myth." To manage effectively in a global environment, managers need to recognize cultural differences and learn to use them to their advantage, rather than either attempting to ignore them or simply allowing them to cause problems.

Applying the above mentioned principles, it may be suggested that since societal values play an important role in determining organizational values, work design of multinationals in India should be compatible with the Indian societal values and allow for relatively high power distance, uncertainty avoidance and individualism, and moderate masculinity. To overcome the constraints of high power distance in India, managers should function as coach and mentor to their subordinates. In order to be compatible with high uncertainty avoidance, clearly defined roles and work procedures are recommended. Further, managerial approaches that emphasize task roles and rewards based on individual performance would suit "individualistic" employees. Finally, moderate masculinity underlines the importance of non-economic rewards that satisfy affiliation needs as well as economic rewards for performance-centeredness and results-orientation. By careful attention to societal culture, managers of multinationals can more effectively help to create an organizational culture in harmony with societal culture.

Managers of multinational organizations must be sensitive to cultural differences in order to succeed in a global economy. This has practical implications for providing enculturation training, particularly for expatriate managers to not only help them adjust to the host country's business and social environment, but also to bridge cultural distance with their native subordinates. The findings also have implications for selection of executives since the commitment of employees has been found to be greater when their societal values match the organizational values. It is therefore suggested that selection and socialisation practices in organizations ought to include considerations of value congruence rather than focusing exclusively on skills, abilities, and non-job-related criteria like goal-orientation, interpersonal skills, etc. This may encourage longer-range planning for human resource needs, especially in MNCs with long career paths.

# Appendix

## LIST OF APPENDICES



### I INTERVIEW SCHEDULE

1. Every organization has certain stories that are a part of its folklore. Through stories we often express our feelings and the organization communicates its morals and what it stands for.

   *(a)* Can you recall any such incident which was widely discussed among you and your colleagues?
   *(b)* Can you narrate any instance/anecdote related to the founder/top management/other central characters that reflect their philosophy, values and beliefs?
   *(c)* Can you recall an incident that made you proud/laugh/concerned/sad etc. at your workplace?

2. What values are important in this company? How would you state the espoused organizational values?
3. What kind of a place is this to work in? Could you explain the cultural characteristics of this organization?
4. What qualities are considered important for success in this organization? Who really gets ahead in the long term and why?
5. What is the biggest mistake one can make here?

## II (i) INDIAN SOCIETAL VALUES SCALE

Please read each of the statement given below and indicate to what extent you agree/disagree with each of them. Please rate the following statements by selecting one of the following numbers:

(5) Agree
(4) Agree to some extent
(3) Undecided
(2) Disagree to some extent, or
(1) Disagree

1. Parents should put high value on children's obedience.
2. Sex roles in our society should be clearly differentiated.
3. Conflict and competition can give rise to aggression and therefore should be avoided.
4. Those in power should try to look less powerful than they are.
5. One should be loyal to his/her community even if one is inconvenienced by the demands of the community.
6. People in authority should be respected because of their position.
7. Deviant ideas are threatening and must be cut off at the root.
8. People at various power levels should not feel threatened and be more prepared to trust other people.
9. One's identity is based in the social system rather than in the individual.
10. Trying to be better than others is neither socially nor materially rewarding.
11. Hierarchy means existential inequality (i.e. those higher in the hierarchy are "in some way superior" than those lower in the hierarchy).
12. One should not be willing to compromise with one's opponents.
13. "I" awareness rules over "We" awareness.
14. Caring for others should be a very important concern in one's life.
15. Power-holders should be entitled to privileges in the society.

16. There is a need for written rules and regulations.
17. One admires the successful achiever.
18. Conservation (preservation) of the environment is a more important problem than economic growth.
19. Time is money.
20. Press should be given a lot of freedom.
21. Achievement is defined in terms of recognition and wealth.
22. All people should have equal rights.
23. Group decisions are better than individual decisions.
24. Social relations are predetermined in terms of in-groups ("*apna*" group).
25. Money and material possessions are more important than warm relationships with people.

## II (ii) INDIAN SOCIETAL VALUES SCALE: ORIGINAL FORM

Please read each of the statement given below and indicate to what extent you agree/disagree with each of them. Please rate the following statements by selecting one of the following numbers:

(5) Agree
(4) Agree to some extent
(3) Undecided
(2) Disagree to some extent, or
(1) Disagree

1. Parents should put high value on children's obedience.
2. People in our society are emotionally resistant to change.
3. Everyone is supposed to take care of himself/herself and his/her immediate family.
4. Sex roles in a society should be clearly differentiated.
5. Youth should put high value on independence.
6. There is greater readiness to live by the day rather than worry about the future.
7. People are born into extended families or clans, which protect them in exchange for loyalty.

8. One should have sympathy for the unfortunate.

9. There should be an order of inequality in this world in which everyone has his/her rightful place; high and low are protected by this order.

10. Conflict and competition can unleash aggression and therefore should be avoided.

11. Enjoyment in life appeals to students.

12. School system in India is performance-oriented (emphasis on marks).

13. Those in power should try to look less powerful than they are.

14. Aggressive behaviour in our society is frowned upon.

15. One should be loyal to his/her community even if one is inconvenienced by the demands of the community.

16. People 'work to live' rather than 'live to work.'

17. People in authority should be respected because of their position.

18. Deviant ideas are threatening and must be cut off at the root.

19. Individual initiative and achievement should be encouraged.

20. People in our society are more oriented towards money and material things.

21. People at various power levels should not feel threatened and be more prepared to trust other people.

22. If rules cannot be kept, we should change them.

23. One's identity is based in the social system rather than in the individual.

24. Trying to be better than others are neither socially nor materially rewarding.

25. Hierarchy means existential inequality (i.e. those higher in the hierarchy are "in some way superior" than those lower in the hierarchy).

26. One should not be willing to compromise with one's opponents.

27. "I" awareness rules over "We" awareness.

28. Caring for others should be a very important concern in one's life.
29. The use of power should be legitimate and subject to the judgement as to whether it is good or evil.
30. The uncertainty inherent in life is easily accepted and each day is taken as it comes.
31. One's private life is invaded by members of the extended family to which one belongs.
32. One should not try one-upmanship (trying to be better) over others.
33. Power holders should be entitled to privileges in our society.
34. There is a need for written rules and regulations.
35. Income inequality exists between various sectors of the economy.
36. One admires the successful achiever.
37. There should be minimal inequality in a society.
38. A small generation gap exists in our society.
39. Friendships are predetermined by stable social relationships, but there is need for prestige within these relationships.
40. Conservation (preservation) of the environment is a more important problem than economic growth.
41. Cooperation among the powerless is difficult to bring about because of low faith in people norm.
42. Time is money.
43. Press should be given a lot of freedom.
44. Achievement is defined in terms of recognition and wealth.
45. Male chauvinism is encouraged in our society.
46. All people should have equal rights.
47. There is a strong need for consensus (agreement) in our society.
48. Value standards of people differ for in-groups ("*apna*" group) and out-groups ("*doosra*" group).

49. Men dominate in all situations.
50. Students show obedience to authority as a societal norm.
51. There should be a great concern with security in life.
52. Group decisions are better than individual ones.
53. One should have belief in the equality of sexes.
54. Showing of emotions should not be preferred.
55. Men and women should take different types of courses for higher-level education.
56. Social relations are predetermined in terms of in-groups ("*apna*" group).
57. Citizens of our country are pessimistic about their ability to control politician's decisions.
58. Money and material possessions are more important than warm relations with people.

## II (iii) INDIAN SOCIETAL VALUES SCALE: RESULTS OF ITEM ANALYSIS

| *Item No.* | *Dimensions* | *t (Above Median, Below Median)* | *t (17, 17)* | *r (Item, Subtotal)* | *Accepted / Rejected* |
|---|---|---|---|---|---|
| 1. | SPD | 1.79* | 2.05* | 0.40** | Accepted |
| 2. | SUA | 1.61 | 1.92* | 0.33** | Rejected |
| 3. | SID | 1.95* | 1.17 | 0.24* | Rejected |
| 4. | SMAS | 1.79* | 5.36** | 0.49** | Accepted |
| 5. | SPD | 0.06 | 0.01 | -0.10 | Rejected |
| 6. | SUA | 0.75 | 1.12 | 0.11 | Rejected |
| 7. | SID | 1.09 | 1.2 | 0.14 | Rejected |
| 8. | SMAS | 1.22 | 1.79* | 0.24* | Rejected |
| 9. | SPD | 1.68 | 1.63 | -0.27* | Rejected |
| 10. | SUA | 5.72** | 3.62** | 0.43** | Accepted |

| | | | | | |
|---|---|---|---|---|---|
| 11. | SID | 0.01 | 0.41 | 0 | Rejected |
| 12. | SMAS | 0.85 | 1.33 | 0.17 | Rejected |
| 13. | SPD | 3.16** | 5.29** | 0.69** | Accepted |
| 14. | SUA | 0 | 0.01 | 0.05 | Rejected |
| 15. | SID | 3.07** | 4.42** | 0.41** | Accepted |
| 16. | SMAS | 0.27 | 0.80 | 0.16 | Rejected |
| 17. | SPD | 2.57** | 2.53** | 0.43** | Accepted |
| 18. | SUA | 2.31* | 3.41** | 0.44** | Accepted |
| 19. | SID | 0.51 | 0.48 | 0.08 | Rejected |
| 20. | SMAS | 1.14 | 0.76 | 0.13 | Rejected |
| 21. | SPD | 3.11** | 4.30** | 0.41** | Accepted |
| 22. | SUA | 0.71 | 0.98 | 0.10 | Rejected |
| 23. | SID | 1.95* | 2.67** | 0.33** | Accepted |
| 24. | SMAS | 3.45** | 2.70** | 0.39** | Accepted |
| 25. | SPD | 1.70* | 2.35* | 0.38** | Accepted |
| 26. | SUA | 2.21* | 4.09** | 0.39** | Accepted |
| 27. | SID | 1.87* | 2.38* | 0.33** | Accepted |
| 28. | SMAS | 2.21* | 4.09** | 0.34** | Accepted |
| 29. | SPD | 1.59 | 2.33* | 0.27* | Rejected |
| 30. | SUA | 0.25 | 0.05 | 0.08 | Rejected |
| 31. | SID | 1.78* | 1.20 | 0.28* | Rejected |
| 32. | SMAS | 1.58 | 2.19* | 0.32* | Rejected |
| 33. | SPD | 4.43** | 4.63** | 0.48** | Accepted |
| 34. | SUA | 2.46** | 2.66** | 0.33** | Accepted |
| 35. | SID | 0.41 | 0.36 | 0.04 | Rejected |
| 36. | SMAS | 3.28** | 2.26* | 0.33** | Accepted |
| 37. | SPD | 0.67 | 1.93* | 0.26* | Rejected |

| | | | | | |
|---|---|---|---|---|---|
| 38. | SUA | 1.61 | 2.44* | 0.27* | Rejected |
| 39. | SID | 1.14 | 2.23* | 0.30* | Rejected |
| 40. | SMAS | 1.69* | 2.75** | 0.34** | Accepted |
| 41. | SPD | 2.94** | 1.28 | 0.22 | Rejected |
| 42. | SUA | 3.33** | 2.77** | 0.37** | Accepted |
| 43. | SID | 1.91* | 1.90* | 0.29* | Accepted |
| 44. | SMAS | 3.13** | 2.92** | 0.44** | Accepted |
| 45. | SMAS | 1.42 | 2.04* | 0.17 | Rejected |
| 46. | SPD | 2.76** | 3.27** | 0.39** | Accepted |
| 47. | SUA | 0.85 | 1.5 | -0.36** | Rejected |
| 48. | SID | 1.58 | 0.90 | 0.15 | Rejected |
| 49. | SMAS | 1.07 | 3.10** | 0.27* | Rejected |
| 50. | SPD | 0.18 | 0.88 | 0.14 | Rejected |
| 51. | SUA | 0.01 | 1.41 | 0.09 | Rejected |
| 52. | SID | 1.67* | 2.77** | 0.42** | Accepted |
| 53. | SMAS | 1.43 | 1.91* | 0.30* | Rejected |
| 54. | SUA | 0.71 | 0.21 | 0 | Rejected |
| 55. | SMAS | 1.01 | 1.14 | 0.21 | Rejected |
| 56. | SID | 3.80** | 3.04** | 0.46** | Accepted |
| 57. | SUA | 0.29 | 2.14* | 0.29* | Rejected |
| 58. | SMAS | 1.68* | 2.95** | 0.33** | Accepted |

*Note:* **p<0.01, *p<0.05.

## III (i) ORGANIZATIONAL VALUES QUESTIONNAIRE

Please read each of the statement given below and indicate to what extent the statement is true of your organization. Please rate the following statements by selecting one of the following numbers:

(5) Agree
(4) Agree to some extent

(3) Undecided
(2) Disagree to some extent, or
(1) Disagree

1. Hierarchical relationships are seen as necessary for running this organization.
2. Group decisions are considered better here than individual decisions.
3. Managers generally make decisions after consulting with their associates.
4. Employees here are quite individualistic; they complete assigned tasks for which they expect to be compensated.
5. Employees do not fear to disagree with their bosses.
6. Employees are emotionally dependent on the company.
7. Managers are more involved in detail rather than strategy.
8. Employees are expected to defend their personal interests.
9. Employees here are willing to make individual and risky decisions.
10. The organizational pyramid is relatively flat.
11. Rules are written and activities are highly structured in this organization.
12. Security of employees is important to the company.
13. There is centralisation of authority in this organization.
14. Employees here give more importance to recognition, challenge and advancement than cooperation.
15. Great value is given here to good relationships and loyalty to the organization.
16. All matters are worked out meticulously, including course of action, and deviations are not liked.
17. Jobs are structured permitting more of group integration than individual achievement.
18. Employees prefer broad guidelines to detailed instructions.
19. In this organization, importance is given to compassion and caring.
20. Superiors are accessible here.

21. Nurturing and helping subordinates is encouraged here.

22. Seniors exercise their authority in most matters, and their authority is accepted by their juniors.

23. Competitiveness and achievement are highly valued here.

24. People here are treated according to their working assignments and not on the basis of kinship, caste, language etc.

25. In this organization, people prefer shorter working hours to more salary.

## III (ii) ORGANIZATIONAL VALUES QUESTIONNAIRE: ORIGINAL FORM

Please read each of the statement given below and indicate to what extent the statement is true of your organization. Please rate the following statements by selecting one of the following numbers:

(5) Agree
(4) Agree to some extent
(3) Undecided
(2) Disagree to some extent, or
(1) Disagree

1. Hierarchical relationships are seen as necessary for running this organization.

2. Group decisions are considered better here than individual decisions.

3. Other things being equal, employees prefer managers of Indian origin to foreign ones.

4. In this organization, employees prefer shorter working hours to more salary.

5. Managers generally make decisions after consulting with their associates.

6. Employees here are quite individualistic; they complete assigned tasks for which they expect to be compensated.

7. Employees in this organization often break company rules.

8. Employees do not fear to disagree with their bosses.

9. Employees are emotionally dependent on the company.

10. Managers are more involved in detail rather than strategy.
11. Employees are expected to defend their personal interests.
12. Employees here are willing to make individual and risky decisions.
13. The organizational pyramid is relatively flat.
14. Training, physical conditions, Facilities, etc. are considered to be important by employees.
15. Rules are written and activities are highly structured in this organization.
16. Security of employees is important to the company.
17. There is centralization of authority in this organization.
18. Organizational policies and practices allow for individual initiative.
19. Managers are more interpersonal-oriented than task-oriented.
20. Employees here give more importance to recognition, challenge and advancement than cooperation.
21. Managers in this organization admit a need for support from their associates.
22. Great value is given here to good relationships and loyalty to the organization.
23. All matters are worked out meticulously, including course of action, and deviations are not liked.
24. Jobs are structured permitting more of group integration than individual achievement.
25. Subordinates here positively evaluate close supervision.
26. Employees prefer broad guidelines to detailed instructions.
27. In this organization, importance is given to compassion and caring.
28. Superiors are accessible here.
29. Organisation encourages variety more than conformity and orderliness.
30. Average age is higher in higher-level jobs.
31. Nurturing and helping subordinates is encouraged here.

32. Seniors exercise their authority in most matters, and their authority is accepted by their juniors.

33. Managers rate autonomy as more important than security in their position.

34. There are fewer specialists than generalists in this organization.

35. Competitiveness and achievement are highly valued here.

36. Different ways of solving problems are encouraged here.

37. Achievement and competence are more important than hierarchical status.

38. People here are treated according to their working assignments and not on the basis of kinship, caste, language etc.

39. Effects of meeting family and social obligations in work performance is given due weight while evaluating employees.

### III (iii) ORGANIZATIONAL VALUES QUESTIONNAIRE: RESULTS OF ITEM ANALYSIS

| *Item No.* | *Dimensions* | *t (27, 27)* | *r (Item, Subtotal)* | *Accepted/ Rejected* |
|---|---|---|---|---|
| 1. | OPD | 4.15** | 0.52** | Accepted |
| 2. | OID | 3.57** | 0.36** | Accepted |
| 3. | OUA | 1.64 | 0.20* | Rejected |
| 4. | OID | 1.39 | 0.48** | Rejected |
| 5. | OPD | 4.39** | 0.49** | Accepted |
| 6. | OID | 4.05** | 0.46** | Accepted |
| 7. | OUA | 1.66 | 0.29** | Rejected |
| 8. | OPD | 5.76** | 0.57** | Accepted |
| 9. | OID | 2.84** | 0.31** | Accepted |
| 10. | OUA | 6.22** | 0.51** | Accepted |
| 11. | OID | 3.83** | 0.40** | Accepted |
| 12. | OUA | 2.66** | 0.32** | Accepted |
| 13. | OPD | 5.32** | 0.56** | Accepted |

| | | | | |
|---|---|---|---|---|
| 14. | OID | 1.98 | 0.27** | Rejected |
| 15. | OUA | 4.03** | 0.48** | Accepted |
| 16. | OMAS | 6.22** | 0.74** | Accepted |
| 17. | OPD | 7.97** | 0.61** | Accepted |
| 18. | OID | 0.13 | 0.02 | Rejected |
| 19. | OUA | 1.21 | 0.37** | Rejected |
| 20. | OMAS | 7.56** | 0.62** | Accepted |
| 21. | OPD | 1.62 | 0.39** | Rejected |
| 22. | OID | 7.41** | 0.63** | Accepted |
| 23. | OUA | 5.88** | 0.59** | Accepted |
| 24. | OMAS | 6.45** | 0.69** | Accepted |
| 25. | OPD | 1.60 | 0.19 | Rejected |
| 26. | OUA | 3.06** | 0.34** | Accepted |
| 27. | OMAS | 7.11** | 0.66** | Accepted |
| 28. | OPD | 6.37** | 0.67** | Accepted |
| 29. | OID | 0.12 | 0.06 | Rejected |
| 30. | OUA | 1.52 | 0.17 | Rejected |
| 31. | OMAS | 4.80** | 0.63** | Accepted |
| 32. | OPD | 5.98** | 0.60** | Accepted |
| 33. | OID | 0.85 | 0.09 | Rejected |
| 34. | OUA | 2.47* | 0.22* | Rejected |
| 35. | OMAS | 2.43* | 0.31** | Accepted |
| 36. | OUA | 1.91 | 0.22* | Rejected |
| 37. | OPD | 2.64* | 0.24* | Rejected |
| 38. | OID | 2.99** | 0.36** | Accepted |
| 39. | OMAS | 2.43** | 0.33** | Accepted |

*Note:* ****p<0.01, *p<0.05.**

# Bibliography


Abrams, D., Ando, K., & Hinkle, S. (1998). Psychological attachment to the group: Cross-cultural differences in organizational identification and subjective norms as predictors of workers, turnover intentions. *Personality and Social Psychology Bulletin, 24*(10), 1027-1039.

Adelman, P.K. (1987). Occupational complexity, control, and personal income: Their relation to psychological well-being in men and women. *Journal of Applied Psychology, 72*, 529-537.

Adler, N.J. (1997). *International dimensions of organizational behaviour*, 3rd ed. Ohio: South-Western College Publishing, International Thomson Publishing.

Adler, N.J., & Jelinek, M. (1986). Is "Organizational Culture" culture bound? *Human Resource Management, 25*(1), 73-90.

Agervold, M. (1985). Office work and psychological stress. *Psychologists Skriftserie Aanhus, 61*(10), 1-29.

Al-Ajmi, R. (2006). The effect of gender on job satisfaction and organizational commitment in Kuwait. *International Journal of Management, 23(4)*, 838-845.

Al-Qarioti, M.Q.A., & Al-Enezi, A. (2004). Organizational commitment of managers in Jordan: A field study. *International Journal of Public Administration, 27(5)*, 331-352.

Allaire, Y., & Firsirotu, M.E. (1984). Theories of organizational culture. *Organizational Studies, 5*, 193-226.

Alvesson, M. (2002). *Understanding organizational culture*. New Delhi: Sage.

Anantharaman, R.N., & John, S. (1983). Job involvement among industrial employees. *Indian Journal of Applied Psychology, 20*, 36-39.

Anantharaman, R.N., & Kalippan, P. (1982). Job involvement and its correlates. *Psychological Studies, 27*(2), 81-82.

Anastasi, A. (1982). *Psychological testing* (5th ed.). New York: Macmillan.

Angle, H.L., & Perry, J.L. (1981). An empirical assessment of organizational commitment and organizational effectiveness. *Administrative Science Quarterly, 26*, 1-14.

Argyris, C. (1951). *Personality fundamentals for administrators*. Yale University: Yale Labour and Management Center.

Argyris, C. (1964). *Integrating the individual and the organization*. New York: Wiley.

Arogyaswamy, B., & Byles, C.M. (1987). Organizational culture: Internal and external fits. *Journal of Management, 13*(4), 647-659.

Arrindell, W.A., Hatzichristou, C., Wensink, J., Rosenberg, E., Van Twillert, B., Stedema, J., & Meijer, D. (1997). Dimensions of national culture as predictors of cross-national differences in subjective well-being. *Personality and Individual Differences, 23*, 37-53.

Aryee, S.W., Wyatt, T., & Ma-Kheng, M. (1991). Antecedents of organizational commitment and turnover intentions among professional accountants in different employment settings in Singapore. *Journal of Social Psychology, 131*(4), 545-556.

Banerjee, R. (1989). *Role stress, organizational effectiveness, and mental health of employees of manufacturing and non-manufacturing organizations*. Unpublished doctoral dissertation, Varanasi: Banaras Hindu University.

Barbara, C.J. (1992). *Exploring complex organizations: A cultural Perspective*. New Delhi: Sage.

Bartol, K.M. (1976). Relationship of sex and professional training area to job orientation. *Journal of Applied Psychology, 61*, 368-370.

Bartolome, F. & Evans, P.A.L. (1979). Professional lives versus private lives: Shifting patterns in managerial commitment. *Organizational Dynamics, 7*(4), 2-29.

Bass, B.M. & Burger, P.C. (1979). *Assessment of managers: An international comparison*. New York: Free Press.

Bateson, G. (1942). Some systematic approaches to the study of culture and personality. *Character and Personality, 11*, 76-84.

Beck, B.E.F., & Moore, L.F. (1985). Linking host culture to organizational variables. In P. J. Frost, L.F. Moore, M.R. Louis, C.C. Lundberg, & J. Martin (Eds.). *Organizational Culture*. Beverly Hills: Sage.

Becker, H.S. (1960). Notes on the concept of commitment. *American Journal of Sociology, 66*, 32-42.

Beehr, T.A., & Newman, J.E. (1978). Job stress, employee health, and organizational effectiveness: A facet analysis, model, and literature review. *Personnel Psychology, 31*(4), 665-669.

Berger, P., & Luckmann, T. (1967). *The social construction of reality.* Harmondsworth: Penguin.

Berkman, L., & Syme, L. (1979). Social networks, host resistance and mortality. *American Journal of Epidemiology, 109,* 186-204.

Bertera, R.I. (1990). The effects of workplace health promotion on absenteeism and employment costs in a large industrial population. *American Journal of Public Health, 80*(9), 1101-1105.

Biswas, S.N., & Tripathi, R.C. (1998). Organizational culture and contextual culture: A Cross-Cultural and Cross-Organizational study of managerial attitudes and perception of organizational climate, *Prajnan, 28*(3), 247-261.

Black, J.S., & Mendenhall, M. (1990). Cross-cultural training effectiveness: A review and theoretical framework for future research. *Academy of Management Review, 15,* 113-136.

Black, J.S., & Porter, L.W. (1991). Managerial behaviour and job performance: A successful manager in Los Angeles may not succeed in Hong Kong. *Journal of International Business Studies, 22,* 99-113.

Blau, G.J. (1985). The meaning and prediction of career commitment. *Journal of Occupational Psychology, 58*(2), 227-237.

Blau, P.M. (1964). *Exchange and power in social life.* New York: Wiley.

Blumberg, R.L. & Winch, R.F. (1972). Societal complexity and familial complexity: Evidence for the curvilinear hypothesis. *American Journal of Sociology, 77,* 898-920.

Bochner, S., & Hesketh, B. (1994). Power Distance, Individualism/ Collectivism, and job-related attitudes in a culturally diverse work group. *Journal of Cross-Cultural Psychology, 25,* 233-257.

Bond, M. (1988). Invitation to a wedding: Chinese values and global economic growth. In P. Sinha & H. Kao (Eds.). *Social values and development.* New Delhi: Sage.

Bond, M.H. (1988). Finding universal dimensions of individual variation in multicultural studies of value: The Rokeach and Chinese Values Surveys. *Journal of Personality and Social Psychology, 55,* 1009-1015.

Bowditch, J.L., & Buono, A.F. (1997). *A primer on organizational behaviour* (4th ed.). New York: John Wiley.

Box, W.R., Odom, R.Y., & Dunn, M.G. (1991). Organizational values and value congruency and their impact on satisfaction, commitment and cohesion: An empirical examination within the public sector. *Public Personnel Management, 20*(2), 195-205.

Brief, A.P., & Motowidlo, S.J. (1988). Prosocial organizational behaviours. *Academy of Management Review, 11,* 710-725.

Brook, A. (1973). Mental stress at work. *The Practitioner, 210*, 500-508.

Brown, A. (1998). *Organizational culture.* (2nd ed.). London: Financial Times.

Bruning, N.A., & Snyder, R.A. (1983). Sex and position as predictors of organizational commitment. *Academy of Management Journal, 26*, 485-491.

Buchanan, B. (1974). Building organizational commitment: The socialization of managers in work organizations. *Administrative Science Quarterly, 19*, 533-546.

Buck, V.K. (1972). *Working under pressure*. London: Staples Press.

Buckley, M.R., Fedor, D.B., Veres, G.J., Weiss, D.S., & Carraher, S.M. (1998). Investigating newcomer expectations and job-related outcomes. *Journal of Applied Psychology, 83*(3), 452-461.

Burke, R.L. & Cooper, C.L. (2002). Introduction: The new world of work. In C.L. Cooper & R.J. Burke (Eds.). *The new world of work: Challenges and opportunities.* Oxford: Blackwell.

*Business International* (1965). Organizing for its world-wide operations, p. 15. New York.

Butler, J.S. & Holmes, M.D. (1984). Race, separatist ideology, and organizational commitment. *Social Science Quarterly, 65*(1), 138-149.

Butler, R. P., Lardent, C. L., & Miner, J. B. (1983). A motivational basis for turnover in military officers education and training. *Journal of Applied Psychology, 68*(3), 496-506.

Cain, K.W., & Bruce, P. (1987). Organizational commitment, satisfaction, professionalism and length of service. *Human Relations, 43*, 781-791.

Calorie, R., & Sarnin, P. (1991). Corporate culture and economic performance: A French study. *Organizational Studies, 12*, 49-74.

Cammann, C., Fichman, M., Jenkins, D., & Klesh, J. (1979). The Michigan Organizational Assessment Questionnaire. Unpublished Manuscript, Ann Arbor, Michigan: University of Michigan.

Campion, M.A. (1991). Meaning and measurement of turnover: Comparison of alternative measures and recommendations for research. *Journal of Applied Psychology, 76*(2), 199-212.

Caplan, R. D., Cobb, S., & French, S.R.P., Jr. (1975). Relation of cessation of smoking and stress, personality, and social support. *Journal of Applied Psychology, 60*, 211-219.

Carstairs, G.M., & Kapur, R.L. (1976). *The great universe of Kota: Stress, change and mental disorders in an Indian village.* London: Hogarth Press.

Carstairs, G.M. (1971). *The Twice-born: A study of the community of high caste Hindu.* Mumbai: Allied Publishers.

Carsten, J.M., & Spector, P.E. (1987). Unemployment, job satisfaction, and employee turnover: A meta-analysis test of the Muchinsky model. *Journal of Applied Psychology, 72*(3), 374-381.

Cascio, W. F. (1982). *Costing human resources: The financial impact of behaviour in organizations.* Boston: Kent.

Chakraborty, S.K. (1991). *Management by values: Towards cultural congruence.* Oxford: Oxford University Press.

Chakraborty, S.K. (1993). *Management transformation by values: A corporate pilgrimage.* New Delhi: Sage.

Chakraborty, S.K. (1999). Social values in organizations: The case for countervailing socialization. In H.S.R. Kao, D. Sinha, & B. Wilpert (Eds.). *Management and cultural values: The indigenization of organizations in Asia.* New Delhi: Sage.

Chao, G.T., O'Leary, A.M., Wolf, S., Klein, H.J., & Gardener, P.D. (1994). Organizational socialization: Its contents and consequences. *Journal of Applied Psychology, 79*(5), 730-743.

Chatman, J.A. (1989). Improving interactional organizational research: A model of person-organization fit. *Academy of Management Review, 14*, 333-349.

Chatman, J. A. (1991). Matching people and organizations: Selection and socialization in public accounting firms. *Administrative Science Quarterly*, 36, 459-484.

Chattopadhyay, G.P. (1975). Dependence in Indian culture: From mud huts to company board rooms. *Economic and Political Weekly, 19*, M30-M38.

Chaturvedi, M.K. (1983). *Human stress and stressors: A sociological study.* New Delhi: Cosmo.

Chaudhuri, A. (2001). *Count your chickens before they hatch.* New Delhi: Vikas Publishing House.

Chen, Z.X. & Francesco, A.M. (2000). Employee demography, organizational commitment, and turnover intentions in China: Do cultural differences matter. *Human Relations*, 53(6), 869-887.

Cheng, B.S. (1995). The relationship between hierarchical fit in organizational value and employee effectiveness. *Chinese Journal of Psychology, 37*(1), 25-44.

Cheng, Y.C. (1994). Locus of control as an indicator of Hong Kong teachers' job attitudes and perceptions of organizational characteristics. *Journal of Educational Research, 87*(3), 180-188.

Chinnappan, N.V. (1996). *A study between organizational culture and employee commitment.* Unpublished doctoral thesis. Bombay: TISS. TC162, New Delhi: ICSSR.

Cho, G.H. (2000). Three essays on the consequences of national and organizational cultures at the United States subsidiaries of Korean multinational corporations. *Dissertation Abstracts International, Section A: Humanities and Social Sciences, 60* (8-A), 3011.

Christopher, B. (1982). Control of emotions, remote stress, and the emergence of breast cancer. *Indian Journal of Clinical Psychology, 6,* 213-220.

Coleman, L. (1941). What is America? A study of alleged American traits. *Social Forces, 19,* 492-499.

Conrad, D.C. (1952). Toward a more productive concept of mental health. *Mental Hygiene, 36,* 455-466.

Cook, J. & Wall, T.D. (1980). Organizational commitment. *Journal of Occupational Psychology, 53,* 34-48.

Cook, J.D., Hepworth, S.J., Wall, T.D., & Warr, P.B. (1981). *The experience of work: A compendium and review of 249 measures and their use.* New York: Academic Press.

Cooke, R.A., & Szumal, J.L. (1993). Measuring normative beliefs and shared behavioural expectations in organizations: The reliability and validity of the Organizational Culture Inventory. *Psychological Reports, 72*(3), 1299-1330.

Cooper, C.L., & Burke, R.J. (2002). *The New World of Work.* Oxford: Blackwell.

Cooper, C.L., & Davidson, M. (1982), *High Pressure: Working Lives of Women Managers.* Glasgow: Fontana.

Cooper, C.L., & Marshall, J. (1976). Occupational sources of stress: A review of the literature relating to coronary heart disease and mental ill health. *Journal of Occupational Psychology, 49,* 11-28.

Cooper, C.L., & Marshall, J. (1980). *White collar and professional stress.* New York: Wiley.

Cooper, R.K., & Sawaf, A. (1997). *Executive EQ: Emotional intelligence in business.* London: Orion.

Coopey, J., & Hartley, J. (1991). Reconsidering the case for organizational commitment. *Human Relations Management Journal, 3,* 18-31.

Cotton, J.L., & Tuttle, J.M. (1986). Employee turnover: A meta-analysis and review of publications for research. *Academy of Management Review, 11,* 55-70.

Cox, T. (1978). *Stress.* London: Macmillan.

Cox, T. (1991). Organizational culture, stress, and stress management. *Work and Stress, 5*(1), 1-4.

Cropanzano, R., Howes, J.C., Grandey, J.C., & Toth, P. (1997). The relationship of organizational politics and support to work behaviours, attitudes, and stress. *Journal of Organizational Behaviour, 18*(2), 159-180.

Crowley, J.E., Levitin, T.E., & Quinn, R.P. (1973). Facts and fictions about the American working woman. In R.P. Quinn & T.W. Mangione (Eds.). *The 1969-1970 survey of working conditions.* Ann Arbor, MI: Institute for Social Research, University of Michigan.

Crozier, M. (1964). *The bureaucratic phenomenon.* Chicago: Univesity of Chicago Press.

Cummings, L.L., Harnett, D.L., & Stevens, O.V. (1971). Risk, fate, conciliation, and trust: An international study of attitudinal differences among executives. *Academy of Management Journal, 14,* 285-304.

d'Iribarne, P. (1989). *La logique de l' honneur: Gestion des enterprises et traditions nationals.* Paris: Edsitions du Seuil.

Dalton, D.R., Krackhardt, D.M., & Porter, L.W. (1981). Functional turnover: An empirical assessment. *Journal of Applied Psychology, 66,* 716-721.

Dandrige, T.C., Mitroff, I., & Joyce, W.F. (1980). Organizational symbolism: A topic to expand organizational analysis. *Academy of Management Review, 5(1),* 77-82.

Dansereau, F., Jr., Cashman, J., & Grean, G. (1974). Expectancy as a moderator of the relationship between job attitudes and turnover. *Journal of Applied Psychology, 59(2),* 228-229.

Davidson, M.J., & Cooper, C.L. (1984). Occupational stress in female managers: A comparative approach. *Journal of Management Studies, 21,* 185- 205.

Davis, K., & Newstorm, J.W. (1989). *Human behaviour at work,* 8th ed. New Delhi: McGraw-Hill.

Dayal, I. (1976). *Cultural factors in designing performance appraisal system.* New Delhi: RC Industrial Relations and Human Resources.

Dayal, I. (2000). *Can organizations develop leaders: A study of effective leaders.* New Delhi: Mittal.

De Gramont (1969). Cited in Peabody, D. (1985). *National characteristics: European monographs in social psychology,* p. 134. Cambridge: The University Press.

De, N. R. (1984). *Alternative designs of human organizations.* New Delhi: Sage.

Deal, T.E., & Kennedy, A.A. (1982). *Corporate Cultures: The rites and rituals of corporate life*. Massachusetts: Addison-Wesley.

Deal, T.E., & Kennedy, A.A. (2000). *The new corporate cultures: Revitalising the workplace after downsizing, mergers and reengineering*. London: Texere.

DeCotiis, T.A., & Summers, T.P. (1987). A path analysis of a model of the antecedents and consequences of OCM. *Human Relations, 40*(7), 445-470.

Delobbe, N., & Vandenberghe, C. (2001). In-house training as an organizational socialization device: A survey in the banking industry. *Travail Humain, 64*(1), 61-89.

Denison, D.R. (1984). Bringing corporate culture to the bottom line. *Organizational Dynamics, 13*, 5-22.

Denison, D.R. (1990). *Corporate culture and organizational effectiveness*. New York: John Wiley.

Dhawan, N., Roseman, I.J., Naidu, R.K., & Rettek, S.I. (1995). Self-concepts across two cultures: India and the United States. *Journal of Cross-Cultural Psychology, 26*, 602-621.

Dick, P. (2000). The social construction of the meaning of acute stressors: A qualitative study of the personal accounts of police officers using a stress counselling service. *Work and Stress, 14*(3), 226-244.

Dornstein, M., & Matalon, Y. (1989). A comprehensive analysis of the predictors of organisational commitment: A study of voluntary army personnel in Israel. *Journal of Vocational Behavior, 34*, 192-203.

Downey, H.K., Hellriegel, D., & Slocum, J.W. (1977). Individual characteristics as sources of perceived uncertainty variability. *Human Relations, 30*, 161-174.

Dunlap, R.E., Gallup, G.H., Jr., & Gallup, A.M. (1993). *Health of the planet: Results of a 1992 International Environmental Opinion Survey of citizens in 24 nations*. Princeton, NJ: The George E. Gallup International Institute.

Ellett, A.J.S. (2000). Human caring, self-efficacy beliefs, and professional organizational culture correlates of employee retention in child welfare. *Dissertation Abstracts International, Section A: Humanities and Social Sciences, 61(8-A)*, 3350.

England, G.W., & Lee, R. (1974). The relationship between managerial values and managerial success in the United States, Japan, India, and Australia. *Journal of Applied Psychology, 59*(4), 411-419.

England, G.W., Agarwal, N.C., & Dhingra, O.P. (1974). *Personal value systems of Indian managers*. Minneapolis: University of Minneapolis Press.

England, G.W., & Negandhi, A.R. (1979). National contexts and technology as determinants of employee's perception. In G.W. England, A.R. Negandhi, & B. Wilpert (Eds.). *Organizational functioning in a cross-cultural perspective*. Kent State University, Kent, Ohio: Comparative Administrative Research Institute.

Enz, C.A. (1988). The role of value congruity in intraorganizational power. *Administrative Science Quarterly, 33*, 284-304.

Erikson, E.H. (1950). *Childhood and society*. New York: Norton.

Evan, W.M., & Damanpour, F. (1988). Societal culture, organizational culture and societal development. In P. N. Khandwalla (Ed.). *Social developments: A new role for the organizational science*. New Delhi: Sage.

Evans, W.A., Hall, K.C., & Schulli, D. (1989). A cross-cultural comparison of managerial styles. *Journal of Management Development, 8*(3), 5-13.

Farrell, D., & Rusbult, C.E. (1981). Exchange variables as predictors of job satisfaction, job commitment, and turnover: The impact of rewards, costs, alternatives, and investments. *Organizational Behaviour and Human Performance, 27*, 78-95.

Fioravanti, M., Gough, H.G. & Frere, L.J. (1981). English, French, and Italian adjective check lists: A social desirability analysis. *Journal of Cross-Cultural Psychology, 12*, 461-472.

Fishbein, M., & Ajzen, I. (1975). Belief, attitude, intention, and behaviour: An introduction to theory and research. Reading, MA: Addison-Wesley.

Fishbein, M. (1967). Attitude and the prediction of behaviour. In M Fishbein (Ed.). *Readings in attitude theory and measurement*. New York: Wiley.

Fleishman, E.A., & Harris, E.F. (1962). Patterns of leadership behaviour related to employee grievances and turnover. *Personnel Psychology, 15*, 43-56.

Fletcher, D.E. (1999). Effects of organizational commitment, job involvement, and organizational culture on the employee voluntary turnover process. *Dissertation Abstracts International, Section B: The Sciences and Engineering, 59(11-B)*, 6101.

Ford, C. (1985). Women in management: The revolution that never happens. *Unilever Magazine, 56*(2), 14-18.

Fontana, D., & Abouserie, R. (1993). Stress levels, gender and personality factors in teachers. *British Journal of Educational Psychology, 63(2)*, 261-270.

Fountain, C.W. (1945). Labour's place in an industrial mental health programme. *Mental Hygiene, 29*, 25.

Fowler, A. (1996). *Employee induction: A good start*, 3rd ed. London: Institute of Personal Development.

Fox, M., Dwyer, D., & Ganster, D. (1993). Effects of stressful demands and control on physiological and attitudinal outcomes in a hospital setting. *Academy of Management Journal, 36*, 289-318.

Frampton, M.R., Norrie, R.T., Recs, A.J., & Williams, B. (1988). *Organizations at work.* (2nd ed.). London: Pitman.

Frese, M. (1978). Patialisierte Handbook and Kontrolle: Zwei Jhemen der industriellen Psychopathologie. In M. Frese, S. Grief, & N. Semmer (Eds.). *Inndustrielle psychopathologis*. Paris: Edsitions du Seuil.

Frese, M. (1982). Occupational socialization and psychological development: An underemphasized research perspective in industrial psychology. *Journal of Occupational Psychology, 55*, 209-224.

Frese, M. (1985). Stress at work and psychosomatic complaints: A casual interpretation. *Journal of Applied Psychology, 70*(2), 314-328.

Fromm, E. (1947). *Man for himself.* New York: Farrar and Rinehart.

Frost, P.J., Moore, L.F., Louis, M.R., Lundberg, C.C., & Martin, J. (1985). (Eds.). *Organization culture.* Newbury Park, California: Sage.

Fukami, C.V., & Larson, E.W. (1984). Commitment to the company and union: Parallel model. *Journal of Applied Psychology, 69*, 367-371.

Furnham, A., & Schaeffer, R. (1984). Person-Environment fit, job satisfaction, and mental health. *Journal of Occupational Stress, 57*(4), 295-307.

Gabriel, Y. (1998). The use of stories. In G. Symon, & C. Cassell (Eds.). *Qualitative methods and analysis in organizational research: A practical guide.* New Delhi: Sage.

Gabrielidis, C., Stephan, W.G., Ybarra, O., Pearson, V.M.S., & Villareal, L. (1997). Preferred styles of conflict resolution: Mexico and the U.S. *Journal of Cross-Cultural Psychology, 28*, 661-677.

Gallie, D. (1978). *In search of new working class: Automation and social interaction within the Capitalistic Enterprise.* London: Cambridge University Press.

Ganesh, S.R. (1982). *Quality of life in Indian organizations: An irrelevant view.* Indian Institute of Management, Ahmedabad, W.P. No. 407.

Ganster, D.C., & Schaubroeck, J. (1991). Work stress and employee health. *Journal of Management, 17(2)*, 235-271.

Ganster, D.C., Fox, M.L., & Dwyer, D.J. (2001). Explaining employee's health care costs: A prospective examination of stressful job demands, personal control and physiological reactivity. *Journal of Applied Psychology, 86*(5), 954-964.

Gardell, B. (1987). *Work organization and human nature: A review of research on man's need to control technology*. Stockholm: Swedish Work Environment Fund.

Garg, P.K., & Parikh, I.J. (1995). *Crossroads of culture: A study in the culture of transience*. New Delhi: Sage.

Garr, M.C. (1998). Organizational culture as a predictor of organizational commitment. *Dissertation Abstracts International, Section B: The Sciences and Engineering, 58(8-B)*, 4500.

Gavin, J.F., & Axelrod, J.H. (1977). Managerial stress and strain in a mining organization. *Journal of Vocational Behaviour, 11*(1), 66-74.

Gbadamosi, G. (1995). An evolution of the relationship among communication, commitment and organizational effectiveness. *Journal of Business, 1*, 112-131.

Gechman, A.S., & Wiener, Y. (1975). Job involvement and satisfaction as related to mental health and personal time devoted to work. *Journal of Applied Psychology, 60*(4), 521-523.

Geertz, C. (1973). *The interpretation of cultures*. New York: Basic books.

Gillin, J. (1960). The middle segments and their values. In R.D. Adams, J.P. Gillin, A.R. Holmberg, O. Lewis, R.W. Patch, C. Wagley (Eds.). *Social change in Latin America today*. New York: Vintage.

Glisson, C., & Durick, M. (1988). Predictors of job satisfaction and organizational commitment in human service organizations. *Administrative Science Quarterly, 33*, 61-81.

Gordon, J.R., Mondy, R.W., Sharplin, A., & Premeaux, S.R. (1990). *Management and organizational behaviour*. London: Allyn & Bacon.

Gorer, G. (1948). *The American people: A study in national character*. New York: Norton.

Gould, S. (1979). An equity-exchange model of organizational involvement. *Academy of Management Review, 4*, 53-62.

Greenberg, J., & Baron, R.A. (2000). *Behaviour in organizations: Understanding and managing the human side of work* (5th ed.). New Delhi: Prentice-Hall of India.

Greenhaus, J., Parasuraman, S., Granrose, C., Rabinowitz, S., & Beutell, N. (1989). Sources of work-family conflict among two-career couples. *Journal of Vocational Behaviour, 34*, 133-153.

Gregersen, H.B., & Black, J.S. (1992). Antecedents of commitment to a parent company and a foreign operation. *Academy of Management Journal, 26*, 485-491.

Gregory, K. (1983). Native-view paradigms: Multiple culture and culture conflicts in organizations. *Administrative Science Quarterly, 28*, 377-97.

Grusky, O. (1966). Career mobility and organizational commitment. *Administrative Science Quarterly, 10*, 488-503.

Gudykunst, W.B., Matsumoto, Y., Ting-Toomey, S., Nishida, T., Kim, K., & Heyman, S. (1996). The influence of cultural individualism-collectivism, self-construals, and individual values on communication styles across cultures. *Human Communication Research, 22*, 510-543.

Guest, E.A. (1991). *Human resource management*. London: McGraw-Hill.

Gunter, B. & Furnham, A. (1996). Biographical and climate predictors of job satisfaction and pride in organization. *Journal of Psychology, 130*(2), 192-208.

Hackman, J.R., & Oldham, G R. (1976). Motivation through the design of work: Test of a theory. *Organizational Behaviour and Human Performance, 16*, 250-276.

Hall, D.T., Schneider, B., & Nygren, H.T. (1970). Personal factors in organizational identification. *Administrative Science Quarterly, 15*, 176-190.

Halman, L. (1991). *Values in the Western world: An international exploration*. Tilburg, Netherlands: Tilburg University Press.

Hampden-Turner, C. (1990). *Corporate culture: From vicious to virtuous circles*. London: Economist Books.

Hansen, C.D., & Kahnweiler, W.M. (1993). Storytelling: an instrument for understanding the dynamics of corporate relationships. *Human Relations, 46*(12), 1391-1409.

Harbison, F., & Meyers, C. (1959). *Management in the Industrial World*. New York: McGraw Hill.

Harbison, F.H., & Burgess, E.W. (1954). Modern management in Western Europe. *American Journal of Sociology, 60*, 15-23.

Harris, S.G., & Mossholder, K.W. (1996). The affective implications of perceived congruence with culture dimensions during organizational transformation. *Journal of Management, 22*(4), 527-547.

Harrison, R. (1972). Understanding your organization's character. *Harvard Business Review, 513*, 119-128.

Heaney, C.A., Price, R.H., & Rafferty, J. (1995). Increasing coping resources at work: A field experiment to increase social support, improve work team functioning, and enhance employee mental health. *Journal of Organizational Behaviour, 16*(4), 335-353.

Hendrix, W.H. (1985). Factors predictive of stress, organizational effectiveness and CHD potential. *Aviation, Space & Environmental Medicine, 56*(7), 654-659.

Henry, D., Keys, C., & Schaumann, R.L. (2001). Value-based job analysis: An approach to human resource management in rehabilitation agencies serving people with developmental disabilities. *Journal of Rehabilitation Administration, 25*(1), 1-17.

Hill, C.W.L., Hitt, M.A., & Hoskisson, R.E. (1988). Declining U.S. competitiveness: Reflection on a crisis. *Academy of Management Executive,* 2, 51-60.

Hitchcock, J. & Minturn, L. (1963). The Rajputs of Khalapur. In B. Whiting (Ed.). *Six Cultures.* New York: John Wiley.

Hofstadler, R. (1965). *The paranoid side of American politics.* London: Kegan Paul.

Hofstede, G. (1980). *Culture's consequences: International differences in work related values.* Beverly Hills, CA: Sage.

Hofstede, G. (1982). *Culture's consequences: International differences in work-related values* (Abridged Version). New Delhi: Sage.

Hofstede, G. (1984). Culture's consequences: *International differences in work-related values* (Abridged ed.). Beverly Hills, CA: Sage.

Hofstede, G. (1991). *Culture and organizations: Software of the mind,* Berkshire: McGraw-Hill.

Hofstede, G. (1995). Managerial values. In T. Jackson (Ed.). *Cross-Cultural management.* Oxford: Butterworth-Heinemann.

Hofstede, G. (1998). *Masculinity and femininity: The taboo dimension of national cultures.* New Delhi: Sage.

Hofstede, G, Neuijen, B., Ohayv, D., & Sanders, G. (1990). Measuring organizational cultures: A qualitative and quantitative study across twenty cases. *Administrative Science Quarterly,* 35, 286-316.

Holenbeck, J.R., & Williams, C.R. (1986). Turnover functionality versus turnover frequency: A note on work attitudes and organizational effectiveness. *Journal of Applied Psychology, 71,* 606-611.

Holsti, O. R. (1968). Content analysis. In G. Lindzey & E. Aronson (Eds.). *The handbook of social psychology, Vol.* 2 (2nd ed.). New York: Amerind.

Hom, P.W., Katerberg, R. Jr., & Hulin, C.L. (1979). Comparative examination of three approaches to the prediction of turnover. *Journal of Applied Psychology, 64,* 280-290.

Hoppe, M.H. (1990). *A comparative study of country elites: International differences in work-related values and learning and their implications for management training and development*. Unpublished doctoral dissertation, University of North Carolina at Chapel Hill.

House, J.S., & Rizzo, J.R. (1972). Role conflict and ambiguity as critical variables in a model of organizational behaviour. *Organizational Behaviour and Human Performance, 7*, 465-505.

House, J.S., Mc Michael, A.J., Wells, J.A., Japlan, B.H., & Landerman, L.H. (1979). Occupational stress and health among factory workers. *Journal of Health and Social Behaviour, 20*(2), 139-160.

Hrebiniak, L.G., & Alutto, J.A. (1972). Personal and role-related factors in the development of organizational commitment. *Administrative Science Quarterly, 17*, 555-572.

Hrebiniak, L.G. (1974). Effects of job level and participation on employee attitudes and perceptions of influence. *Academy of Management Journal, 17*, 649-662.

Hsu, F. (1985). The self in cross-cultural perspective. In A. Marsella, G. DeVos, & F. Hsu (Eds.). *Culture and self*. New York: Tavistock.

Inglehart, R. (1990). *Culture shift in advanced industrial society*. Princeton, NJ: Princeton University Press.

Inkeles, A. (1960). Industrial man: the relation of status to experience, perception, and value. *American Journal of Sociology, 66*, 1-31.

Irving, P.G., & Meyer, J.P. (1994). Reexamination of the met-expectations hypothesis: A longitudinal analysis. *Journal of Applied Psychology, 79*, 937-949.

Israel, B.A., House, J.S., Schurman, S.J., & Heaney, C.A. (1989). The relation of personal resources, participation, influence, interpersonal relations and coping strategies to occupational stress, job strains and health: A multivariate analysis. *Work and Stress, 3*(2), 163-194.

Jaeger, A.M. (1990). The applicability of Western management techniques in developing countries: a cultural perspective. In A.M. Jaeger, & R.N. Kanungo (Eds.). *Management In Developing Countries*. New York: Routledge.

Jaffe, D.T., Scott, C.D., & Tobe, G.R. (1994). *How to revitalize yourself, your work and your organization: Rekindling commitment*. San Francisco: Jossey-Bass.

Jagdish, & Srivastava, A. K. (1989). Buffering effect of job satisfaction and job stress-strain (mental ill health) relationship. *Advances in psychology, 4*(2), 89-96.

Jahoda, M. (1958). *Current concepts of positive mental health*. New York: Basic Books.

Jelinek, M., Smircich, L., & Hirsch, P. (1983). Introduction: A code of many colours. *Administrative Science Quarterly, 28,* 331-338.

Jick, T.D., & Mitz, L.F. (1985). Sex differences in work stress. *Academy of Management Review, 10*(3), 408-420.

Johnson, F. (1985). The Western concept of self. In A.J. Marsella, G. Devos, & F L K. Hsu (Eds.). *Culture and self: Asian and Western perspectives.* New York: Tavistock.

Johnson, M.P. (1973). Commitment: A conceptual structure and empirical application. *Sociological Quarterly, 14,* 395-406.

Johnson, T.W., & Stinson, J.E. (1975). Role ambiguity, role conflict, and satisfaction· Moderating effects of individual differences. *Journal of Applied Psychology, 60*(3), 329-333.

Juvonen, J. (2000). The social functions of attributional face-saving tactics among early adolescents. *Educational Psychology Review. 12*(1), 15-32.

Kakar, S. (1971). Authority patterns and subordinate behaviour in Indian organizations. *Administrative Science Quarterly, 16,* 298-307.

Kakar, S. (1978). *The inner experience: A psychoanalytic study of childhood and society in India.* New Delhi: Oxford University Press.

Kanungo, R.N. (1979). The concept of alienation and involvement revisited. *Psychological Bulletin, 86,* 119-138.

Kanungo, R.N. (1990). Culture and work alienation: Western models and Eastern realities. *International Journal of Psychology, 25,* 795-812.

Kanungo, R.N., & Jaeger, A.M. (1990). Introduction: The need for indigenous management in developing countries. In A.M. Jaeger, & R.N. Kanungo (Eds.) *Management in Developing Countries.* New York: Routledge.

Kanungo, R.N., & Mendonca, M. (1994). Introduction: Motivational models for developing societies. In R.N. Kanungo, & M. Mendonca (Eds.). *Work Motivation: Models for developing countries.* New Delhi: Sage.

Kao, H.S.R., Sinha, D., & Sek-Hong, N. (Eds.) (1994). *Effective organizations and social values.* New Delhi: Sage.

Kao, H.S.R., Sinha, D., & Wilpert, B. (1999) *Management and cultural values: The indigenization of organizations in Asia.* New Delhi: Sage.

Kapp, W.K. (1963). *Hindu culture, economic development and economic planning in India.* Bombay: Asia Publishing House.

Karasek, R. (1979). Job demands, job decision, latitude, and mental strain: Implications for job redesign. *Administrative Science Quarterly, 24,* 285-306.

Karasek, R., & Theorell, T. (1991). *Healthy work*. New York: Basic Books.

Karlins, M., Coffman, T.L., & Walters, G. (1969). On the fading of social stereotypes: studies in three generations of college students. *Journal of Personality and Social Psychology, 13*, 1-16.

Kasl, S.V. (1978). Epidemiological contributions to the study of work stress. In C.L. Cooper & R. Payne (Eds.). *Stress at work*. Chichester: Wiley.

Kasl, S.V. & Cooper, C.L. (Eds.). (1987). *Stress and health: Issues in research methodology*. Chichester: Wiley.

Katju, P. (1986). *Certain factors related to member integration in a multinational organization*. Unpublished doctoral dissertation, Allahabad: University of Allahbad.

Katz, D., & Kahn, R.L. (1966). *The social psychology of organizations*. New York: John Wiley.

Katzell, R.A. (1998). Contemporary meta-trends in Industrial and Organizational Psychology. In H.C. Triandis, M.D. Dunnette, & L.M. Hough (Eds.). *Handbook of Industrial and Organizational Psychology*, Vol. 4. Mumbai: Jaico.

Keesing, R.M. (1974). Theories of culture. *Annual Review of Anthropology, 3*, 73-97.

Kelley, L., & Reeser, C. (1973). The persistence of culture as a determinant of differentiated attitudes on the part of American managers of Japanese ancestry. *Academy of Management Journal, 16*(1), 67-76.

Kelley, S.W. (1992). Developing customer orientation among service employees. *Journal of the Academy of Marketing Science, 20*(1), 27-36.

Kelley, T.L. (1939). The selection of upper and lower groups for the validation of test items. *Journal of Educational Psychology, 30*, 17-24.

Kerr, J.H. (1996). Employee Fitness Programmes and Reduced Absenteeism: A Case Study. In J. Kerr, A. Griffiths, & T. Cox (Eds.). *Workplace Health: Employee fitness and exercise*. London: Taylor & Francis.

Khandelwal, K.A., & Dhillon, P K. (2003). Development of Indian Societal Values Scale. *Journal of Personality and Clinical Studies, 19*(2), 221-228.

Khandwalla, P.N. (1988). Organizational Effectiveness. In J. Pandy (Ed.). *Psychology in India: The state-of-the-art*, Vol.3. New Delhi: Sage.

Khatib, T.M. (1997). Organizational culture, subcultures, and organizational commitment. *Dissertation Abstracts International, Section A: Humanities and Social Sciences, 57(11-A)*, 4952.

Kidron, A. (1978). Work values and organizational commitment. *Academy of Management Journal, 21*, 239-247.

Kiesler, C.A., & Sakumura, J. (1966). A test of a model for commitment. *Journal of Personality and Social Psychology, 3*, 349-353.

Kilmann, R.M., Saxton, M.J., & Serpa, R. (Eds.). (1985). *Gaining control of the corporate culture.* San Francisco: Jossey - Bass.

Kim, S.U. (1999). Determinants and characteristics of the corporate culture of Korean enterprises. In Kao, H.S.R., Sinha, D., & Wilpert, B. (Eds.). *Management and cultural values.* New Delhi: Sage.

Kinicki, A., McKee, F., & Wade, K. (1996). Annual Review, 1991-1995: Occupational health. *Journal of Vocational Behaviour, 49*, 190-220.

Kirkbridge, P.S., Tang, S.F., & Westwood, R.I. (1991). Chinese conflict resolution preferences and negotiating behaviour: Cultural and psychological preferences. *Organization Studies, 12*(3), 365-386.

Kirkcaldy, B. (1993). Job stress and satisfaction: International police officers. *Psychological Reports, 72*(2), 386.

Kirkman, B.L., Gibson, C.B., & Shapiro, D.L. (2001). "Exporting' teams: Enhancing the implementation and effectiveness of work teams in global affiliates. *Organizational Dynamics, 30*(1), 12-29.

Kluckhohn, C.K. (1951). Values and Value Orientations in the Theory of Action. In T. Parsons and E.A. Shils (Eds.). *Toward a General Theory of Action.* Cambridge, MA: Harvard University Press.

Koch, J.L., & Steers, R.M. (1978). Job attachment, satisfaction and turnover among public sector employees. *Journal of Vocational Behaviour, 12*, 119-128.

Koestler, A. (1960). *The lotus and the robot.* New York: Harper & Row.

Kogan, H. (1997). Workplace health promotion: Providing a rationale. In H. Kogan (Ed.). *The corporate healthcare handbook.* London: Koran Page.

Komarovsky, M. (1976). *Dilemmas of masculinity: A study of college youth.* New York: Norton.

Konovsky, H.A., Folger, R., & Cropanzano, R. (1987). Relative effects of procedural and distributive justice on employee attitudes. *Representative Research in Social Psychology, 17*, 15-24.

Kornhauser, A. (1962). Mental health of factory workers: A Detroit study. *Human Organization, 21*, 43-46.

Kornhauser, A. (1965). *Mental health of the industrial worker.* New York: Wiley.

Kraut, A.I. (1975). Predicting turnover of employees from measured job attitudes. *Organizational Behaviour and Human Performance, 13*, 233-243.

Krecker, M.L. (1994). Work careers and organizational careers: The effects of age and tenure on worker attachment to the employment relation. *Work and Occupations, 21*(3), 251-283.

Kroeber, A.L., & Kluckhohn, C. (1952). *Culture: A critical review of concepts and definitions* (Vol. 47, No. 1). Cambridge, MA: Peabody Museum.

Kumar, U. (1981). The successful executives: A study of the Indian manager in an industrial organization. *Interpersonal Development, 1*, 39-70.

Laurent, A. (1981). Matrix organization and Latin cultures. *International Studies of Management and Organization, 10*(4), 101-114.

Lauter, G. P. (1969). Sociological-cultural and legal factors impeding decentralization of authority in developing countries. *Academy of Management Journal, 12*, 367-378.

Lawson, R.B., & Shen, Z. (1998). *Organizational psychology: Foundations and applications.* New York: Oxford.

Lee, S.M. (1971). An empirical analysis of organizational identification. *Academy of Management Journal, 14*, 213-226.

Lee, J.C., Song, K.J., & Lee, H.K. (1997). The study on the relationship of organizational commitment with occupational stress and stress coping ability. *Korean Journal of Industrial and Organizational Psychology, 10*(1), 21-38.

Lee, T.W., Ashforth, S.J., Walsh, J.P., & Mowday, R.T. (1992). Commitment propensity, organizational commitment, and voluntary turnover: A longitudinal study of organizational entry processes. *Journal of Management, 18*, 15-32.

Leiter, M.P. (1991). Coping patterns as predictors of burnout: The function of control and escape patterns. *Journal of Occupational Behaviour, 12*, 123-144.

Leites, N. (1969). *The rules of the game in Paris.* Chicago: University of Chicago Press.

Leong, C.S., Furnham, A., & Cooper, C.L. (1996). The moderating effect of organizational commitment on the occupational stress outcome relationship. *Human Relations, 49*(10), 1345-1363.

Levi, L. (1984). Work stress and health. *Scandinavian Journal of Work Environment and Health, 10*(6), 494-500.

Levi, L. (1990). Occupational stress: Spice of life or kiss of death? *American Psychologist, 45*(10), 1142-1145.

Lewin, K., Lippitt, R., & White, R.K. (1939). Patterns of aggressive behaviour in experimentally created social climates. *Journal of Social Psychology, 10*, 271-299.

Lewis (1962). Cited in Sinha, J. B. P. (1997). *Cultural context of leadership and power*. A national fellowship (ICSSR) Report. Patna: ANS Institute of Social Studies.

Lilienthal, D. (1960). The Multinational Corporation. In A. Melvin & G.L. Bach (Eds.). *Management and Corporations (1985)*. New York: McGraw-Hill.

Lieb, P.S. (2000). Culture and performance appraisal systems: How does this relationship effect organizational commitment, job satisfaction, and turnover intention? *Dissertation Abstracts International, Section A: Humanities and Social Sciences, 61(1-A)*, 262.

Lincoln, J.R., Hanada, M., & Olsen, J. (1981). Cultural orientations and individual reactions to organizations: A study of employees of Japanese-owned firms. *Administrative Science Quarterly, 26*, 93-115.

Lind, E.A., & Tyler, T.R. (1988). *The social psychology of procedural justice*. New York: Plenum.

Lindstrom, K. (1994). Psychosocial criteria for good work organization. *Scandinavian Journal of Work, Environment and Health, 20*, 123-133.

Lippitt, R., & White, R.K. (1958). An experimental study of leadership and group life. In E.E. Maccoby, T.M. Newcomb, & E.E. Hartley (Eds.). *Readings in social psychology*. New York: Holt, Rinehart & Winston.

Lipset, S.M. (1963). *The first new nation*. New York: Basic Books.

Lipset, S.M. (1960). *Political man*. New York: Doubleday.

Locke, E.A. (1968). Toward a theory of task motivation and incentives. *Organizational Behaviour and Human Performance, 3*, 157-189.

Locke, E.A. (1976). The nature and causes of job satisfaction. In M D. Dunnette (Ed.). *Handbook of industrial and organizational psychology*. Chicago: Rand-McNally.

Lodahl, T., & Kejner, M. (1965). The definition and measurement of job involvement. *Journal of Applied Psychology, 49*, 24-33.

Louis, M. (1980). Surprise and sense making: What newcomers experience when entering the unfamiliar organizational settings. *Administrative Science Quarterly, 25*, 226-251.

Louis, M.L., Posner, B.Z., & Powell, G.N. (1983). The availability and helpfulness of socilaisation practices. *Personnel Psychology, 36*, 857-866.

Luthans, F. (1995). *Organizational Behaviour* (7th ed.). New Delhi: McGraw Hill.

Luthans, F., Baack, D., & Taylor, L. (1987). Organizational Commitment: Analysis of antecedents. *Human Relations, 40*(4), 219-236.

Luthans, F., McCaul, H.S., & Dodd, N.G. (1985). Organizational commitment: A comparison of American, Japanese, and Korean employees. *Academy of Management Journal, 28*(1), 213-219.

Luthans, F., Wahl, L.V.K., & Steinhaus, C.S. (1992). The importance of social support for employee commitment: A quantitative and qualitative analysis of bank tellers. *Organization Development Journal, 10*(4), 1-10.

Lynn, R. (1991). *The secret of the miracle economy: Different national attitudes to competitiveness and saving money*. Exeter, UK: Social Affairs Unit.

Lyons, T.E. (1971). Role clarity, need for clarity, satisfaction, tension, and withdrawal. *Organizational Behaviour and Human Performance, 6*, 99-110.

MacDonald, S., & Parker, A. (1965). Creating a strategy for international growth. *International Enterprises*, 17-19.

Macy, B.A., & Mirvis, P.H. (1983). Assessing rates and costs of individual work behaviours. In S.E. Seashore, E.E. Lawler, P.H. Mirvis, & C. Cammann (Eds.). *Assessing organizational change*. New York: Wiley.

Maddi, S., & Kobasa, S. (1984). *The hardy executive: Health under stress*. New York: Dow Jones Irwin.

Maeher, M.L. (1987). Managing organizational culture to enhance motivation. In M.L. Maeher & D.A. Kleiber (Eds.). *Advances in motivation and achievement: Enhancing motivation*, Vol. 5. Greenwich: Jai Press.

Mahler, J. (1988). The quest for organizational meaning: identifying and interpreting the symbolism in organizational stories. *Administration and Society, 20*, 344-368.

Major D.A., Kozlowski, S.W.J., Chao, G.T., & Gardner, P.D. (1995). A longitudinal investigation of newcomer expectations, early socialization outcomes, and the moderating effects of role development factors. *Journal of Applied Psychology, 80*(3), 418-431.

Manhardt, P.J. (1972). Job orientation of male and female college graduates in business. *Personnel Psychology, 25*, 361-368.

Marceau, J. (1977). *Class and status in France: Economic change and social immobility 1945-1975*. Oxford: Clarendon Press.

March, J.G., & Simon, H. A. (1958). *Organizations*. New York: Wiley.

Margolis, B.L., Kroes, W.H., & Quinn, R.P. (1974). Job stress: An unlisted occupational hazard. *Journal of Occupational Medicine, 16*, 654-661.

Mark, E. (1999). *Breaking through culture shock: What you need to succeed in international business*. London: Nicholas Brealey.

Markus, H.R., & Kitayama, S. (1991). Culture and self: Implications for cognition, emotion, and motivation. *Psychological Review, 28*, 224-253.

Marriott, M. (1976). Hindu transactions: Diversity without dualism. In B. Kapferef (Ed.). *Transaction and meaning: Directions in the anthropology of exchange and symbolic behaviour*. Philadelphia: ISHI Publishing.

Marsden, P.V., Kalleberg, A.L., & Cook, C.R. Gender differences in organizational commitment. *Work and Occupations, 20*(3), 368-390.

Marsh, R.M., & Mannari, H. (1977). A new look at lifetime commitment in Japanese industry. *Economic Development and Cultural Change, 20*(4), 611-630.

Marshall, J., & Cooper, C. L. (1979). *Executive under pressure: A psychological study*. London: McMillan.

Martin, J., & Siehl, C. (1983). Organizational culture and counterculture: An uneasy symbiosis. *Organizational Dynamics, 12*(2), 52-64.

Martin, J., Feldman, M.S., Hatch, M.J., & Sitkin, S.B. (1983). The uniqueness paradox in organizational stories. *Administrative Science Quarterly, 28*, 438-53.

Martin, J., Sitkin, S.B., & Boehm, M. (1985). Founders and the elusiveness of a cultural legacy. In P.J. Frost, L.F. Moore, M.R. Louis, C.C. Lundberg, & J. Martin (Eds.). *Organizational culture*. London: Sage.

Martin, T.N. (1984). Role stress and inability to leave as predictors of mental health. *Human Relations, 37*(11), 969-983.

Maslow, A.H., & Mittelman, B. (1951). *Principles of abnormal psychology*. New York: Harper.

Mathieu, J.E. & Hamel, K. (1989). A causal model of the antecedents of organizational commitment among professionals and nonprofessionals. *Journal of Vocational Behavior, 34*, 299-317.

Mathieu, J.E., & Zajac, D.M. (1990). A review and meta-analysis of the antecedents, correlates, and consequences of organizational commitment. *Psychological Bulletin, 108*, 171-194.

Mathur, P., Aycan, Z., & Kanungo, R.N. (1996). Work cultures in India organizations: A comparison between public and private sector. *Psychology and Developing Society, 8*(2), 199-222.

Mattis, M.C. (2002). Best practices for advancing women in business organizations. In C.L. Cooper, & R.J. Burke (Eds.). *The new world of work: Challenges and opportunities*. Oxford: Blackwell.

McCann-Erickson (1977). De Volwassen Jeugd van de Zeventiger Jaren. Amsterdam: McCann-Erickson. Cited in Hofstede (1982). *Culture's consequences: International differences in work-related values* (Abridged Version. New Delhi: Sage.

McClelland, D.C. (1975). *Power: The inner experience*. New York: Free Press.

McClosky, H., & Schaar, J.H. (1965). Psychological dimensions of anomy. *American Sociological Review, 30*(1), 14-40.

McCormick, I.A., & Cooper, C.L. (1988). Executive stress: Extending the international comparison. *Human Relations, 41*(1), 65-72.

McEvoy, G.M., & Cascio, W.F. (1985). Strategies for reducing employee turnover: A meta-analysis. *Journal of Applied Psychology, 70*(2), 342-353.

McEvoy, G.M., & Cascio, W.F. (1987). Do good or poor performers leave? A met-analysis of the relationship between performance and turnover. *Academy of Management Journal, 30*, 744-762.

McFarlin, D.B., & Sweeney, P.D. (1992). Distributive and procedural justice as predictors of satisfaction with personal and organizational outcomes. *Academy of Management Journal, 35*, 626-637.

McGee, G.W. & Ford, R.C. (1987). Two (or more?) dimensions of organizational commitment: Reexamination of the affective and continuance commitment scales. *Journal of Applied Psychology, 72*, 638-642.

Mead, M. (1940). Social change and cultural surrogates. *Journal of Educational Psychology, 14*, 92-110.

Meade, R.D. (1967). An experimental study of leadership in India. *Journal of Social Psychology, 72*, 35-43.

Meek, V.L. (1988). Organizational culture: Origins and weaknesses. *Organization Studies, 9*(4), 453-73.

Meglino, B.M., Ravlin, E.C., & Adkins, C.L. (1989). A work values approach to corporate culture: A field test of the value congruence process and its relationship to individual outcomes. *Journal of Applied Psychology, 75*(3), 424-432.

Mendenhall, M., & Oddou, G. (1985). The dimensions of expatriate acculturation: A review. *Academy of Management Review, 10*(1), 39-47.

Mendonca, M., & Kanungo, R.N. (1990). Performance management in developing countries. In A.M. Jaeger & R.N. Kanungo (Eds.). *Management in developing countries*. New York: Routledge.

Mendonca, M., & Kanungo, R. N. (1992). Managing human resources: The issue of cultural fit. *Human resource management in developing countries proceedings*. Montreal, Canada: McGill University.

Menon, S.T. (1994). Designing work in developing countries. In R.N. Kanungo & M. Mendonca (Eds.). *Work motivation: Models for developing countries.* New Delhi: Sage.

Meyer, J.P., & Allen, N.J. (1984). Testing the 'side-bet' theory of organizational commitment: Some methodological considerations. *Journal of Applied Psychology, 69,* 372-378.

Meyer, J.P. & Allen, N.J. (1991). A three-component conceptualization of organizational commitment. *Human Resource Management Review, 1,* 61-89.

Meyer, J.P., Paunonen, S.V., Gellatly, I.R., Goffin, R.D., & Jackson, D.N. (1989). Organizational commitment and job performance: It's the nature of commitment that counts. *Journal of Applied Psychology, 74,* 152-156.

Michaels, C.E., & Spector, P.E. (1982). Causes of employee turnover: A test of the Mobley, Griffeth, Hand, & Meglino model. *Journal of Applied Psychology, 67,* 53-59.

Miles, R.E., & Snow, C.C. (1984). Fit, failure, and the Hall of Fame. *California Management Review, 26,* 10-28.

Miller, H.E., Katerberg, R., & Hulin, C.L. (1979). Evaluation of the Mobley, Horner, and Hollingsworth model of employee turnover. *Journal of Applied Psychology, 64*(5), 509-517.

Minium, E.W., King, B.M., & Bear, G. (1995). *Statistical reasoning in psychology and education* (3rd ed.). New York: John Wiley.

Mintzberg, H. (1983). *Structure in fives: Designing effective organizations.* Englewood Cliffs, NJ: Prentice Hall.

Mirvis, P.H. & Lawler, E.E., III. (1977). Measuring the financial impact of employee attitudes. *Journal of Applied Psychology, 62,* 1-8.

Mishra, P.K. (1992). Does organizational climate help improving climate? *Social Science International, 8* (1-2), 37-43.

Mishra, P.K., Das, B.K., Mishra, C., & Dash, M. (1989). Work culture and organizational role behaviour. *Social Science International, 5*(1-2), 49-55.

Misra, S., & Kanungo, R.N. (1994). Bases of work motivation in developing societies: A framework for performance management. In R.N. Kanungo & M. Mendonca (Eds.). *Work motivation: Models for developing countries.* New Delhi: Sage.

Mobley, W.H. (1982). *Employee turnover: Causes, consequences and control.* Reading, MA: Addison-Wesley.

Mobley, W.H., Griffeth, R.W., Hand, H.H., & Meglino, B.M. (1979). Review and conceptual analysis of the employee turnover process. *Psychological Bulletin, 86,* 493-522.

Mobley, W.H., Horner, S.O., & Hollingsworth, A.T. (1978). An evaluation of the precursors of hospital employee turnover. *Journal of Applied Psychology, 63,* 408-414.

Moddie, A.D. (1987). *India in search of values.* New Delhi: Allied.

Moilanen, I., Kunelius, A., Tirkkonen, T., & Crittenden, P. (2000). Attachment in Finnish Twins. In P. Crittenden, & Claussen, A. H. (Eds.) *The organization of attachment relationships: Maturation, culture, and context.* New York: Cambridge University Press.

Monopolis, S., Moraitis, J., Kouvaris, M., & Golanopoulou, P. (1977). Health as a human value. *Transnational Mental Health Research, 19(4),* 5-9.

Moore, W. E. (1961). The social framework of economic development. In R. Braibanti & J.J. Spenglers (Eds.). *The traditional values and socio-economic development.* Durnham: Duke University.

Morgan, G. (1986). *Images of organizations.* New Delhi: Sage.

Morris, C.W. (1956). *Varieties of human value.* Chicago: University of Chicago Press.

Morris, J., & Sherman, J. (1981). Generalizability of an organizational commitment model. *Academy of Management Journal, 24,* 512-526.

Morris, J., & Steers, R. (1980). Structural influences on organizational commitment. *Journal of Vocational Behaviour, 17,* 50-57.

Motowidlo, S.J. (1983). Predicting sales turnover from pay satisfaction and expectations. *Journal of Applied Psychology, 68,* 484-489.

Mottaz, C.J. (1988). Determinants of organizational commitment. *Human Relations, 41,* 467-482.

Mowday, R., Porter, L., & Steers, R. (1982). *Employee-Organization linkages: The psychology of commitment, absenteeism and turnover.* London: Academic Press.

Muchinsky, P.M. (1997). *Psychology applied to work: An introduction to industrial and organizational psychology,* 5th ed. New York: Brooks/Cole.

Muchinsky, P.M., & Tuttle, M.L. (1979). Employee turnover: An empirical and methodological assessment. *Journal of Vocational Behaviour, 14,* 43-77.

Munroe, N. (1994). *Worksite wellness: The financial justification of corporate health promotion schemes.* London Business School, Unpublished research.

Murphy, K.R., & Davidshofer, C.O. (2001). *Psychological testing: Principles and applications* (5th ed.). New Delhi: Prentice Hall of India.

Murphy, L.B. (1953). Roots of tolerance and tension in Indian child development. In G. Murphy (Ed.). *In the minds of men*. New York: Basic Books.

Murrell, K.F.H. (1978). *Ergonomics: Man and his working environment.* London: Chapman and Hall.

Murrell, H. (1978). *Work stress and mental strain: A review of some of the literature*. Work Research Unit Occasional Paper No. 6.

Naidoo, J.C. (1999). The experience of contrasting subjective cultures. In J. Adamapoulous, & Y. Kashima (Eds.). *Social psychology and cultural context*. New Delhi: Sage.

Nambudiri, C., & Saiyadain, M. (1978). Management problems and practices: India and Nigeria. *Columbia Journal of World Business, 13*(2), 62-69.

Nandy, A., & Kakar, S. (1976). Culture and personality. In U. Pareek (Ed.). *A survey of research in psychology, 1971-76*. Bombay: Popular Prakashan.

Narain, D. (1957). *Hindu character*. Bombay: University of Bombay.

Narain, D. (1967). Indian national character in the twentieth century. *Annals*, 124-132.

Near, J.P. (1989). Organizational commitment among Japanese and U.S. workers. *Organization Studies, 10*(3), 281-300.

Nunnally, J.C. (1982). *Psychometric theory* (2nd ed.). New York: McGraw Hill.

O'Driscoll, M.P. (2001). The interface between job and off-job roles: Enhancement and conflict. In C. Cooper & I. Robertson (Eds.). *Well-Being in organizations*. New York: John Wiley.

O'Driscoll, M.P., Bhagat, R.S., Chookar, J., Fernandez, M.J.G., Mahanyele, M., Ninokumar, B.H., Pate, L.E., Ryder, P., & Harnisch, D. (1998). Employee-supportive organizational values and job-related attitudes and affective reactions. *Journal of Applied Social Behaviour, 4*(2), 1-11.

O'Reilly, C., & Caldwell, R. (1987). Personality-Job fit: Replications for individual attitudes and performance. *Organizational Behaviour and Human Performance, 18*, 36-46.

O'Reilly, C., & Chatman, J. A. (1986). Organizational commitment and psychological attachment: The effects of compliance, identification and internalization on prosocial behaviour. *Academy of Management Journal, 34*, 487-516.

O'Reilly, C.A., III, Chatman, J., & Caldwell, D.F. (1991). People and organizational culture: A profile comparison approach to assessing person-organization fit. *Academy of Management Journal, 34,* 487-516.

Oberg, W. (1963). Cross-cultural perspectives on management principles. *Academy of Management Journal, 6,* 129-143.

O'Driscoll, M.P., & Randall, D.M. (1999). Perceived organizational support, satisfaction with rewards, and employee job involvement and organizational commitment. *Applied Psychology: An International Review, 48*(2), 197-209.

Ohbuchi, K.I., & Takahashi, Y. (1994). Cultural styles of conflict management in Japanese and Americans: Passivity, covertness, and effectiveness of strategies. *Journal of Applied Social Psychology, 24,* 1345-1366.

Omundson, J.S., Schroeder, R.G., & Stevens, M.B. (1996). Type A personality, job satisfaction, and turnover intention among certified public accountants: A comparison of Euro-Americans and Hispanics. *Hispanic Journal of Behavioural Sciences, 18*(1), 39-50.

Ornstein, S., & Isabella, L. (1990). Age versus stage models of career attitudes of women: A partial replication and extension. *Journal of Vocational Behaviour, 36,* 1-19.

Orpen, C. (1993). The effect of organizational cultural norms on the relationships between personnel practices and employee commitment. *Journal of Psychology, 127*(5), 577-579.

Orpen, C. (1994). Organizational level as a moderator of the relationship between perceived political climate and employees' work attitudes. *Psychological Reports, 75*(2), 769-770.

Orpen, C. (1995). The effect of organizational commitment on the relationship between communication quality and managerial attitudes. *Psychological Studies, 40*(1), 60-64.

Ostroff, C. (1993). The effects of climate and personal influences on individual behaviour and attitudes in organizations. *Organizational Behaviour and Human Decision Processes, 56*(1), 56-90.

Ott. J. S. (1989). *The organizational culture perspective.* California: Brookes/ Cole.

Ouchi, W.G. (1981). *Theory Z: How American business can meet the Japanese challenge.* New York: Avon.

Pages, M., Michael. B. Vincent, G., & Daniel, D. (1979). *L'emprise de l' organization.* Paris: Presses Universitaries de France.

Pandey, J. (1986). Sociocultural perspectives on ingratiation. In B. Maher & W. Maher (Eds.). *Progress in Experimental Personality Research,* Vol. 14. New York: Academic Press.

Pareek, U. (1981). *Beyond Management: Essays on the processes of institution building*. New Delhi: Oxford and IBH.

Pareek, U. (1988). *Organizational behaviour processes*. Jaipur: Rawat.

Pareek, U. (1994). *Beyond Management: Essays on institution building and related topics*. New Delhi: Oxford and IBH.

Parker, M. (2000). *Organizational culture and identity: Unity and division at work*. New Delhi: Sage.

Parkes, L.P., Bochner, S., & Schneider, S.K. (2001). Person-organization fit across cultures: An empirical investigation of individualism and collectivism. *Applied Psychology: An International Review, 50*(1), 81-108.

Parsons, C.K., Herold, D.M., & Leatherwood, M.L. (1985). Turnover during initial employment: A longitudinal study of the role of causal attributions. *Journal of Applied Psychology, 70*(2), 337-341.

Parsons, T. (1949). *Essays in sociological theory*. Glencoe, III: Free Press.

Pascale, R.T., & Athos, A.G. (1981). *The art of Japanese management*. New York: Simon and Schuster.

Patel, M.K. (1999). A study of impact of age on job involvement and OCM of nationalized and co-operative bank employees. *Journal of the Indian Academy of Applied Psychology, 25*(1-2), 65-70.

Peabody, D. (1985). *National Characteristics*. Cambridge: Cambridge University Press.

Pelissolo, A., & Lepine, J.P. (2000). Normative data and factor structure of the Temperament and Character Inventory (TCI) in the French version. *Psychiatry Research, 94*(1), 67-76.

Perlmutter, H. V. (1969). The tortuous evolution of the multinational corporation. *Columbia Journal of World Business, 4*, 9-18.

Peters, B.J. (2000). Organizational stress in a selected group of males and females consulting personnel. *Dissertation Abstracts-International: Section B: The Sciences and Engineering, 60(11-B)*, 5819.

Peters, J., & Waterman, R. (1982). *In search of excellence: Lessons from America's best-run companies*. New York: Harper and Row.

Peterson, K.D., & Martin, J.L. (1990). Developing teacher commitment: The role of the administrator. In P. Reyes (Ed.). *Teachers and their workplace: Commitment, performance, and productivity*. Thousand Oaks, CA: Sage.

Peterson, M., & Wilson, J. (1998). A culture-work-health model: A theoretical conceptualization. *American Journal of Health Behavior, 22*(5), 378-390.

Pettigrew, A (1979). On studying organizational cultures. *Administrative Science Quarterly, 24,* 570-581.

Pfeffer, J. (1981). *Power in organizations.* Marshfield, MA: Pittman.

Phelan, J., Schwartz, J.E., Bromet, E.J., Dew, M.A., Parkinson, D.K., Schulberg, H.C., Dunn, C.O., Balane, H., & Curtis, E.C. (1991). Work stress, family stress and depression in professional and managerial employees. *Psychological Medicine, 21,* 999-1012.

Pondy, L.R. (1983). The role of metaphors and myths in organizations and in the facilitation of change. In L.R. Pondy, P.J. Frost, G. Morgan, & T.C. Dandridge (Eds.). *Organizational symbolism.* Greenwich CT: JAI Press.

Pool, S.W. (2000). Organizational culture and its relationship between job tension in measuring outcomes among business executives. *Journal of Management Development, 19*(1), 32-49.

Porter, L.W., Crampon, W.J., & Smith, F.J. (1976). Organizational commitment and managerial turnover: A longitudinal study. *Organizational Behaviour and Human Performance, 15,* 87-98.

Porter, L.W., & Lawler, E.E. (1965). Properties of organizational structure in relation to job attitudes and work behaviour. *Psychological Bulletin, 64,* 23-51.

Porter, L.W., Lawler, III, E.E., & Hackman, J.R. (1975). *Behaviour in organizations.* New York: McGraw Hill.

Porter, L.W., & Steers, R.M. (1973). Organizational, work, and personal factors in employee turnover and absenteeism. *Psychological Bulletin, 80,* 151-176.

Porter, L.W., Steers, R.M., Mowday, R.T., & Boulian, P.V. (1974). Organizational commitment, job satisfaction, and turnover among psychiatric technicians. *Journal of Applied Psychology,59,* 603-609.

Posner, B.Z., Kouzes, J.M., & Schmidt, W.H. (1985). Shared values make a difference: An empirical test of corporate culture. *Human Resource Management,* 24(3), 293-309.

Prakash, A. (1994). Organizational functioning and values in the Indian context. In H.S. R. Kao, Sinha, D., & N. Sek-Hong (Eds.) *Effective organizations and social values.* New Delhi: Sage.

Presthold, P.H., Lane, I.N., & Mathews, R.C. (1987). Nurse turnover as reasoned action. Development of a process model. *Journal of Applied Psychology, 72,* 221-228.

Price, J.L. (1977). *The study of turnover.* Ames: Iowa State University Press.

Price, J.L., & Mueller, C.W. (1981). A causal model of turnover for nurses. *Academy of Management Journal, 24,* 543-565.

Putti, J.M., Aryee, S., & Liang, T.K. (1989). Work values and organisatioanl commitment: A study in the Asian context. *Human Relations, 42*, 275-288.

Quarles, R. (1994). An examination of promotion opportunities and evaluation criteria as mechanisms for affecting internal auditor commitment, job satisfaction and turnover intentions. *Journal of Managerial Issues, 6*(2), 176-194.

Quinn, R.E., & McGrath, M.R. (1985). The transformation of organizational cultures: A competing values perspective. In P.J. Frost, L.F. Moore, M.R. Louis, C.C. Lundberg, & J. Martin (Eds.). *Orgnaisational culture.* Newbury Park, California: Sage.

Quinn, R.P., & Shepard, L.J. (1974). *The 1972-73 Quality of Employment Survey.* Ann Arbor, Michigan: Institute for Social Research, University of Michigan.

Quinn, R.P., Seashore, S., & Mangione, I. (1971). *Survey of working conditions.* US Government Printing Office.

Rahman, M. (1989). Job stress, satisfaction, and mental health of factory workers in Bangladesh. *Work and Stress, 3*(2), 155-162.

Randall, D.M. (1990). The consequences of organizational commitment: A methodological investigation. *Journal of Organizational Behaviour, 11*, 361-378.

Reddy, K.P. (1988). *Influence of organizational culture on organizational structure.* Unpublished thesis. Anand: Institute of Rural Management.

Reichers, A.E. (1985). A review and reconceptualization of organizational commitment. *Academy of Management Review, 10*, 465-476.

Reiger, F., & Durhane, W.R. (1990). Organization and culture in developing countries: a configurational model. In A.M. Jaeger, & R.N. Kanungo (Eds.). *Management in developing countries.* London: Routledge.

Rennie, J.A.C., Swackhamer, G., & Woodwar, L.E. (1947). Toward industrial mental health: An historical review. *Mental Hygiene, 31*, 66-68.

Repetti, R.L., & Cosmos, K.A. (1991). The quality of the social environment at work and job satisfaction. *Journal of Applied Social Psychology, 21*(10), 840-854.

Repetti, R.L. (1987). Individual and common components of the social environment at work and psychological well-being. *Journal of Personality and Social Psychology, 52*, 710-720.

Rice, A.K., Hill, J.M., & Trist, E.L. (1950). The representation of labour turnover as a social process. *Human Relations, 3*, 349-372.

Riesman, D. (1950). *The lonely crowd*. New Haven: Yale University Press.

Robinowitz, S., & Hall, D. (1977). Organizational research on job involvement. *Psychological Bulletin, 84*, 265-288.

Rogg, K.L. (1998). Organizational commitment in the post-loyalty era: Perceived organizational support, multiple commitments, and other antecedents' effects on 3turnover intentions and job performance. *Dissertation Abstracts International, Section B: The Sciences and Engineering, 58(8-B)*, 4503.

Rohner, R.P. (1984). Towards a conception of culture for cross-cultural psychology. *Journal of Cross-Cultural Psychology, 15*(2), 111-138.

Roland, A. (1987). The familial self, the individualized self, and the transcendental self: Psychoanalytic reflections on India and America. *Psychoanalytic Review, 74*, 237-250.

Roland, A. (1988). *In search of self in India and Japan: Toward a cross-cultural psychology*. Princeton, NJ: Princeton University Press.

Rollinson, D. & Broadfield, D. (2002). *Organizational behaviour and analysis: An integrated approach* (2nd ed.). New York: Prentice-Hall.

Romzek, B.S. (1989). Personal consequences of employee commitment. *Academy of Management Journal, 39*, 641-661.

Rosen, R. (1984). Worksite health promotion: fact or fantasy? *Corporation Commentary, 1*(1), 1-8.

Rosse, J.G., & Hulin, C.L. (1985). Adaptation to work: An analysis of employee health, withdrawal, and change. *Organizational Behaviour and Human Decision Processes, 36*(3), 324-347.

Rotter, J.B. (1966). Generalized expectancies for internal versus external control of reinforcement. *Psychological Monograph, 80*(1), 1-28.

Rumke, H.C. (1955). Solved and unsolved problems in mental health. *Mental Hygiene, 39*, 386-398.

Rusbult, C.E., & Farrell, D. (1983). A longitudinal test of the investment model: The impact on job satisfaction, job commitment, and turnover of variations in rewards, costs, alternatives, and investments. *Journal of Applied Psychology, 68*(3), 429-438.

Saffold, G.S. (1988). Culture traits, strength, and organizational performance: Moving beyond "strong" culture. *Academy of Management Review, 13*(4), 546-58.

Salancik, G.R. (1977). Commitment and contest of organizational behaviour and belief. In B.W. Staw, & G.H. Salacik (Eds.). *New directions in organizational behaviour*. London: Academic Press.

Sanden, P.O., & Johansson, G. (1991). *Job content and technology in process control consequences for mental load and job involvement.* Sweden: Stockholm University.

Sandhu, S. (1993). *A study of burnout, career commitment, social support and coping strategies: A comparative study between a private and a government hospital.* Unpublished Masters dissertation, New Delhi: University of Delhi, South Campus.

Sarker, S., Crossman, A., & Chinmeteepituck, P. (2003). The relationships of age and length of service with job satisfaction: An examination of hotel employees in Thailand. *Journal of Managerial Psychology, 18*(7/8), 745-775.

Schein, E.H. (1968). Organizational socialization and the profession of management. *Industrial Management Review, 9,* 1-16.

Schein, E.H. (1983). The role of the founder in creating organizational cultures. *Organizational Dynamics, 12*(1), 13-28.

Schein, E.H. (1984). Coming to a new awareness of organizational culture: *Sloan Management Review, 25,* 3-16.

Schein, E.H. (1985). Organizational *culture and leadership: A dynamic view.* San Francisco: Jossey-Bass.

Schein, E. H. (1990). Organizational culture. *American Psychologist, 45,* 109-111.

Schein, E. H. (1992). *Organizational culture and leadership,* 2nd Ed. San Francisco: Jossey-Bass.

Schneider, B. (1985). Organizational Behaviour. *Annual Review of Psychology, 36,* 573-611.

Schultz, D. (1977). *Growth psychology: Model of the healthy personality.* New York: Van Nostrand Reinhold.

Schultz, R., Greenley, J.R., & Brown, R. (1995). Organization, management, and client effects on staff burnout. *Journal of health and social behaviour, 36*(4), 333-345.

Schwartz, H., & Davis, S.M. (1981). Matching corporate culture and business strategy. *Organizational Dynamics, 10,* 30-48.

Schwartz, S.H. (1990). Individualism-collectivism: Critique and proposed refinements. *Journal of Cross-Cultural Psychology, 21,* 139-157.

Schwartz, S.H., & Bardi, A. (2001). Value hierarchies across cultures: Taking a similarities perspective. *Journal of Cross-Cultural Psychology, 32*(3), 268-290.

Schwartz, S.H. (1999). A theory of cultural values and some implications for work. *Applied Psychology: An international review, 98*(1), 23-47.

Schwepker, C.H. (1999). Research note: The relationship between ethical conflict, organizational commitment and turnover intentions in the salesforce. *Journal of Personal Selling and Sales Management, 19*(1), 43-49.

Seashore, S.E., Lawler, E.E., Mirvis, P. & Cammann, C. (Eds.) (1982). *Observing and measuring organizational change: A guide to field practice.* New York: Wiley.

Segall, M.H. (1984). On the search for the independent variable in cross-cultural psychology. In S.H. Irvine & J.W. Berry (Eds.). *Human assessment and cultural factors.* New York: Plenum Press.

Sekaran (1986). Significant differences in quality-of-life factors and their correlates: A function of differences in career orientations or gender? *Sex Roles, 14,* 261-279.

Selznick, P. (1957) *Leadership in Administration: A Sociological Interpretation.* Berkeley: University of California Press.

Seth, N. R. (1988). *The social framework of an Indian factory.* Manchester: University of Manchester Press.

Sharma, C.S. (1998). Organizational commitment: A test of predictor models. *Productivity, 31*(2), 179-191.

Sharma, S. (1999). Social support, stress and psychological well-being. In G. Misra (Ed.). *Psychological perspectives on stress and health.* New Delhi: Concept.

Sharma, S., & Sharma, S. (1987). Job involvement in relation to demographic variables. *Indian Journal of Industrial Relations, 14*(1), 141-148.

Shaw, J., & Reyes, P. (1992). School cultures: Organizational value orientation and commitment. *Journal of Educational Research, 85*(5), 295-302.

Shaw, J.D. (1999). Job satisfaction and turnover intentions: The moderating role of positive affect. *Journal of Social Psychology, 139*(2), 242-244.

Sheldon, M.E. (1971). Investments and involvements as mechanisms producing commitment to the organization. *Administrative Science Quarterly, 16,* 143-150.

Sheridan, J.E. (1992). Organizational culture and employee retention. *Academy of Management journal, 35*(5), 1036-1056.

Siehl, C., & Martin, J. (1984). The role of symbolic management: How can managers effectively transmit organizational culture? In J.G. Hunt (Ed.). *Leaders and managers: International perspective on managerial behaviour and leadership.* New York: Pegamon Press.

Singh, N.K., & Paul, O. (1985). *The corporate soul: Dynamics of effective management.* New Delhi: Vikas.

Singh, P., & Bhandarkar, A. (1990). *Corporate success and transformational leadership.* New Delhi: Wiley Eastern.

Singh, S. (1990). *Organizational stress and executive behaviour*. New Delhi: Shriram Centre for Industrial Relations and Human Resources.

Sinha, D. (1988). Basic Indian values and behaviour dispositions in the context of national development. In D. Sinha & H.S.R. Kao (Eds.). *Social values and development: Asian perspectives*. New Delhi: Sage.

Sinha, D. (1999). Studying the psychology of the Indian people. In U.N. Dash & U. Jain (Eds.). *Perspectives on psychology and social development*. New Delhi: Concept.

Sinha, D., & Kao, H.S.R. (1988). *Social values and development: Asian perspectives*. New Delhi: Sage.

Sinha, D., Kao, H.S.R., & Wilpert, B. (1999). Introduction: The emergence of Indigenization. In H.S.R. Kao, D. Sinha & B. Wilpert (Eds.). *Management and cultural values: The Indigenization of organizations in Asia*. New Delhi: Sage.

Sinha, D., & Sinha, M. (1990). Dissonance in work culture in India. In A. Moddie (Ed.), *The concept of work in Indian society*. Shimla: Indian Institute of Advanced Study.

Sinha, D., & Tripathi, R.C. (1994). Individualism in a collectivist culture: A case of coexistence of opposites. In U. Kim, H.C. Triandis, C. Kagitcibasi, S. Choi, & G. Yoon (Eds.). *Individualism and collectivism: Theory, method and applications*. London: Sage.

Sinha, J.B.P. (1970). *Development through behaviour modification*. Bombay: Allied.

Sinha, J.B.P. (1973). *Some problems of public-sector organizations*. New Delhi: National.

Sinha, J.B.P. (1980). *The Nurturant Task Leader*. New Delhi: Concept.

Sinha, J.B.P. (1982). Power in Indian organizations. *Indian Journal of Industrial Relations, 17*(3), 339-52.

Sinha, J.B.P. (1985). Psychic relevance of work in Indian culture. *Dynamic Psychiatry, 18*, 134-41.

Sinha, J.B.P. (1990a). *Work culture in the Indian context*. New Delhi: Sage.

Sinha, J.B.P. (1990b). The salient Indian values and their socio-cultural roots. *The Indian Journal of Social Science*, 3(4), 477-488.

Sinha, J.B.P. (1997). *Exploitative work culture*. ICSSR Report, Assert Institute of Management Studies, Patna.

Sinha, J.B.P. (1998). Cultural embeddedness and the developmental role of industrial organizations in India. In H.C. Triandis, M D. Dunnette, & L.M. Hough (Eds.). *Handbook of Industrial and Organizational psychology*. New Delhi: Jaico.

Sinha, J.B.P., Daftaur, C.N., Gupta, R.K., Mishra, R.C., Jayaseetha, R., Jha, S.S., Verma, J., Vijaykumar, V.S.R. (1994). Regional similarities and differences in people's beliefs, practices and preferences. *Psychology and Developing Societies, 6*(2), 131-150.

Sinha, J.B.P., & R.N. Kanungo (1997). Context Sensitivity and Balancing in Organizational Behaviour. *International Journal of Psychology, 32*, 93-105.

Sinha, J.B.P., & Sinha, D. (1990). Role of Indian social values in Indian organizations. *International Journal of Psychology, 25*, 705-714.

Sinha, J.B.P., & Verma, J. (1987). Structure of collectivism. In C. Kagitcibasi (Ed.). *Growth and progress in cross-cultural psychology*. Lisse, the Netherlands: Swets & Zeitlinger.

Sinisalo, P. (1995). Changes in occupational plans: Two Finnish cohorts, 1977 and 1989. *Orientation-Scolaire-et-Professionnelle, 24*(1), 39-53.

Siu, O.L., & Cooper, C.L. (1998). A study of occupational stress, job satisfaction and quitting intention in Hong Kong firms: The role of locus of control and organizational commitment. *Stress Medicine, 14*(1), 55-66.

Slocum, J.W., Jr., (1971). A comparative study of the satisfaction of American and Mexican operatives. *Academy of Management Journal, 14*, 89-97.

Smircich, L. (1983). Concepts of culture and organizational analysis. *Administrative Science Quarterly, 28*, 339-358.

Smith, M., Beck, J., Cooper, C.L., Cox, C., Ottaway, D., & Talbot, R. (1986). *Introducing Organizational Behaviour*. London: Macmillan.

Soddy, K. (1950). *Mental health*. Institute of Health Bulletin. League of Redcross Societies.

Soh, S. (2001). Organizational socialization of newcomers: A longitudinal study of organizational enculturation processes and outcomes. *Dissertation Abstracts International, Section B: The Sciences and Engineering, 61(8-B)*, 4460.

Sommer, S.M., Bae, S.H., & Luthans, F. (1996). Organizational commitment across cultures: The impact of antecedents on Korean employees. *Human Relations, 49*(7), 977-993.

Sopachitwattana, P. (2000). An examination of the effects of participative management and cultural values on organizational commitment for American and Thai managers. *Dissertation Abstracts International, Section A: Humanities and Social Sciences, 61(3-A)*, 1075.

Soyibo, K. (1994). Occupational stress factors and coping strategies among Jamaican high school teachers. *Research in Science and Technological Education, 12*(2), 187-192.

Spector, P.E., & Jex, S.M. (1991). Reactions of job characteristics from multiple data sources with employee affect, absence, turnover intentions and health. *Journal of Applied Psychology, 76*(1), 46-53.

Spiro, M.E. (1951). Culture and personality: The natural history of a false dichotomy. *Psychiatry, 14*, 19-46.

Splinder, G.D. (1948). American character structure as revealed by the military. *Psychiatry, 11*, 275-281.

Spratt, P. (1966). *Hindu culture and personality*. Bombay: Manaktala.

Srivastava, A.K., & Singh, H.S. (1988). Modifying effects of coping strategies on the relation of organizational role stress and mental health. *Psychological Reports, 62*, 1007-1009.

Srivastava, A.K. (1983). Role-based stress and mental health of white-collar employees. *Indian Journal of Clinical Psychology, 10*, 343-347.

Staw, B.M. (1984). Organizational behaviour: A review and reformulation of the field's outcome variables. *Annual Review of Psychology, 35*, 627-666.

Steel, R.P., & Ovalle, N.K. (1984). A review and meta-analysis of research on the relationship between behavioural intentions and employee turnover. *Journal of Applied Psychology, 69*, 673-686.

Steel, R.P., Shane, G.S., & Kennedy, K.A. (1990). Effects of social-system factors on absenteeism, turnover, and job performance. *Journal of Business and Psychology, 4*(4), 423-430.

Steers, R.M., & Black, J.S. (1994) *Organizational Behaviour* (5th ed.). New York: Harper Collins.

Steers, R.M., & Mowday, R.T. (1981). Employee turnover and post-decision accommodation processes. In L.L. Cummings, & B.M. Staw (Eds.). *Research in organizational behaviour*, Vol. 3. Greenwich, CT: JAI Press.

Steers, R.M., & Rhodes, S.R. (1978). Major influences on employee attendance: A process model. *Journal of Applied Psychology, 63*, 391-407.

Steers, R.M. (1977). Antecedents and outcomes of organizational commitment. *Administrative Science Quarterly, 22*, 46-56.

Stevens, J., Beyer, J., & Trice, H. (1978). Assessing personal, role and organizational predictors of managerial commitment. *Academy of Management Journal, 21*, 380-396.

Stoetzel, J. (1983). *Present-day values: A European survey*. Paris: Presses Universitaries de France.

Stone, P.J. (1972). Child care in twelve countries. In A. Szalai (Ed.). *The use of time*. Mouton: The Hague.

Sutherland, V., & Davidson, M.J. (1993). Using a stress audit: The construction site manager experience in the UK. *Work and Stress, 7*(3), 273-286.

Tain, C.C. (2000). A study of the individual, the organization, and the cultural match in Taiwan. *Dissertation Abstracts International, Section A: Humanities and Social Sciences, 60(8-A)*, 3020.

Tantratian, M. (1996). Police organizational culture and commitment: The relationship between the individual's perception of organizational culture and continuance, instrumental, and normative commitment in police personnel. *Dissertation Abstracts International, Section A: Humanities and Social Sciences, 57(2 A)*, 861.

Taylor, W.S. (1948). Basic personality in orthodox Hindu cultural patterns. *Journal of Abnormal and Social Psychology, 43*, 3-125.

Theorell, T., Tsutsumi, A., Hallquist, J., Reuterwall, C., Hogstedt, C., Fredlund, P., Emlund, M., & Johnson, J.V. (1998). Decision latitude, job strain, and myocardial infarction: A study of working men in Stockholm. *American Journal of Public Health, 88*, 382-388.

Thibaut, J.W., & Kelley, H.H. (1959). *The social psychology of groups*. New York: Wiley.

Thomas, D.C., & Ravlin, E.C. (1995). Responses of employees to cultural adaptation by a foreign manager. *Journal of Applied Psychology, 80*(1), 133-146.

Thompson, M.S., & Page, S.L. (1992). Psychological determinants of occupational burnout. *Stress Medicine, 8*(3), 151-159.

Thompson, N., Stradling, S., Murphy, M., & O'Neill, P. (1996). Stress and organizational culture. *British Journal of Social Work, 26*(5), 647-665.

Tinsley, C.H., & Brett, J.M. (2001). Managing workplace conflict in the United States and Hong Kong. *Organizational Behavior and Human Decision Processes, 85*(2), 360-381.

Tonnies, F. (1963). *Community and society*. New York: Harper & Row.

Triandis, H.C. (1977). *Interpersonal behaviour*. Monterey, CA: Brooks/Cole.

Triandis, H.C. (1982). Review of culture's consequences: international differences in work related values. *Human Organization, 41*, 86-90.

Triandis, H.C. (1994). *Culture and social behaviour*. New York: McGraw Hill.

Triandis, H.C. (1995). *Individualism and Collectivism*. Boulder, CO: Westview.

Triandis, H.C. (1999). Cross-cultural industrial and organizational psychology. In H.C. Triandis, M. Dunnette & L.M. Hough (Eds.). *Handbook of industrial and organizational psychology*. New Delhi: Jaico.

Triandis, H.C., Bontempo, R., Betancourt, H., Bond, M., Leung, K., Brenes, A., Georgas, J., Hui, C.H., Matin, G., Setiadi, B., Sinha, J., Verma, J., Spangenberg, J., Touzard, H. & Montmollin, G. (1986). The measurement of the etic aspects of individualism and collectivism across cultures. *Australian Journal of Psychology, 38*, 257-267.

Triandis, H.C., Bontempo, R., Villareal, M.J., Asai, M., & Lucca, N. (1988). Individualism and collectivism: Cross-cultural perspectives on self-ingroup relationships. *Journal of Personality and Social Psychology, 54*, 328-338.

Triandis, H.C., McCusker, C., & Hui, C.H. (1990). Multimethod probes of individualism and collectivism. *Journal of Personality and Social Psychology, 59*, 1006-1020.

Trice, H.M., & Beyer, J.M. (1984). Studying organizational cultures through rites and ceremonies. *Academy of Management Review, 9*, 653-659.

Tripathi, R.C. (1988). Aligning development to values in India. In D. Sinha & H.S.R. Kao (Eds.). *Social values and development.* New Delhi: Sage.

Tripathi, R.C. (1990). Interplay of values in the functioning of Indian organizations. *International Journal of Psychology, 25*, 715-734.

Tudor, T.R. (1997). The effects of self-efficacy, work locus of control, and job involvement on perceived work stressors and strains. *Dissertation Abstracts International-Section-A: Humanities and Social Sciences, 58(6-A)*, 2297.

Turner, B.A. (1986). Sociological aspects of organizational symbolism. *Organization Studies, 7*(2), 101-115.

Udy, S.H. (1970). *Work in traditional and modern society*. Englewood Cliffs, New Jersey: Prentice-Hall.

United Nations (1973). *Multinationals Corporations in World Development.* Retrieved March 28, 2008 from http://unctc.unctad.org/data/e73iia.pdf.

United States Tariff Commission (1973). *Implications of multinational firms for world trade and investment sand for US Trade and Labor*. Washington, D.C.: US Government Printing Office.

U. N. Document, F/5300, Rev 1:ST/ESA/6. *The impact of multinational corporation on development and international relations*, p. 25.

United Nations Development Project. (1996). *Human development report 1996*. New York: Oxford University Press.

Van Maanen, J. (1976). Breaking in: Socialization to work. In R. Dubin (Ed.). *Handbook of Work, Organization and Society*. Chicago: Rand McNally.

Van Maanen, J. (Ed.). (1983). *Qualitative methodology*. Beverly Hills: Sage.

Van, V., & Annelies, E.M. (2000). Person-organization fit: The match between newcomers' and recruiters' preferences for organizational cultures. *Personnel Psychology, 53(1)*, 113-149.

Vandenberghe, C. (1999). Organizational culture, Person-Culture fit, and turnover: A replication in the health care industry. *Journal of Organizational Behaviour, 20*(2), 175-184.

Vardi, Y., Weiner, Y., & Popper, M. (1989). The value content of organizational mission as a factor in the commitment of members. *Psychological Reports, 65*, 27-34.

Vashishtha, A. & Mishra, P.C. (1998). Social support as a moderator variable on occupational stress and organizational commitment relationship. *Psychological Studies, 43*(1-2), 33-36.

Verma, J. (1986). Perceived causes of norm violation as a function of Individualism and Collectivism. *Psychological Studies, 31*, 169-176.

Vernon, R. (1971). *Sovereignty at bay*. The Multinational spread of U.S. enterprises. New York: Basic Books.

Virmani, B. R., & Guptan, S. U. (1991). *Indian management*. New Delhi: Vision.

Vukotich, G. (1996). Organizational culture: A view of the enculturation process and its relation to turnover. *Dissertation Abstracts International, Section A: Humanities and Social Sciences, 56(12-A)*, 4856.

Wagner, J.A., & Hollenback, J.R. (1995). *Management of organizational behaviour*. Michigan: Michigan State University, Prentice-Hall.

Wahn, J.C. (1998). Sex differences in the continuance component of organizational commitment. *Group and Organization Management, 23*(3), 256-266.

Walker, C.R., & Guest, R.H. (1952). *The man on the assembly line*. Cambridge: Harvard University Press.

Wallace, J.E. (1993). Professional and organizational commitment: Compatible or incompatible? *Journal of Vocational Behaviour, 42*, 333-349.

Wanous, J.P., Poland, T.D., Premack, S.L., & Davis, K.S. (1992). The effects of met expectations on newcomers attitudes and behaviours: A review and meta-analysis. *Journal of Applied Psychology, 72*, 288-297.

Warren, N.D. (1997). The organizational and psychosocial bases of cumulative trauma and stress disorders. *Dissertation Abstracts International, Section B: The Sciences and Engineering, 58(3-B)*, 1224.

Warren, T.R. (1997). Person-organization fit and organizational outcomes.

*Dissertation Abstracts International, Section B: The Sciences and Engineering, 57(7-B)*, 4765.

Watts, C.R., & White, H.C. (1988). Assessing employee turnover. *Personnel Administrator, 33*(4), 80-85.

Weber, M. (1958). *The religion of India: The sociology of Hinduism and Buddhism* (Trs. and Eds. H.H. Greth & D. Martindale). Glencoe: Free Press.

Weiner, Y. (1982). Commitment in organizations: A normative view. *Academy of Management Review, 7*, 418-428.

Wells, D.L., & Muchinsky, P.M. (1985). Performance antecedents of voluntary and involuntary turnover. *Journal of Applied Psychology, 70*(2), 329-336.

Welsh, H.P., & Laven, H. (1981). Interrelationship between organizational commitment and job characteristics, job satisfaction, professional behaviour and organizational climate. *Human Relations, 34*, 1079-1089.

Werbel, J.D., & Gould, S. (1984). A comparison of the relationship of commitment to turnover in recent hires and tenured employees. *Journal of Applied Psychology, 69*, 687-690.

White, L. (1948). Man's control over civilization. *Scientific Monthly, 66*, 235-247.

Whitener, E.M., & Waltz, P.M. (1993). Exchange theory determinants of affective and continuance commitment and turnover. *Journal of Vocational Behaviour, 42*, 265-281.

Whyte, W.F. (1969). Culture and work. In R.A. Webber (Ed.). *Culture and management.* Homewood: IL: Irwin.

Wig, N.N. (1979). Mental health and population growth. *Indian Journal of Psychiatry, 21*, 12-33.

Wilkins, A., & Ouchi W. (1983). Efficient cultures: Exploring the relationship between culture and organizational performance. *Administrative Science Quarterly, 28*, 468-481.

Wilkins, A.L. (1983). Organizational stories as symbols which control the organization. In L.R. Pondy, P.J. Frost, G. Morgan, & T.C. Dandridge (Eds.). *Organizational symbolism.* Greenwich, Conn.: JAI.

Wilkinson, C. (1997). *Managing health at work: A guide for managers and workplace health specialists.* London: Chapman & Hall.

Williams, A., Dodson, P., & Walters, M. (1993). *Changing culture, new organizational approaches* (2nd ed.). London: Institute of Personnel Management.

Williams, J.E., & Best, D.L. (1990). *Measuring sex stereotypes: A multination study.* Newbury Park, CA: Sage.

Williams, L.K., Whyte, W.F., & Green, C.S. (1966). Do cultural differences affect workers' attitudes? *Industrial Relations, 5*, 105-117.

Worrall, L., Cooper, C.L., & Campbell, F. (2000). The impact of organizational change on UK managers' perceptions of their working lives. In R.J. Burke & C.L. Cooper (Eds.). *The organization in crisis: Downsizing, restructuring, and privatization.* Oxford: Blackwell.

Yoder, D. (1962). *Personnel management and industrial relations.* Englewood Cliffs, NJ: Prentice-Hall.

Youngblood, S.A., Mobley, W.H., & Meglino, B.M. (1983). A longitudinal analysis of the turnover process. *Journal of Applied Psychology, 68,* 507-516.

Zedeck, S., & Mosier, K.L. (1990). Work in the family and employing organization. *American Psychologist, 45,* 240-251.

Zippo, M. (1982). Dealing with absenteeism and turnover: Some current problems. *Personnel, 59,* 43-45.

# Index